REFUGEES IN INTERNATIONAL POLITICS

Refugees in International Politics

LEON GORDENKER

New York   Columbia University Press   1987

Printed in Great Britain

Library of Congress Cataloging-in-Publication Data
Gordenker, Leon, 1923–
    Refugees in international politics.

    Bibliography: p.
    Includes index.
    1. Refugees, Political. 2. Political
persecution. 3. International relations.
4. Refugees — International cooperation. I. Title.
HV640.G65   1987   362.8'7   87-11688
ISBN 0-231-06624-4

Contents

Preface   5
Foreword   9
1. Introduction   11
Unprecedented difficulties   12
An international network   15
2. Organisational and Conceptual Development   19
The heritage of the League of Nations   20
The first UN efforts for refugees   22
An operating agency for refugees   25
Continuing agencies for refugees   27
Conceptual bases   29
Functional expansion   33
Conceptual expansion   36
Expansion of executive roles   42
3. The Novel Nature of Recent Refugee Incidents   49
New technology and new nationalism   50
Remarkable aspects of contemporary refugee incidents   52
    Numbers   52
    Location and development   53
    Large-scale migration   55
    Organised transnational programmes   56
Definitional insufficiencies   59
4. Causal Elements in Contemporary Refugee Incidents   62
International war   64
    Fighting phase   65
        Ground fighting   65
        Aerial bombardment   66
        Propaganda and political warfare   66
    Liquidation phase   67
Internal turbulence   68
    Violent governmental change   68
    Revolution   69
    Coups d'état   70
    Insurrectionary social structures   71
    National loyalties   72
        Divided nations   72
        Minorities   72
    Brutal government   74

Positive brutality 74
Self-serving, repressive dictatorship 75
Incompetent government 76
Deliberately undertaken change of social structures 77
Violent or repressive liquidation of elites 78
Legitimate replacement of elites 79
Economic obsolescence 81
International political tension 82
Ideological opposition 82
Political warfare 84
Propaganda 84
Support of opposition groups 85
Economic pressure 85
Organised international political action 86
Dispute-handling 86
Political attacks 87
Protection of human rights 87
5. Responses to Movements of Refugees 89
Urgent assistance 90
Responses within a state 90
Modest numbers 91
Large numbers 92
Obligations of states 93
Transnational responses 95
Bilateral governmental responses 95
Intergovernmental responses 96
Voluntary organisations 103
Continuing assistance 105
Shelter and food 107
Medical and social care 108
Schools 109
Limitations and inhibitions 111
Structural 111
Legal 112
Financial and administrative 113
6. Resolving Forced Migrations 125
Repatriation 126
Repatriation and causes of flight 127
Negotiating repatriation 128
Resettlement in first-asylum locations 131
Asylum and the causes of flight 132
Limiting effects of on-the-spot settlement 133
Jealousy 134
Approach of receiving government 134

Costs   135
Conceptual issues   135
Third-country resettlement   138
  Refugees and immigration policies   138
  Preparation for resettlement   141
  Reception   144
Emerging issues   146
  Fair shares   146
  Economic and social development   149
  Unresolved refugee situations   155
  Prevention   158
7. Looking Ahead   168
Forecasting refugee flows   168
  A general standard   169
  Existing machinery   171
  Additional capacity   173
Early warning   174
  Fundamental factors   175
  Warning for relief   175
  Warning, prevention and politics   176
Preventing forced migration   177
  Obviating departure   177
  Preventing departure   180
  Discouraging entry   183
  Preventing entry   184
  'Push' and 'pull'   186
  Expulsion as a weapon   188
8. Conclusions   195
Limitations on responses   197
An obsolete standard?   201
The benefits of internationalisation   206
Limits and potentials in organising internationally   208
Bibliography   215
Index   221

Preface

A challenge by an otherwise well-informed friend in the United States to point out where multilateral co-operation can be seen to work well eventually led to this study of what international organisation does for forced migrants and what effect such people have on governments. The presence in the world of refugees, of which I, like others of my generation, have been conscious since childhood, has in fact called forth a real effort on the part of individuals, their associations and their governments. The resulting co-operation saves many millions of human lives. In doing so, it provides a rare example of co-operation among governments for the purpose of giving direct assistance to individuals.

Is international organisation for the purpose of coping with refugees satisfactory? Of course not. Nothing could entirely make up for the pain of persecution, the burden of fear, the detachment from roots that refugee status implies. Even more deeply refugees represent a failure on the part of society to care for its own. International co-operation that repairs the damage to at least some victims is, in my opinion, far better than nothing. The institutions that have been created, the networks of helping individuals and associations, the appeals for aid, the donations of funds gathered through taxes and gifts have come to symbolise human decency in a world where blood is shed unceasingly. Yet binding up the wounds of victims — and of only some of them at that — does not prevent the continual production of more.

Nevertheless, as this study shows, a rudimentary system can be seen to function. It remains distant from perfection, from brilliant efficiency, from faultless timing, from peerless leadership. But it is not my purpose to expose the shortcomings of this primitive organisation or to fill in a blueprint of reform. Rather, this study emphasises the reasons why the system came into being, how it operates and where its limits are to be found. Its purpose is to add to our understanding of when and why co-operation develops in a world where conflict is becoming more visible.

It would be an error to assume that the co-operation needed to cope with forced migration either stands as an unparalleled example or that the techniques it employs are in any way unique. In fact much of the business among states has been of an organised nature, and that organisation functions day in, day out, hardly to the satisfaction of every government or every observer but at a level well above that of sheer anarchy. It has not achieved a stage where the brutishness of international relations has become a distant memory; nor is it uniformly developed among different issues. But as this study shows, government officials and a large number of private individuals understand how such co-operation works and know how to use it when refugees appear.

What they do for forced migrants, it can be argued, could be done in no other way. The misery of refugees thus dulls the glitter of unilateral, short-term campaigning by governments. The homeless, persecuted, hungry, confused people who turn up at border posts and distant airports signify the costs of conflict within and among societies and states. They are living monuments to war, disorder, long-term social collapse, governmental failure, prejudice and sheer malice. They pay directly for the militaristic swaggering of their leaders, for the intolerance of political and religious orthodoxy and for the short-term successes of mindless power-seekers. As I feel pride that my fellow men can aid some — alas, only some — of these victims, I feel shame that their suffering exists at all.

This work is the result of a lengthy career spent observing attempts to organise international relations. Sources consulted include official documents of intergovernmental organisations, especially the United Nations, of which the documentation of the High Commissioner for Refugees forms a part; official and informal publications of intergovernmental agencies, including press releases and other public information materials; secondary studies of a scholarly nature; journalistic books; and newspapers and magazines. Fuller information is set out in the bibliographical note below.

While all of these sources provided valuable bases for studying refugee issues, their richness was brought out by interviews with officials of international organisations, national governments, local governments, voluntary agencies and refugees and former refugees. These interviews took place in Geneva, New York, Washington, London, The Hague, Bangkok, Islamabad and Peshawar, New Delhi, Hong Kong, Guangzhou, Beijing, Singapore, Nairobi, Mogadishu, Khartoum and in refugee camps or resettlement locations near many of these places. There, refugees were asked to tell their stories and air their views. Some did so with evident conviction, others with practised glibness and some in bewilderment that their words were heard at all. Altogether several hundred interviews were conducted and many dozens of officials, willingly or unwittingly, helped to inform me. Among those interviewed were August Lindt, Felix Schnyder, and Prince Sadruddin Aga Khan, all former High Commissioners for Refugees, as well as Poul Hartling, then High Commissioner. Senior officials, including James Carlin, Director of the Intergovernmental Commission for Migration, and others in the International Committee of the Red Cross and the League of Red Cross Societies, also were consulted. Numerous senior national officials of several countries and diplomatic representatives of many more were interviewed. Important insights and information were willingly given me by several dozen representatives of transnational voluntary organisations.

As the locations of interviews and the levels of knowledge and information, not to speak of language, varied so greatly, it seemed unlikely that a systematic form of interview could be worked out. Consequently, interviews provided a mixture of concrete information, expert opinion, intuitive comment, deliberate evasion and evident ignorance. Yet on the whole these interviews illuminated the more formally presented information and highlighted the conceptual and human significance of written documents. The text does not cite specific interviews for the simple reason that most talks, especially with senior organisational officials, were undertaken with the express reservation that no attribution of specific information or views would be made. I have respected this undertaking, even if it means that some controversial material in the text is not attributed. One rejected alternative would have led to a plethora of unhelpful references to sources identified only by initials. I have also tried to restrict the amount of annotation as far as possible and in particular not to cite sources of commonly known facts. The interpretations of documentary materials and of interviews are my responsibility. Those interviewed helped me greatly to come to conclusions, to understand subtleties and partly to overcome the unevenness — indeed, too often the secrecy and bureaucratic defensiveness — of access to the archives and working papers of organisations. No doubt some specialists on refugee affairs would quarrel with my estimates: neither they nor I are likely to have a monopoly on wisdom, and further discussion will help us all, including the refugees whose presence originally stimulated what is written here.

It is also a pleasure to acknowledge the scholarly, administrative and financial support of several organisations. Princeton University, where I am professor emeritus after serving as a faculty member for 28 years, provided a generous infrastructure and the indispensable leaves of absence for research. Its Center of International

Studies, where I was faculty associate, offered me vital summer support and opened the way for some of my travels, especially that to China. Professor C.E. Black, its director when this study was undertaken, sustained my work in many indispensable ways. The Institute for the Study of World Politics extended financial support that made possible my first extended period of field research. Without that assistance, this study would have been stopped before it started. The Long-Range Assessments Office of the United States Department of State commissioned a paper — made available to the public free of charge — which underlies a considerable part of this work. A temporary association with the Institut Universitaire de Hautes Études Internationales in Geneva, where I am now a faculty member, gave me an opportunity to reach East Africa. A Fulbright Research Professorship at Leiden University helped deepen some of my research and encouraged me to a more cosmopolitan understanding of governmental policies. Officials of the UN High Commissioner for Refugees generously aided my visits to refugees in Kenya, Somalia, Sudan, Pakistan, Thailand, China, Singapore, Hong Kong and a few less critical sites. ICM officers in the field and ICRC personnel also instructed me about their work. All these officials, some of them working on overwhelming tasks in grim conditions, helped to keep me in contact with the network concerned with refugees. The Refugee Policy Group in Washington also kept me in touch with the networks. The Independent Commission on International Humanitarian Issues commissioned my exploration of the opportunities in early warning. Students in my classes at Princeton helpfully filtered my gathering thoughts on the subject of forced migrants and international co-operation. To all those organisations and people mentioned here, and to many more whose advice and memories helped me understand better, I acknowledge my debt.

Leon Gordenker, July 1986, Grijpskerke, Netherlands

This book was written under the auspices of the Center of International Studies, Princeton University.

Foreword

1985 marked the fortieth anniversary of the foundation of the United Nations. It is very appropriate that at this time we should look back over the last 40 years to see what has been achieved, and where we might go in the future. The Geneva International Peace Research Institute (GIPRI) and the International Peace Academy (IPA) are very happy to assist in this process by being associated with a series of volumes evaluating the work of the United Nations. Our object is solid analysis, based on pluridisciplinary contributions. We seek to draw on the experience of those who have studied, know well and are objective about the work of the United Nations. We propose constructive, well-informed criticism that will inform future policy and planning, and also be more generally educational. This second volume in our series focuses on the international community's ability to ease the plight of refugees, which is central to the future work of the United Nations and to its reform. It must be more responsive to human needs as well as governmental demands. We welcome discussion and comments from readers and friends so that there can be a wide, as well as scientific, discussion on a United Nations that can pursue peace and development more effectively.

Alexandre Berenstein,
President
Geneva International Peace Research Institute,
Geneva, Switzerland.

Major-General Indar Jit Rikhye (Retd.),
President
International Peace Academy,
New York.

For R.J.M., H.W.P., E.E.S.

1

Introduction

Millions of refugees, huddled together in overflowing camps or tucked away in the obscure corners of towns, constitute a poignant element of human hope and desperation in our time. No one knows precisely how many refugees scrabble for survival and pride in a world that seems to drive people from their homes with unprecedented ease. Estimates of their numbers range from 8 to over 15 million in all continents. While the number of refugees in a locality may wax and wane, the total estimates have remained remarkably stable for several years.[1] Indeed, refugee populations seem likely to be a permanent feature of an international landscape already disfigured by the machinery of war.

Yet the wholesale mistreatment of human beings which impels a sudden spiralling, as well as uneven trickles, of refugee populations calls forth a mixture of humane and expedient responses. The existence of refugees has never been better understood, their needs never more completely registered. They receive help on a scale which often surprises those who have little contact with international institutions or with voluntary agencies that provide compassionate aid for the victims of actions perpetrated by governments, their servants and associated groups. The effort to assist refugees to stay alive through their initial peril, to return to their homes if circumstances permit, to resettle in new lands if only that way is open and to avoid a squandering of human energy while their fates are determined reflects large-scale organised, transnational activity. In the first instance, it owes its existence to the willingness of governments — not all, but a substantial, well-endowed number of them — to co-operate. This co-operation achieves organisational continuity through a corps of international civil servants as well as officials of the sprawling network of non-governmental agencies. The latter work with intergovernmental bodies and with national authorities that frequently serve as executive arms. A substantial foundation of international law and concomitant international practice reflects the successful efforts made in the past and offers a footing for the future.

If refugees have become a permanent feature of the international scene or so frequent an outcrop of it that their tenuous existence enters the consciousness of a substantial public, the international arrangements for serving those who are forced to flee need to be understood. So do the causes of flight. This study aims at furthering such understanding. It begins with a historical sketch of issues involving refugees. It then argues that twentieth-century refugee incidents possess certain novel characteristics. A substantial part of the study is concerned with developing a causal analysis of contemporary refugee situations. It then traces the effects of such situations, giving special attention to the reactions of governmental, intergovernmental and other social institutions. Finally, it takes up unresolved issues concerning refugees, including prevention, definitional difficulties and possible alternative policies available to governments and other organisations. The study aims at analytical precision and penetration, rather than at prescription of specific policies. The political origins of refugees cannot, however, be brushed aside; as a result any conclusions necessarily have implications for governmental policies.

Unprecedented difficulties

Migration has always formed part of human life. People have left their homes for both material and spiritual reasons, because of faith and religion and in spite of them, in bad times and in good. Wars have driven some from their homes and have been caused by others seeking to expand their homelands. Some have fled from tyrants and others to join them. Droughts, earthquakes, floods and climatic shifts have all induced migrations. In a broad sense, all of those who felt themselves *forced* to migrate were refugees. Forced migrations thus include a psychological element, a perceived fear.

Contemporary understanding of the concept of refugee, whatever the antecedents, rests on a deliberate conceptual exclusion and a search for precision. It begins with the separation of natural disasters from those brought about by human beings. Refugees, it is said, are those who flee man-made disasters. They fear the threatened

consequences of staying in their homes even more than strange surroundings, uncertainty and insecurity. Such disasters are not spontaneous; they require decisions, failure to decide or dereliction and
misfeasance on the part of a particular set of social authorities.
Because authoritative decisions on the part of the state apparatus
so often underlie man-made disasters, the creation of refugees —
as the concept is now understood — is political.

Flight for political reasons is nothing new. Threatened princes
and defeated pretenders of old sought shelter in neighbouring courts
and, frequently under codes of royal courtesy, got what they wanted.
Individuals who became political refugees either foreshadowed or
were reacting to changes of regime and social order, as did Voltaire,
Marx, Kossuth, Mazzini, Bolivar, Trotsky and thousands of others.
Force used for international political ends — wars — generally produced a certain amount of forced migration. When the nomad way
of life was still common, whole tribes continually shifted from one
realm to another without changing loyalty or custom. Religious conflicts induced by political decisions bred numerous refugees, such
as the Jews who left Spain during the Inquisition or the Huguenots
who sought safety in the Netherlands or South Africa. All these
movements entailed human suffering and social change, some of
it leading to the implantation of important technological and intellectual innovation in the host countries. All embodied conceptual elements which contribute to the contemporary perception of
refugees.[2]

In magnitude and cause, several incidents around the time of
the First World War more closely foreshadowed the refugee situations that exist at present. The movement of opposed military forces
deeply affected very large civilian populations. A striking example
is that of the approximately half-million Belgians who fled the German attack and received organised assistance in France, Britain and
the Netherlands.

Soon afterwards, the Russian Revolution and resulting civil war
produced a heavy stream of refugees from the former elite. They
were estimated to number 1,500,000, scattered around the edges
of the Czarist empire from China to Western Europe. The new
revolutionary government employed its authority, force and
ideological pressure in the effort to change society. This combination tended to rule out repatriation for most of the refugees and
to make their exile a permanent one. Meanwhile, communal antag-
onism produced another vast flow of post-war refugees from Turkey:
these were the some 250,000 Armenians who suffered violent

repression on the part of the revolutionary Turkish government. Another huge batch of refugees, these of Greek origin, also poured out of Turkey after the defeat of the Greek forces in Anatolia in 1922. Remaining ethnic Greeks in Turkey, and Turks in Greece, were dealt with in an official exchange of population under international auspices. As both incidents were used by the Turkish government to nurture nationalism, any repatriation of the refugees was effectively ruled out.

At the same time, the Fascist regime in Italy was dealing with its opposition in a heavy-handed manner. The result was a stream of individual political refugees abroad. Many escapees would have been liable to persecution had they returned. During these same years a similar stream of solitary political refugees departed from the Soviet Union for similar reasons.

The government of Adolf Hitler that took power in Germany in 1933 soon augmented the number of refugees in the world. The first to depart were political enemies of the new government, which made it clear that it would more than match the ruthlessness of the Italian Fascists and the Soviet revolutionaries. No one can doubt that it made good its promise. When it extended its attention to the Jews, gypsies and yet others considered undesirable, the Hitler government produced a heavy flow of people seeking refuge. And by the end of the Second World War, the German government had scattered Eastern Europeans far and wide over Western Europe, ensured that the few surviving Jews could not even dream of returning to their former lives and left the victorious military forces of the United Nations with a massive relief problem.

Since then, both the numbers of refugees and the regions of the world affected by them have multiplied.[3] Refugees left East Germany for the West; North Korea for the South; Czechoslovakia, Poland, Hungary and Yugoslavia for shelter in Western Europe, North America and Israel; North Africa and the Middle East for Israel; and Israel for the surrounding lands. The 1970s and 1980s saw even more dramatic movements in some of the poorest parts of the world. For example, the conflicts which in 1971 resulted in the creation of the state of Bangladesh produced as many as ten million refugees who fled to India. The increasingly severe guerrilla warfare which preceded the independence of Zimbabwe in 1980 drove some 200,000 people into exile in Mozambique and others into Zambia. The 1976 Soweto riots in South Africa and the subsequent repression sent several thousand people, most of them young, into the precarious economies of Botswana, Swaziland and Lesotho.

The war in Kampuchea between the China-oriented Pol Pot regime
— which, unaided, had already butchered its population — and
the Vietnamese-backed Heng Semrin government put several hundred thousands into the border areas and into camps in Thailand.
Other refugees came from Vietnam — over a million spilt into China
and South-East Asia, from where substantial numbers were resettled
in other parts of the world, especially the United States. More than
100,000 Lao were sheltered in camps in Thailand. Ethiopia produced at least 350,000 Eritrean refugees, given asylum in Sudan;
and camps in Somalia in 1980 housed some 800,000, who had left
Ogaden Province. The Soviet Union's invasion of Afghanistan and
its aftermath of guerrilla warfare sent more than 2,000,000 people
into refugee camps and other forms of asylum in Pakistan and
numerous others to temporary shelter in family and other unofficial
locations. In 1980 Cuba encouraged some 80,000 of its nationals
to flee to the United States in a matter of weeks; this followed a
spontaneous movement of 10,000 refugee-seekers into the Peruvian
embassy in Havana. Over 100,000 Jews, most of whom were able
to claim at least some consideration as refugees, left the Soviet Union
during the seventies. Over 30,000 Chileans, 50,000 Nicaraguans and
some tens of thousands of Argentinians and Salvadorans fled
political upheaval and violence in their countries.

The very existence of such numbers of people adrift is enough
to indicate a crisis of humanity. As the analysis that follows will suggest, additional reasons point to such a crisis, certainly from a
humanitarian point of view, and from other standpoints as well.
Moreover, the vast dimensions of forced migrations and asylum-
seeking suggest this crisis is neither short-lived nor merely eccen-
tric; rather, it seems likely to continue. This likelihood has its
counterpart in the international regime that has grown up for the
protection and relief of refugees and certain others in similar
circumstances.

An international network

Social, political and personal upheavals of the breadth and depth
of current refugee crises lie beyond the capacity of any one government to deal with, either as non-recurring incidents or largely
foreseeable events for which preparations can be made. It is a —
perhaps ironic — fact that the supposedly temporary refugee populations which have appeared since the First World War have left the

world a legacy of elaborate international framework for responding to current situations. Part of this framework, formed either by institutions or by national commitment to international legal norms, antedates that war. Shortly afterwards came the Geneva Convention and the attendant machinery of the International Red Cross movement. The League of Nations endorsed a durable concept of, and the setting up of rudimentary machinery for, international protection of refugees, based on intergovernmental commitment and supervision. The Second World War induced the creation of large-scale intergovernmental machinery in the UN Relief and Rehabilitation Administration (UNRRA)[4] and its successor, the International Refugee Organization (IRO).[5] Both these organisations had vanished by 1951, but their successors, the UN High Commissioner for Refugees (UNHCR) and the Intergovernmental Committee for European Migration (ICEM), vigorously carry out activities on a scale which their governmental sponsors entirely failed to anticipate. The International Red Cross movement has never before been so much engaged in offering help to refugees. A ring of older organisations, such as the American Catholic Relief Services and the International Catholic Migration Commission and the World Council of Churches, has been joined by newer creations, among them OXFAM, in acting both on behalf of intergovernmental organisations and themselves. At one side, almost irrelevant to activities elsewhere, the UN Relief and Works Agency for Palestine Refugees (UNRWA)[6] was created to fit into a framework of political settlements around the new-born state of Israel. This framework failed to stand, and the care of Palestinian refugees turned into a permanent dole for succeeding generations of people who were neither resettled nor returned.

That these organised efforts to deal with refugee situations, as will be seen in more detail in the following pages, have expanded and become more elaborate in their potential services is indisputable. Yet the international approach to refugee matters rests on concepts developed in different circumstances and at various times. These concepts, like the organisations that apply them, have been reinterpreted and adapted; that much is certain from the most cursory examination. But the question remains as to the degree to which either conceptual foundations or organisational structures at the international level fit current needs. Moreover, organisational adaptation required the making of new decisions. This requirement raises the question as to how and to what effect the decision-making structures react to changing circumstances. Such decisions involve expansion and contraction of activities, increases and decreases in expenditure, the appointment and release of employees and the engagement and release of sister organisations from their functions. The means for managing such an ebb and flow of activity also raise questions.

In addition, the enormous growth in refugee populations and their financial requirements has led to new varieties of governmental involvement. The scale of refugee flows and their effects on international security encourage an upgrading of the political level at which these matters are considered. For example, the UN Secretary-General has increasingly involved his office in refugee affairs. Affected governments, as was the case in Thailand or Somalia, must react to refugee affairs as matters of survival, or war or peace, for their polities. Both these refugee situations, moreover, engage the interests of the superpowers, the Soviet Union and the United States.[7] The acts of their military and political clients bore directly on the production of refugees and condition their treatment. Therefore, the approach to international machinery contains a political tone which in the recent past has sometimes been muted. On the other hand, the principal donor governments, facing budgets for the UN High Commissioner for Refugees that have exceeded $500 million per year and covering expenditures on their own resettlement and bilateral programmes, also treat their involvement with refugees as an issue of general importance. A significant piece of evidence of such national concern is the appointment by the then President Jimmy Carter of a National Refugee Co-ordinator for the United States and the continuation of that office under President Ronald Reagan.

Notes

1. A typical approximation appears in *World Refugee Crisis: the International Community's Response*, Report to the Committee on the Judiciary, United States Senate, Ninety-Sixth Congress, First Session, by Congressional Research Service (Government Printing Office, Washington, 1979) [hereafter referred to as *Judiciary Committee Report*], p. xi, which gives a low estimate of over 8 million and a high estimate of over 10 million. In US Committee for Refugees, *World Refugee Survey 1982* (US Committee on Refugees, New York, 1982), the ten-million figure is used again. The same estimate is made for 1985 in US Committee for Refugees, *World Refugee Survey 1985* (American Council for Nationalities Services, Washington, 1986). The *Judiciary Committee Report*, p. xi, mentions that American officials gave estimates of over

13 million for 1978. See discussion in Charles B. Keely, *Global Refugee Policy: The Case for a Development-Oriented Strategy*, (The Population Council, New York, 1981), pp. 14-15, 28-38. The numbers depend on definitions and accuracy of data.

2. Gunther Beyer, 'The Political Refugee; 35 Years Later', *International Migration Review*, 15, 53/54 (spring/summer 1981), pp. 26-8.

3. Ibid., *Judiciary Committee Report, passim* and the series of annual reports by the US Committee on Refugees, cited in note 1 above.

4. A complete account of UNRRA exists in George Woodbridge, *The History of UNRRA*, 3 vols (Columbia University Press, New York, 1950).

5. A comprehensive study is Louise W. Holborn, *The International Refugee Organization, Its History and Work, 1946-1952* (Oxford University Press, London, 1956).

6. For an account of this organisation, see Edward H. Buehrig, *The UN and Palestinian Refugees: A Study in Nonterritorial Administration* (Indiana University Press, Bloomington, 1971).

7. Gilburt D. Loescher and John Scanlan, *Calculated Kindness: Refugees and the Half-Opened Door, 1945 to the Present* (Free Press, New York, 1986), Chapter 3, part III.

2

Organisational and Conceptual Development

As victory for the Allies drew closer during the Second World War, so too did a time of concerted attention to refugees on a scale never before seen. It has not yet ended. This period of unprecedented construction included a great deal of transnational organisation. It also produced political and administrative experience which gave distinctive form to a set of concepts defining refugees and delimiting organisational tasks. These concepts still serve as the fundamental basis for contemporary treatment of refugee issues.

Even before the war was seen to be obviously going in favour of the Allies, plans were being drawn up to provide relief for those in the liberated territories. Millions — perhaps as many as 20 — of men, women and children, driven from their homes, would be encountered as the United Nations armies advanced. At first they would all be designated displaced persons, if they were not in their land of origin. Some would be anxious to return to their homelands. It also soon became apparent, however, that among those who had been deliberately transported by the German government or had picked their way westward through the military lines of Eastern Europe, many thousands would resist returning. To these could be added the pitiful survivors of the German death camps. These footloose millions, moreover, got in the way of military action and burdened the sometimes bewildered military commanders charged with responsibility for the liberated territories. Thus, broadly speaking, both humanitarian and military-political reasons lay behind the attention given to refugee issues.

The heritage of the League of Nations

Arrangements bequeathed by the League of Nations gave some guidance to the UN allies for dealing with refugee situations.[1] The earlier experience demonstrated that those without homes or governmental protection would need both immediate material assistance and legal arrangements for continuing their lives. Yet the League had never handled anything of the scale that faced the UN governments during 1943. The main activities of the Nansen offices and the commissioners for refugees in various legal guises created by the League had to do with narrow categories of asylum-seekers; for instance, they gave legal protection to White Russians after the revolution in that country or to Turkey's fleeing Armenians. When considerable material assistance had to be provided, as in the case of the Greek refugees from Turkey, the League was nevertheless spared anything more than a high-level organising role: the administration of material assistance fell to governments and to philanthropic organisations. The role of the League with regard to the Jewish refugees from Germany remained very restricted, even after the Nazi government had withdrawn from the organisation.

However modest the League's efforts and practice may seem in the light of contemporary handling of refugee issues, they did require basic distinctions and definitions. After the First World War, in a world that now universally required passports and administrative approval of varied kinds for foreigners to work and to enjoy benefits, refugees were non-persons. They usually had no valid legal identification. The governments from which they had fled were generally unprepared to offer help. Refugees were not even able to prove, for instance, that they were married or the children of those claiming to be their parents, for to obtain such proofs from outside the country in question generally requires the services of a consulate of one's country of origin; as a rule such services would neither be requested nor offered. Nor could a refugee simply travel farther, for without valid documents he would be unable to obtain legal admission to another country. And in his place of asylum, whether the first or a later one, he usually had no legal right to accept employment and was forced to be a burden on someone else. Host governments often declined to carry such burdens unless prior arrangements had been made; they generally failed to facilitate such arrangements.

Following initiatives by the International Committee of the Red Cross and Dr Fridtjof Nansen, Norwegian political leader and Arctic explorer, who in 1921 became the first High Commissioner for

Refugees, the League took steps which resulted in practical legal protection specifically for Russian refugees. This programme broke the necessary legal ground for future developments. League activities after Nansen's death in 1930 added incrementally to the growing body of legal and political practice. These efforts involved the political act of persuading governments to register refugees who could not be returned to their homelands and to provide them with valid legal documents for additional travel or residence in a country of present refuge, often that of first asylum. Equipped with such documents, refugees were able to become self-sufficient and also to travel to a country of ultimate resettlement. While such documents were issued as a result of international agreements, the actual administrative actions remained a responsibility of governments, not of any international agency. International functionaries appointed in one or another manner as a result of decisions by the League were able only to observe the application of the international agreements by governments, to persuade more governments to adhere to the agreements and to propose alterations, improvements and extensions.[2] Thus, the international machinery had primarily political and technical functions but very restricted executive tasks.

Given the primitive nature of international facilities for dealing with refugees at the beginning of the League's efforts, the results were substantial. Yet there was anything but an enthusiastic adoption of its proposals. 'The more binding and comprehensive the nature of the agreements,' Louise Holborn notes, 'the fewer tended to be the states which ratified them'.[3] Her survey shows that only eight governments ratified the comprehensive convention on international status for refugees, recommended in 1933 to fill out the previous agreement of 1922 on documents for Russian refugees, to which 56 governments had adhered. A convention on the status of refugees coming from Germany, proposed in 1938, obtained only three ratifications.

The outbreak of war in 1939 virtually eliminated the League as an effective supervisor of legal protection for refugees. Even before then, however, President Franklin Roosevelt had proposed an international conference on refugees, which convened in Évian-les-Bains, France, in 1938. It created an Inter-governmental Committee on Refugees (IGCR) as an instrument to deal with the flight of political and Jewish refugees from Germany and Austria and to seek their resettlement. Its work could scarcely have begun under more forbidding circumstances, for the barriers to immigration — a matter for decision by national governments — had been strengthened during the Great Depression and by the political suspicion that was a hallmark of the time of Fascist governments. In 1943, the scope of the IGCR was broadened to include refugees from the Spanish Civil War and also those whose flight resulted from the then raging global war. The IGCR co-operated with voluntary agencies that operated underground railways for Jewish escapees during the war. Only a pitiful four thousand Jews thus were helped to safety. IGCR also worked with the League of Nations High Commissioner for Refugees until the ghostly functions of that organisation came to an end in 1946, when IGCR took over some of the remaining responsibilities for protection. It also chartered three ships to be used for a gigantic expansion in operations. Nevertheless, the IGCR never became a powerhouse of assistance and protection, though its member governments never expected it to do so. Indeed, its very existence owed something to the willingness of governments to tuck the problem of refugees somewhere out of sight. IGCR's record was therefore one of preserving the skills of the past more than of expanding to meet the needs of the present.

The first UN efforts for refugees

The first of the post-war institutions of what later became the United Nations system was created by many of the same governments which had been content to keep IGCR within modest bounds. The new agency, intended to bring relief to the liberated territories, was the UN Relief and Rehabilitation Administration (UNRRA).[4] It was established in November 1943 by 44 governments. A major part of its anticipated work had to do with displaced persons, not refugees with political fears. Its origins can be found in intergovernmental planning exercises that began as early as 1942, and in emergency relief programmes for liberated areas that the British and American governments undertook as the African campaigns during 1942 brought their forces into contact with uprooted people. UNRRA was designed as a temporary agency and obviously had short-term tasks to perform in caring for those people left adrift by the retreat of the Germans and their allies. It had no mandate to give aid to nationals of enemy states. Its most important sphere of operation was Europe, although it had a Far Eastern operation.

UNRRA possessed many of the characteristics of the functional agencies later to be created within the UN system. It had its own membership list, an international civil service headed by a Director-General who was responsible for its work, supervisory commissions and a periodic general meeting of all members for the purpose of laying down its general policies. Its budget was shared among the members, although in practice by far the largest contribution came from the United States, the only one that had sufficient resources. In fact, the organisation owed a great deal to American initiatives, as did the entire UN system. UNRRA remained responsive to Washington's demands, which nevertheless sometimes could not be satisfied. The Director-General was always an American, first the former governor and senator from New York, Herbert H. Lehman, and later the ebullient former mayor of New York City, Fiorello H. LaGuardia. The operations they directed were guided by a written constitution, approved by all member governments.

Partly because of its conventional design and partly because of its mandate, UNRRA differed considerably from those organisations that were later charged by the UN system with the care of refugees. To begin with, UNRRA only incidentally provided assistance for refugees escaping from untenable political situations. It primarily aided those — the vast majority — who had simply been displaced by the war and its ramifications. Furthermore, UNRRA had no mandate to resettle refugees outside their country of origin; it was expected that displaced persons would be repatriated, and that their dependence on assistance would therefore end. UNRRA took the position that no one should be forced to return to his country of origin, but it did not emphasise legal protection as the basis of its work. If they were anywhere, resettlement and legal protection remained within the province of the IGCR. UNRRA actually had responsibility, which it shared with voluntary organisations that specialised in such tasks, for the operation and management of camps and assembly centres. At one period, these installations numbered several hundred. Displaced persons could depart from them for settlement under other than UNRRA auspices.

UNRRA helped some seven million people return to their homes. This mainly voluntary repatriation followed the pattern that international agencies, beginning with Nansen's effort, had set out as the best possible end to refugee situations. The great wave of repatriation came immediately after the end of fighting in Europe in 1945 and later declined until it became a mere trickle. The pool of the uprooted, however, still did not go dry. Initially some 100,000 people, mainly Eastern European or Soviet nationals, declined offers of repatriation. Then their numbers began to swell. More and more people pushed their way from Eastern Europe, especially to Germany and Austria before the escape routes were sealed by the Soviet authorities. By the beginning of 1946, approximately two million people who sought refuge, not repatriation, were in camps and other temporary quarters. In hope or desperation, there they awaited new homes, often seeking to go to the United States or elsewhere outside Europe. As usual for such populations, life was mean, precarious and filled with psychological pressure. In war-defiled cities and rural areas, some of the life-giving supplies furnished to refugees by UNRRA and other relief organisations became the stuff of black marketeering. It enabled some who depended on relief to increase their own choices, better meeting individual needs, and others simply to profit from misery. As the source of some supplies, UNRRA received strong criticism when journalists and other observers described what was happening as scandalous. Furthermore, some UNRRA employees were corrupted by what they saw as the chance to make an easy profit.

The occasional scandal could be understood in retrospect as the concomitant of the social confusion and disintegration caused by war. At the time, this was one of several elements that were seized on by critics of UNRRA, particularly in the United States. As UNRRA's principal originator and donor, the United States and its public had a special importance. Its government, however, hardly had a clear view of the future of displaced persons and refugees, partly because the vacillating but generally forbidding American policy on pre-war refugees for the most part endured. Furthermore, UNRRA included the Soviet Union, which would not let the organisation operate in its German zone and sought the forced repatriation of its nationals wherever they were. Earlier UNRRA operations in territories under Soviet control had been so strictly limited as to be unsatisfactory to the agency's leadership. In addition, the financial contributions by the United States were enormous when seen within the cramped framework of American experience with international agencies or in comparison with donations of other states. Finally, numerous pressure groups, some of them of Eastern European origin, made UNRRA the butt of their dissatisfactions with temporary assistance, repatriation and immigration. Despite impassioned pleas for continued work and even a broader mandate for UNRRA by Director-General LaGuardia, the Truman administration decided to withdraw its support, to treat UNRRA's temporary mission as largely fulfilled and to handle refugee affairs in a different manner. Not all members of UNRRA agreed completely or even mainly with the American decision, but it prevailed. UNRRA ceased operations in mid-1947.

An operating agency for refugees

Out of UNRRA's experience emerged two main issues with regard to refugees. First, how could the problem of supported refugees be liquidated? UNRRA had in effect cleared the camps of displaced persons who had either to be repatriated or helped to return to homes elsewhere in the country where they were given assistance. This legacy of the war was thus dealt with; it suggested that the remnant refugees could also be dealt with as a short-term measure. Second, how could the rights of refugees be protected and a system developed which would allow them to find places in society? The UNRRA leadership had responded to American and Western European moral precepts by formally refusing to repatriate those who did not want to leave. With some unhappy exceptions,[5] this policy was executed. But the inmates of the camps, the new refugees of that era, were still unable either to travel or to settle on a permanent basis without having a base in the form of some legal regime from which to ease their way back into society. IGCR was supposed to provide such protection, but in fact was hardly capable of doing so. Accordingly, it was dissolved along with UNRRA.

As a result of British and American initiative, the first session of the new UN General Assembly in 1946 took up these issues, seeking an organisational route to resolving them. After a study by the Economic and Social Council and a special committee, the General Assembly decided at the end of 1946 to establish within the UN framework another temporary agency which, unlike UNRRA, would have a direct mandate to care for and assist refugees. This new body, the International Refugee Organization,[6] received 30 votes in its favour when its constitution came before the General Assembly. It was a mark of the limited popularity of refugee issues that 18 governments abstained and five (the Soviet group) opposed. An interim agreement continued the care offered by UNRRA until the IRO came into official existence on 20 August 1948. Only 18 states became members of IRO, and of these one, Switzerland, declined to join the United Nations. Four of the five permanent members of the Security Council joined the IRO, but, apart from China, no Asian state did so. Only three Latin American governments were represented; the remaining members were the smaller Western European countries plus Australia, New Zealand

and Canada. The United States — by far the largest donor — and the United Kingdom together contributed some 60 per cent of the budget.

Because IRO was designed in the light of the two main immediate post-war refugee issues and because its work was limited to refugees, it combined past experience with a present need to develop a sophisticated approach to its task. Its subjects — unlike the majority of displaced persons in 1945 — were rather widely scattered over the face of the earth. Not counting refugees in the Far East, some one-and-a-half million persons were capable of inclusion in the IRO mandate. The majority, however, were in Germany (except for the eastern, Soviet-occupied zone, which IRO was unable to enter), Austria and Italy. Certain others were in places as far afield as Kenya and India, while a group of Russians and Jews were stranded in Shanghai. Some 30 original nationalities were represented. Their prospects individually and as a group were hardly to be defined, but the presence of the countries of greatest immigration among the IRO membership hinted at an implied promise. At the same time, the United Kingdom had progressively narrowed the oppor-tunity for legal immigration into Palestine, the League of Nations mandate which it still administered, in reaction to a growing influx of Jewish war survivors.

IRO's mandate carefully avoided permanent obligations for governments. To begin with, IRO was given only three years of life; this was later extended by a further eighteen months. IRO worked under the direction of a policy-making body from which an executive committee of member-states was drawn. To this committee, a Director-General, J. Donald Kingsley, an American ex-professor, reported frequently and had responsibility for a staff which at its most numerous exceeded 2,800. Both the international civil servants and the governmental representatives within the General Council and the Executive Committee kept the notion of a temporary agency constantly in mind. IRO was also implicitly limited by the lack of any comprehensive set of legal arrangements with regard to refugees. It had inherited from the League and IGCR certain undertakings on the part of governments, but these related either to distinct groups of refugees or to certain persons able to demonstrate that they were stateless, which was not necessarily the case with most refugees. Yet because the agency was a temporary one, there was little incentive for either IRO or the supporting governments to use it as a forum for exploring wider permanent legal protections. It did, however, ask the UN Commission on Human Rights for action to give legal protection to stateless persons and thus engaged the mechanism of the Economic and Social Council.

IRO operations were indeed designed to conform to a short-term pattern. The organisation's main functions were those of assisting refugees to maintain their lives and then finding places of settlement for them. It had behind it a widespread sympathy on the part of its member countries for those thousands who had suffered during the war or fled from what they considered a repressive political system in the Soviet zones of Eastern Europe. The growing tension of the Cold War both dramatised the existence of large numbers of refugees and smoothed the way to their resettlement. In addition, the low population growths of Western Europe pushed up demands for certain categories of skill, as did the economic expansion of countries of overseas settlement such as Canada and Australia. Such background factors aided IRO in finding suitable operating methods. It was in fact the first agency to 'approach the refugee problem in all its phases'.[7]

Continuing agencies for refugees

However comprehensive IRO may have been, its supporting governments sought less, not better, involvement with refugee issues. Consequently, they pushed aside the opportunity offered by IRO's demise to incorporate its experience in a permanent, central, operating institution. Instead, using the machinery of the United Nations, they rescued some bits and pieces of IRO practice while allowing others to disappear. From the rubble was constructed, slowly and at irregular intervals, the present transnational structure for dealing with refugees. This tends to centre around the United Nations High Commissioner for Refugees.[8]

The original design for this intergovernmental office rested firmly on the notion of legal protection for refugees. This was no novelty, for its roots reached back to the Nansen office in the League of Nations and subsequent practice. The creation of the Office of High Commissioner was coupled with the drafting of the United Nations Convention on Refugees,[9] a multinational treaty that set out the obligation of acceding states with regard to refugees. In general, both the creation of the office and the recommendation of the convention by the UN General Assembly to governments assumed that refugees would occasionally and in relatively small numbers come into sight only on the edges of governmental agendas. The marginal character of governmental concern with refugees was emphasised by omitting any provision in the Statute of the Office of the High Commissioner for operations. They were left to governments.[10] The High Commissioner was thus able to serve as the guardian of the rights of refugees and as the promoter of further accessions to the Convention but had no authority to establish the camps and transportation systems that IRO had operated.

Although IRO had done its job well enough to reduce drastically camp populations and substantially the numbers of dependent refugees, some thousands yet remained. For part of this remnant, settlement in a third country was available. To provide for their transportation, some of the IRO-supporting governments created another agency quite outside the United Nations structure. This was the Intergovernmental Committee for European Migration (ICEM),[11] whose very title indicated a strong difference in approach from that of IRO. The remaining refugee departures would be merged for settlement outside Europe with a flow of emigrants whose skills were superfluous to the damaged European economies and were travelling to countries of immigration that welcomed their capacities. ICEM was then given duties that reached beyond IRO's concern with refugees. As for those refugees, such as the incurably infirm or insane, for whom resettlement was either difficult or impossible, UNHCR was able to offer them some help, based partly on the liquidation of remaining IRO resources, until governments took over the responsibility.

Thus by 1951, the large-scale programmes for refugees and displaced persons that the prosecution of the war and its aftermath had called into being had been completely overhauled. In place of central operating agencies came a decentralised system. Legal protection of the rights of refugees rested on a new treaty that was separated from operations. What there was of the latter was to be kept outside the United Nations structure and related only to emigration from Europe. The scale of international concern was unmistakeably reduced by the UN General Assembly.

This reformed institutionalisation embodied not only the earlier legal approaches of the League of Nations but also the political sensitivities of the world following the Second World War. In seeking the dissolution of UNRRA, the United States reflected the growing Soviet-American animosity. The United States wanted to eliminate the Soviet voice from refugee policy, to prevent the forcible repatriation of displaced persons and refugees to the Soviet Union and to cut off the dribble of economic aid to the USSR that

UNRRA provided. As the IRO represented principles — such as free choice by individuals as to emigration — that the Soviet Union rejected, it also had some tint of the Cold War.[12] The Soviet Union nevertheless remained a member of the United Nations and able to criticise the handling of refugee issues. But the establishment of ICEM beyond the reach of the United Nations meant that the excluded Soviet Union would have no voice in matters of migration from Western Europe, whether or not refugees or displaced persons were among the emigrants. The UN Convention on Refugees emerged from the American-led policy process of the United Nations. During the deliberations, the Soviet Union made clear its determined opposition to the draft document: it would never accede to such a treaty. As for UNHCR, the Soviet Union also opposed its establishment but was unable to summon the support necessary to prevent it. UNHCR was intended to have only a limited task — connected with the Convention — and a minuscule budget. The Soviet Union would not be able to find in the new structures the dramatic, large-scale material needed for the building of an organised opposition. In fact, during the years of the Cold War the United States and its allies succeeded in excluding the Soviet Union from any significant influence on the international treatment of refugee affairs.

Conceptual bases

The drafting of the Convention on Refugees and the establishment of UNHCR reaffirmed the principle, already adopted in the creation of IRO, that the international responsibilities for general relief and protection of refugees would be limited in both time and place. The Convention expressly confined its attention to refugees in Europe who claimed asylum before 1951. UNHCR could therefore possibly show an interest, as a matter of administrative discretion, in refugees generally but could not claim the legal authority to take up the cause of refugees unconnected with Europe or, in essence, with the Second World War and its aftermath. The mandate of UNHCR actually had broader overtones, but it could hardly be claimed that the UN General Assembly intended to create an administrative agency whose concern would be refugees and displaced persons in general. The minuscule budget provided for the UN High Commissioner re-emphasised the point.[13] Furthermore, the High Commissioner at first received no authority to raise funds on his own. As for duration, the new office was initially established for three years: either the phenomenon of refugees would decline to a level that needed little international attention or else the office would fail and simply be allowed to disappear.

Even more fundamental limitations were inherent in the new regime as a result of both national policies and the nature of international politics. No government has ever shown itself eager to surrender authority over immigration. Some governments, such as those of the United States and the United Kingdom, have had to deal with immigration policies as leading issues in national political life. The experience with refugees and displaced persons after the Second World War demonstrated the expediency of resettlement as a means of coping with accumulations of refugees. But resettlement means that refugees become immigrants. Granting general rights to refugees or allowing a large number of people formally to become refugees could thus diminish national control over immigration policies. Therefore, governments approached refugee matters with some tentativeness and showed a clear resistance to handing over even minor decisions to an international agency. As a result. the Convention enables a person outside his own country to enter a claim to a government for asylum but gives him no right to it. The rights of refugees are based in the first instance on protection from being sent into danger or persecution, either in their original homes or in a third country. Thus, the doctrine of *non-refoulement* to protect refugees may promote the granting of long-term asylum but does not ensure it. Governments acceding to the Convention maintain their authority over immigration and nationality.

Furthermore, protection for refugees derives legally from a multilateral treaty. This document is binding only on states that ratify it. They execute its provisions. They make their own specific, executive decisions with regard to what is done and for whom. As governments usually respect their international legal obligations — and any treaty embodies obligations — the Convention certainly has real significance for asylum-seekers and for other governments. The UN High Commissioner can make representations on behalf of refugees and try to convince governments to carry out their obligations according to a specific pattern that he sets out or to improve existing practices. Nevertheless it is governments that bear the ultimate responsibility. Moreover, they can decide to abandon the legal obligations designed to protect refugees. However much the decisions by the United Nations may appear to centralise the handling of refugees, the ways in which individual cases are determined remain decentralised.

Consonant with the political and systemic limitations giving tone to the new arrangements, the definition of a refugee adopted in the Convention and repeated in the Statute of the Office of High Commissioner was also a narrow one. Geographical and temporal limitations apart, the Convention defined a refugee as someone outside his country of nationality, unprotected by his own government and having a well-founded fear of persecution on political, religious or racial grounds should he return.[14] A person fitting this definition had legal protection against *refoulement*. The definition effectively excluded attention to persecuted individuals who were still in their own country: they need to have escaped their tormentors in order to be of international concern under the Convention and Statute. Usually a person who flees his homeland out of fear of persecution neither seeks nor is offered protection by his own government. This provision is therefore probably always of secondary importance in determining the status of an asylum-seeker.

Whether the fear that usually is demonstrated by asylum-seekers is well founded remains a crucial question. The answer has psychological, legal, political and administrative dimensions. The refugee who tries to demonstrate that his safety would be endangered if he were returned to his homeland has little access to supporting information; only his word and the conviction of his claim provide initial support. Thus, the test of a well-founded fear relates to the nature of the refugee's perception of danger. Such a perception may or may not be shared by those who have to decide on asylum. The political elements of decisions on persecution are linked to the question of how openly a receiving state wishes to criticise the behavior of the refugee-producing government. Such a decision also necessarily relates to internal political settings and controversies, interest groups and social values. Conceivably, those engaged in controversy over such issues will place high values on the protection of forced migrants; yet they may not do so, preferring to support such other aims as a cordial relationship with a refugee-producing government or limitations on the immigration of persons from specific countries or of certain religions or colours, whether or not they openly admit it.

Formal refugee status involves benefits for the individual concerned and also imposes certain responsibiliities. The certified refugee acquires the legal right to travel documents, which usually includes the right to return to the country of first asylum. He is given the legal right to reside in the land of asylum. The opportunity for education and training within the national framework is open to the refugee. Other social services, such as medical care, are also extended. In order that the refugee may become self-sufficient, he may enter the labour market on at least the same terms as other foreigners. If he works, he pays taxes; but given the sensitivity of some labour unions and other groups to foreign workers, the importance of this sign of normal social participation may be brushed aside for political reasons. At the same time, refugees may have to depend on financial and other support from the asylum-giving government and in many instances from UNHCR for a considerable period of adjustment. This expectation does not differ from the social provisions made in many countries for those workers who are displaced from their normal employment as the result of the government's economic policies or market operations.

The role of UNHCR is conceived in the Statute of the Office as primarily diplomatic and bureaucratic. Its diplomatic function depends fundamentally on the Convention, which the office is instructed to promote and supervise, and on the Statute adopted by the General Assembly. The High Commissioner is nominated by the UN Secretary-General, appointed by the General Assembly and is formally part of the UN Secretariat. As an international civil servant, the High Commissioner depends on the General Assembly for instructions and in principle can set out little in the way of an independent policy. He and his subordinates can, however, discuss particular cases with governments and have a specific instruction to promote accessions to the Statute. As a bureaucratic organisation, UNHCR prepares reports to the Economic and Social Council and through it to the General Assembly. It keeps the records of its own work and maintains contacts with other organisations, including non-governmental agencies. It also responds to government requests for information and posts officials to the field to represent the common standard for refugees. In an initial conceptual sense, UNHCR figures as only one part of the international civil service.

Explicit but not sharply defined limits set out in the UN documents of the early 1950s affect both the diplomatic and bureaucratic functions. The Office is instructed to base its work on humanitarian concerns; in other words, it is directed to exclude political activities. Precisely how actions undertaken to give succour to persons suffering from the results of political acts can always be understood as non-political is nowhere explained. Nor is it clear that persuading governments to accede to the Convention can be classed as a humanitarian action, even though the outcome may be beneficial to refugees.

The limitation on the bureaucratic functions of the Office was originally stated as a prohibition against operations and a denial of authority to appeal to governments for money. If it is assumed that the natural tendency of a supervisory organisation would be to step into operational breaches, this conceptual dimension sharply restricts bureaucratic development. It also raises questions, just as the restriction on political activity does, as to where the precise boundaries lie. In fact, both of these conceptual limitations proved highly elastic.

Functional expansion

The stretching of the conceptual limitations depended both on the perceived needs of governments and the readiness of bureaucratic responses. If governments deliberately designed UNHCR and its parallel organisation, ICEM, in a narrow manner, they did so presumably because they saw little need, or felt only avoidable pressure, to support wider services and because they sought to reduce their responsibilities to refugees and to a broader community of states. These policies were designed by national bureaucracies which had every reason to be aware of the tendency for organisations to seek to improve their performances by means of structural growth. The policies hardly fitted the concrete context of international affairs as it developed during the succeeding years.

To begin with, refugee populations did not disappear as a result of resettlement overseas or absorption in place in Europe. As for the refugees from Palestine, their fate depended on a political settlement between Israel and her neighbours;[15] it lay farther away with each advancing year, and local absorption was for the most part prevented by host governments. In such circumstances, the international bureaucracies necessarily sought to convince governments that assistance and camps had to continue. Given their past claims of humanitarian intentions, many governments no doubt found it easier to accede to the proposals of the international staffs than to pay the price of scorn from other governments and from domestic interest groups, including sections of their own bureaucracies. Furthermore, the first UN High Commissioner, G.J. van Heuven Goedhart, a Dutch activist, took his job seriously and did his best to create publicity and support for protection for refugees. He quickly found it possible, moreover, to raise some non-governmental money through a grant from the Ford Foundation in the United States for training and other projects related to resettlement. UNHCR was awarded the Nobel Prize for Peace in 1955, an honour that brought with it more publicity. Meantime, a steady — if thin — stream of refugees continued to flow out of Eastern Europe and to get attention from a broad public in Western Europe and North America. Migrations, such as the large-scale departures from East Germany to the Federal Republic, were handled as national matters but had wide transnational implications.

Events in Eastern Europe encouraged the first burst of expansion in the international handling of refugees after the limiting decisions of the early 1950s. In 1953, the riots in East Berlin and in 1961 the construction of the Berlin Wall by the East German government provided a clear demonstration, if one were needed, of the explosive pressures that existed in Eastern Europe. Three years later, the revolt in Hungary and its suppression by Soviet military forces was accompanied by the first mass exodus to be treated strictly as a refugee incident. Some quarter-million Hungarians, including whole families as well as solitary individuals, poured over the border into Austria in particular, and into Yugoslavia. These fugitives claimed to be seeking freedom from political oppression, an oppression of which Western governments had earlier openly complained. Whether the emigrés would have been persecuted on their return could perhaps have been questioned, but it was certain that the Hungarian government had earlier dealt with political dissidents in a tough manner that violated procedural civil rights as described in the UN Universal Declaration of Human Rights of 1948.[16] Furthermore, a Soviet military force had control of the country and could hardly be expected to welcome the fugitives — who claimed to oppose both the Soviet presence and its political methods — back to their homes. In addition, the Western countries and especially the United States had earlier provided asylum for large numbers of fugitives from Communist-governed countries. The Hungarian refugees, whose humanitarian needs were unquestionable, also fortuitously fitted an ideological pattern acceptable to asylum-givers.

In this context, the UN High Commissioner for Refugees took strong initiatives in organising assistance and then permanent asylum for the Hungarians. This leadership was — somewhat opportunistically — welcomed and urged on by the United States and the Western governments. Most of the small staff of the High Commissioner's office were veterans of the post-war refugee programmes.

They quickly reactivated the networks of voluntary agencies which had served earlier and mobilised experienced personnel. The Austrian government was equally active and sympathetic. Within days, the refugees had a safe margin of food and shelter. Within a few weeks, the first groups proceeded to permanent resettlement, most of them in the United States, whose government found an exceptional legal means of admitting them as immigrants. The Soviet Union thundered against this activity on the part of an agency of the United Nations, but it achieved nothing more than publicity for the claims of the Hungarian fugitives. Later, the Hungarian government publicly expressed its gratitude for the activities of UNHCR on behalf of its countrymen.

From the time of the Hungarian refugees onwards, the notion that the United Nations and other intergovernmental organisations, together with voluntary agencies of many kinds should be concerned with refugees has never faded, even if it has only occasionally figured high on the international political agenda. UNHCR has been engaged in helping refugees from Algeria in North Africa, Chinese and Westerners in Hong Kong, displaced persons in Cyprus, Angolans in Zaïre, Zaïreans in Sudan, Ethiopians of several national backgrounds in the Horn of Africa, Sudanese in Ethiopia and Uganda, Ugandans in neighbouring countries, Afghans in Pakistan, Nicaraguans and Guatemalans in Mexico, Chileans in Spain, Cubans in the United States, Vietnamese in China and Thailand and Bangladeshi in India, among others. Each of these incidents contained by now familiar elements. Some persons who claimed protection as refugees were denied that status, while others whose claims were controversial achieved it. Some refugees received rations and medical care in camps, and others received a small dole disbursed by a government or UNHCR office. When travel to new homelands was needed, ICEM sometimes joined in the process. Voluntary agencies raised small funds on their own, but many of them who took on the major tasks of operating camps, preparing refugees for moves to new homes as legal migrants or return to their own countries or caring for the education of the young and the retraining of adults worked on contracts from UNHCR. The local governments continued to bear the main legal responsibility for the refugees within their borders, while taxpayers in distant lands supported their own governments' contributions. By 1981, UNHCR had budgets as large as $500 million, mostly made up of governmental contributions, for which the High Commissioner by then was allowed to appeal directly. In the Middle East, however,

35

UNRWA could neither expand its work nor liquidate its woefully long client list. Its budget declined in real terms and in other respects over the years, and it made no telling contribution to the politics of the Israeli area, even if its training programmes did furnish at least some skilled personnel to the several Palestinian nationalist movements that made so heavy an impression on Israeli opinion and Lebanese politics.

The historical record can thus be summed up — with the partial exception of UNRWA — as one of unbroken expansion of functions on behalf of refugees. This expansion took place in terms of geographical location, numbers and variety of services offered. The nature of the expansion can be seen from bureaucratic constructions employed by UNHCR. The handful of lawyers specialising in legal protection have long since been overshadowed in number by the bureau concerned with assistance to refugees.[17] This far outstrips every other in expenditures. Moreover, UNHCR has built up a formidable money-raising capacity. Its officials now benefit from advance planning for emergency intervention in a refugee crisis, and the directorate in Geneva can despatch people to the field at short notice. Its 90 branch offices girdle the earth, underlining the extent of refugee activity.

Conceptual expansion

The expansion of concrete functions on behalf of refugees was accompanied by a series of changes and adjustments in the conceptual basis for transnational co-operation. Crises and reactions to them impelled the process of change; so did efforts on the part of bureaucracies and their leaders to rationalise their practices and set out explicit — and preferably more liberal — provisions governing their work. The formal expansion of the earlier conceptual foundations for the handling of refugees thus involved a series of decisions of a political nature. These political elements included choices of policies by governments, by international organisations and by other parts of the refugee network. These policies sometimes provided for the placing of limitations on the behaviour of national governments and the creation of obligations under international law. They also comprised asymmetrically mutual but influential relationships among officials of international, national and private transnational organisations. Thus, however much the eventual policies may have borne on humanitarian needs, they nevertheless depended on choices made from among several claims. The fact that choices made by governments and others had a significant quality is implied by the size of contributions for refugee programmes.

The conceptual expansion proceeded along related lines. The first of these had to do with the scope of concern of UNHCR and the time span for its existence. The second related to the legal definition of refugees and their protection in international law. A third line had to do with finances and internal operations. Little of this expansion took place without some controversy, and all of it was affected by crises that either produced refugees or placed persons in similar circumstances.

Private transnational organisations concerned with refugees had generally extended their concern to a wider group of asylum-seekers than did UNHCR. Thus, the most remarkble broadening of the scope of concern occurred at the intergovernmental level.

The extension of the life of UNHCR after its first three-year term signalled the initial step towards accepting concern with refugees as a permanent task of international organisations. This action on the part of the UN General Assembly followed the successful participation of UNHCR in helping Hungarian refugees of 1956. The Assembly underlined the conceptual change with regard to the Office by abandoning the three-year limit on its authorisation in favour of five years. Since then, each prolongation of UNHCR has taken place with only slight opposition and a great deal of praise from representatives to the General Assembly.

The extremely limited capacity for financing UNHCR that the UN General Assembly originally adopted also began to crumble under the impact of the flood of Hungarian refugees. It became clearer than ever that the European camps could not simply be cleared despite the progressive resettlement of the remaining IRO clients. The High Commissioner was authorised to appeal to governments for material support and to establish an emergency fund. This authorisation paved the way to appeals for funds on a large scale, compared to anything sought earlier.

The geographical limitation of UNHCR's concern to Europe also began to weaken after the Hungarian episode. The first expansion related to European and Chinese refugees who were left without support in Hong Kong. It was followed by provision of services by UNHCR to refugees from the war in Algeria. In both cases, the High Commissioner took the lead. He informed the General Assembly of the plight of the people involved and sought formal instructions, which he suggested, to assist them. The General

Assembly kept the old geographical limitation but as an exceptional matter directed UNHCR to undertake the programme that the High Commissioner proposed. Both these incidents highlighted a conceptual anomaly in the framework designed by the General Assembly in 1950. The Convention, which created legal obligations on the states that acceded, had to do with refugees caused by events in Europe before 1951. The Statute of UNHCR, which was not a treaty but a recommendation to governments by the General Assembly and an instruction to the UN Secretariat, contained a broader definition of refugees who would be of concern to the office. To those who met the Convention's strict criteria with regard to time and place, it added all those others who were outside their country of nationality as a result of a well-founded fear of persecution. Thus UNHCR had the duty of protecting all refugees from persecution, even if states undertook no legal obligations in that regard. UNHCR was in the curious position of promoting accessions to a Convention whose scope of concern was narrower than that of the constitutional document of the Office.

Nor did the Convention fit the emerging configuration of the post-war world. The steady emergence of new groups of refugees — especially in Africa and Latin America during the late 1950s and early 1960s — underlined how inadequate the scope of the Convention was. Successive High Commissioners began to take up this shortcoming with governments and, following a series of consultations and meetings both within and outside the UN structure, a draft of a new protocol to the Convention was placed by the High Commissioner before the General Assembly with a recommendation from the Economic and Social Council. It was adopted in late 1966 and came into force in October 1967 for those states that acceded to it.[18] In essence, the Protocol of 31 January 1967 eliminated from the Convention, for those states that agreed, the limitations with regard to time and place in the definition of refugees. Moreover, it provided for the automatic accession to the Convention of those states which agreed only to the Protocol and also included some clarifications with regard to federal states. This latter set of provisions made it possible to overcome earlier objections from the United States to the Convention. The document was widely accepted and therefore effectively broadened the scope of protection of refugees to all persons anywhere with a well-founded fear of persecution who were outside their own countries. It eliminated the anomaly in the relationship between the Statute of UNHCR and the Convention and lent much greater force to the application of the doctrine of *non-refoulement*.

Even so, large numbers of asylum-seekers were excluded from the purview of UNHCR and could come to the notice of the United Nations system only through the fragmented net of concern with human rights generally. But that conceptual restrictiveness did nothing to make the presence of people in flight from their homes any less painful to themselves or any less noticeable. The refugees in Hong Kong and those in North Africa as a result of the Algerian revolt against France had offered an opportunity to stretch the limitations contained in the definition of refugees. In both cases, the political context militated against treating the asylum-seekers as refugees in the classic sense of victims of persecution. China and France would brook no accusations that they persecuted their subjects, and at the time few governments were prepared to support such a claim openly. Yet the people involved resembled refugees in all but formal ways and needed help. In these circumstances, the High Commissioner let it be known that he was prepared to help if he were given the authority to do so. In the same action that permitted UNHCR to deal with the refugees in Hong Kong — despite their location outside Europe — the General Assembly asked the High Commissioner to 'use his good offices' to arrange aid for the asylum-seekers in Hong Kong. This 'good offices' formula provided new conceptual elasticity in the definition of refugees. High Commissioner Lindt used it on his own initiative to bring assistance to refugees from Algeria and only later obtained an explicit sanction from the General Assembly. By 1959, the General Assembly had accepted the idea that 'good offices' might be employed to assist refugees who did not fit the definition of the Covenant. The same formula was later applied in the case of Angolans in Zaïre and elseswhere.

In another respect, the High Commissioner successfully sought to broaden his authority so as to assist persons claiming to be refugees. The wording of the Covenant and the Statute, with its emphasis on a 'well-founded fear of persecution', could be taken to imply that a separate investigation had to be made into the circumstances of each person seeking asylum before UNHCR could offer him assistance and provide full protection. But refugees began to appear in masses, especially during the decolonisation process in Africa. UNHCR responded by accepting prima facie evidence of refugee status for large groups, basing its practice on the precedent of the Hungarian refugees. If individual determinations were needed, they could be made later.

A further stretching of the original concepts developed around the 'good offices' approach. The UNHCR began to seek means of extending the legal protection to persons given assistance under 'good offices' programmes. Refugees granted status under the Convention could be given travel documents and permitted to seek employment, education and other benefits in their countries of refuge with the backing of UNHCR and on the basis of legal right where the Convention was in force. Others assisted by UNHCR had no such rights. Nevertheless, the High Commissioner began campaigning early in the sixties for an end to this sharp distinction with regard to legal protection for the Convention and 'good offices' categories. Although the legal reasoning involved much sophistication, the plain intention was to enlarge the conceptual range of UNHCR's activity.

Closely related to the good offices concept is the broadening of the concern of UNHCR to 'refugee-like' situations. These may involve persons who are displaced in their own country or who otherwise do not obviously fit the Convention's definition. Yet in other respects they resemble refugees, fleeing possible or actual persecution possibly in addition to war or social upheaval.

The clearest instance of such expansion can be seen in the response to the large-scale displacement of Greek inhabitants of Cyprus during the fighting of 1974, after a *coup d'état* against the government of President Makarios and the subsequent invasion by a force from Turkey. Greek-speakers numbering several tens of thousands fled from their villages. In the circumstances, Secretary-General Kurt Waldheim, who had responsibility for the UN peacekeeping forces on the island, asked High Commissioner Sadruddin Aga Khan to co-ordinate assistance to displaced persons. An appeal to governments, following the High Commissioner's inspection of the situation, raised $20 million at once. The General Assembly specifically referred to the people assisted as refugees.[19]

A similar co-ordinative role involving displaced persons had earlier been undertaken by UNHCR in connection with the disintegration of East Pakistan and the formation of Bangladesh in 1971.[20] While this was an immense operation, many of the refugees had crossed the border to India and were arguably encompassed by the UN Convention on Refugees. In the case of Cyprus the displaced persons actually remained on their home island.

The global conceptual basis for defining refugees was surpassed in breadth, if not in the scope of actual operations, by states co-operating in the Organization for African Unity. This regional redefinition relied on advice and participation from UNHCR as well as five years of consultations among African governments. Thus, the global and the African regional systems for assisting and protecting refugees were closely linked. The result was the OAU Refugee Convention of 1969,[21] which generally follows the UN Convention but in one important respect far surpasses its range. It adds to the definition of refugees in the Convention those persons who, 'owing to external aggression, occupation, foreign domination or events seriously disturbing public order' in the home country are compelled to flee abroad. This broadening of the definition of refugees with regard to Africa, in a Convention which is in force, anticipated important causes of massive displacements of people in several actual refugee situations. The broader concept has also received favourable attention from many international officials concerned with refugees; they regard it as something of a model for the future expansion of formal definitions.

The widening scope of concern for refugee situations on the part of the organised international community never overcame the restrained positions of governments. To begin with, the Convention still has far less than universal acceptance. The Protocol did help to broaden the engagement of states, but even as late as 1984 more than 50 governments remained outside the regime. Initiatives by the UN High Commissioner almost always resulted in only recommendatory action by the General Assembly, rather than formal extension of treaty obligations which became part of national legal structures.

In one important instance where UNHCR sought to create new obligations on states, the result was failure. This effort sought a right of asylum, recognised by governments as part of their obligation to refugees. The refugee convention obliged acceding states to avoid *refoulement* and to extend certain benefits; it did not establish any right of asylum or to protection during the time that a government took to make a decision as to whether a claimant were a refugee under the standard definition. In fact, the drafters of the Convention expressly declined to include a right to asylum. Moreover, the Universal Declaration of Human Rights and the Covenants that give it legal effect spoke of a right to leave one's country but not to enter another.[22] Consequently a great deal of uncertainty attended the granting of asylum, even in regions such as Latin America where political asylum has a long history. In order to close this gap in protection, the High Commissioner and his staff spent more than two decades in convincing a series of international deliberative organs to put forward a draft convention on the right of asylum.

Despite the stately procession of meetings, drafts, declarations and consultations, a conference summoned by the General Assembly in 1977 was unable to agree on the draft convention.[23] This document mainly reiterated the doctrine of *non-refoulement* and set out the Convention definition of refugees. It bound the contracting states to use their best endeavors to grant asylum to refugees. Perhaps the most important practical advance could be found in an article providing for a provisional stay, pending a decision on a request for asylum. Such a decision was to be made by a designated, competent authority from which an appeal could be made. Other provisions set out undertakings by governments to co-operate in the event of a massive movement of refugees. Yet these additional protections were too strong to be acceptable to governments. They remained jealous, as always, of any international supervision over decisions that touched on immigration.

Expansion of executive roles

The same reservations that apply to the internationalisation of immigration policy tend to inhibit the formation of a strong bureaucratic structure to deal with refugee problems. At the same time acceptance of, and insistence on, broader international responsibility for specific refugee incidents encourages the growth of organised staffs whose members can cope with the specialised demands that asylum-seekers create. As the air of emergency hangs so heavily over refugee incidents, governments may have to put aside the niceties of national jurisdiction in order to prevent chaos. They also often require outside assistance in the process. Thus, the sheer weight of refugee concerns has led to enhanced roles for senior officials, increased their numbers and made their work more visible.

The push and pull between national reservations and international bureaucratic requirements has resulted in a characteristic role and mode of operation on the part of officials. Striking personal leadership of the kind exercised by Nansen has hardly ever emerged in refugee affairs since the end of the Second World War. The High Commissioners generally work behind the diplomatic scenes, and their staff members try to cope with both emergency situations and the need for policy changes by persuasion at the technical levels of government. For issues requiring directives from the United Nations, the complex, ponderous deliberative mechanism offered international civil servants a standing framework within which to attempt to influence policy in contexts ranging from obscurity to full publicity. At the same time, the modest role planned originally for the High Commissioner underlines the formal subordination of international officials to the decisional committees made up of governmental representatives.

The High Commissioners did take personal initiatives, some of them of real importance. Thus, Van Heuven Goedhart succeeded in expanding the amount of material assistance, Lindt and his successor, Felix Schnyder, undertook deliberate campaigns to stretch the geographical and substantive limits of their office. Sadruddin Aga Khan offered new levels of assistance in refugee-like situations and made little secret of his interest in trying to offer services in connection with selected tense political situations, for instance Cyprus. Poul Hartling presided over the creation of programmes for mass exoduses from Somalia, Afghanistan, Indo-China and Cuba, expanding the size of UNHCR and raising vast amounts of money. These efforts won striking public recognition in the form of two Nobel Peace prizes and other tokens of praise and trust. Yet none of this could be understood as leadership in the form of direct charismatic behaviour or appeals to masses of people. Rather, those to be influenced were governmental officials and ministers, not constituents *en masse*. The form of approach was diplomatic and technical, rather than demagogic and judgemental. And always the High Commissioners insisted that their ideas represented better means of providing humanitarian services rather than political departures.

As for other international organisations dealing with refugees, UNRWA never operated in a political context that favoured much initiative, except in the direction of lowering costs. Budget-cutting perforce followed an insistence on the part of donors on lowering contributions; the UNRWA Agent-General usually had to exercise his ability in making less money do more. ICM meanwhile remained primarily a technical-level agency. Its initiatives took the form of the efficient operation and recruitment of needed skilled immigrants for governments that wished them, rather than as a leader at the policy level. Even when its initiatives were greeted favourably by governments, they were marginal to more important concerns. Its operations and membership gradually diminished. ICM none the less later proved enterprising in developing the technical systems needed to prepare and transport the refugees of the late seventies and early eighties from South-East Asia to new homes.

The non-governmental organisations interested in refugees might conceivably have offered fertile ground for developing popular leadership. Yet none of those that specialise in refugees was large or famous in relation to broader-purpose organisations or governments. For the most part, the voluntary agencies that worked under contracts with UNHCR had functions in other areas of humanitarian or social affairs. The League of Red Cross Societies or Médecins sans Frontières, for example, also sent assistance to those suffering in emergencies quite different from the man-made disasters that overcome refugees. Moreover, none of the organisations was of the size to command immediate attention, except perhaps the Roman Catholic Church together with its various humanitarian bodies. Roman Catholic popes from the end of the Second World War onwards did sometimes speak out on behalf of refugees, but for them the item was only one on a long agenda. Nor did any of the voluntary organisations produce a brilliant leader whose talents could not be ignored by large governments and mass opinion. Rather, the efforts of leaders usually were directed to the membership of organisations that required enthusiastic reactions in order to continue.

Despite the stateliness of the diplomatic quadrille that leads to treaty commitments by governments, initiatives in the field of refugees have in fact produced visible results. These results could not have emerged without the constant attention of international officials whose memories, skills and ambitions gave continuity to the efforts to create a stronger regime. UNHCR, for instance, sponsors elaborate discussions of its initiatives, both in its own informal and formal consultative organs, including the Executive Committee and its sub-committees, and also helps to build coalitions in the General Assembly.[24] The long succession of General Assembly resolutions in commending its efforts signals genuine political success. Such success certainly cannot be understood as assured, for the General Assembly still has to renew the mandate of UNHCR every five years. The UN member governments have ultimate influence on the appointment of the High Commissioner, whatever the wishes of the international bureaucracy may be.

Considerable bureaucratic adroitness has been summoned up by UNHCR as its budget grew so large as to become an issue of serious interest to some governments. The largest donors, including the United States, the United Kingdom, France and the smaller

Western European countries, have occasionally criticised the operation. The United States has closely observed the expansion and has pressed for its own version of more efficient accounting and staff policies. During the major crises of the late seventies and early eighties, the United States maintained a staff of skilled specialists in its mission in Geneva. Their demands for detailed information revealed a willingness to go beyond bland official reports and to submit specific criticisms. Together with that from other governments, this pressure has increased the degree of advance consultation between them and UNHCR. It has given rise to a series of informal meetings with principal donors, not to mention a certain degree of friction. ICM, meanwhile, continued to respond with enthusiasm to American ideas. As the ICM director has always been an American whose candidacy was put forward officially, the liaison is an understandably smooth one. ICM has also developed new bureaucratic confidence as its task has once more expanded, although its initiatives fall within much narrower bounds than those of UNHCR.

Voluntary organisations have also reacted significantly on the bureaucratic plane.[25] They have repeatedly suggested to UNHCR that more consultation in advance of establishing programmes would be helpful and have sometimes criticised the nature of the relationship that has developed. Generally, the voluntary organisations have sought more influence than occasional consultation and formal representation than the meetings of the Executive Committee produce. As a step in the direction of a minimum common position, most of the major agencies have joined the committee on refugees and migration of the International Confederation of Voluntary Agencies in Geneva. Headed by a former UNHCR official, ICVA has actively consulted with intergovernmental agencies and built up a standing communications network in the refugee field. It publishes informative periodicals and has created a computerised data bank. Although none of this will do much to sway a determined government, it can have a significant effect in specific bureaucratic relationships.

Above all, the role of executive staffs in refugee affairs depends on skill, information, memory and willingness to react to needs of governments in refugee issues. In a real sense, the international policies and programmes concerning refugees offer governments a way out of difficulties caused by emergencies and their own lack of competence in issues that cannot be resolved within one national jurisdiction. Nor is the willingness to employ international mechanisms a matter of timely, deliberate advance decisions on the part of governments. In terms of trained officials and fixed procedures, few governments have much capacity to deal with a mass exodus or other kind of refugee emergency. Even a government as large and as well-financed as that of the United States had visible difficulties in dealing with the flood of Cubans who arrived in 1979-80. Thus, the international mechanisms can both fill a void and make national decision-making simpler and less pioneering. By serving in this context, officials dealing with refugees on behalf of transnational organisations have developed a significant influence on general policies. Nevertheless, such policies ultimately depend on the willingness of governments to be persuaded.

Notes

1. For a brief, authoritative account of the League's activities, see Louise W. Holborn, *Refugees: a Problem of Our Time: The Work of the United Nations High Commissioner for Refugees, 1951-1972* 2 vols. (NJ, Methuen, Scarecrow Press, 1975), pp. 3-20.

2. Ibid.

3. Loc. cit.

4. Woodbridge, *The History of UNRWA*; and Holborn, *Refugees*, gives brief account, pp. 23-8.

5. Full accounts of these events, in which more than 2,000,000 war prisoners, refugees, forced labourers and turncoat soldiers were forced back to the Soviet Union are to be found in Nicholas Bethell, *The Last Secret: Forcible Repatriation to Russia 1944-47* (André Deutsch, London, 1974) and Nikolai Tolstoi, *The Silent Betrayal* (Scribner, New York, 1978).

6. For a full account, see Holborn, *The International Refugee Organization*.

7. Holborn, *Refugees*, p. 31.

8. Strictly speaking, the term 'High Commissioner for Refugees' refers to the senior official of the Office of the High Commissioner, while 'the Office' refers to the establishment as a whole. In this study 'UNHCR' refers to the Office, while the full title 'High Commissioner' refers to the individual heading that office.

9. UN Treaty Series no. 2545, vol. 189, p. 137, adopted by the UN Conference of Plenipotentiaries on the Status of Refugees and Stateless Persons on 28 July 1951. It came into force for those states that ratified it on 22 April 1954, hereafter referred to as UN Convention on Refugees.

10. UN General Assembly Resolution 428 (V), 14 December 1950, contains the Statute. Until recently it was a firm doctrine of the Office that it is not operational.

11. ICEM was based on an intergovernmental treaty setting out its structure and purposes. It is therefore not a creature of another international organ (*UN Treaty Series*, vol. 207, p. 189). The limitation of operations to Europe was dropped 20 years later and ICEM became ICM.

12. As the effects of the Cold War spilt over on to all forms of international co-operation, criticisms of the handling of refugee issues by either side emerged in numerous organisational contexts. Holborn, *Refugees*, provides a very brief summary of this contention, p. 58-62. See also Loescher and Scanlan, *Calculated Kindness*, for further evidence of the direct effect of the Cold War on the American policies towards refugees about to immigrate to the United States.

13. The UNHCR budget for 1951 was $254,000 out of a total budget of $47,788, 600, proposed by the Secretary-General for the UN as a whole. *Yearbook of the United Nations* (UN Department of Public Information, New York, 1951), pp. 156-7.

14. The relevant paragraph [A(2)] of the UN Convention on Refugees reads: 'As a result of events occurring before 1 January 1951 and owing to a well-founded fear of being persecuted for reasons of race, religion, nationality, membership of a particular social group or political opinion, is outside the country of his nationality and is unable or, owing to such fear, is unwilling to avail himself of the protection of that country; or now, not having a nationality and being outside the country of his former habitual residence as a result of such events, is unable or, owing to such fear, is unwilling to return to it.' Adherents to the Convention could choose whether the events referred to were those of Europe exclusively or also those elsewhere [paragraph B].

15. David P. Forsythe, 'UNRWA, the Palestine Refugees and World Politics', *International Organization* 25 (winter 1971), pp. 26-45; and Forsythe, 'The Palestine Question: Dealing with a Long-Term Refugee Situation', *The Annals*, 467 (May 1983), pp. 89-101.

16. UN General Assembly Resolution 217 A (III), 10 December 1948.

17. Plans for manning the relevant bureaus of UNHCR make this clear. For 1984-85, the Geneva-based bureau directing and co-ordinating protection was to have 14 professional officers, while the counterpart bureau for assistance planned for 30 professionals. In addition, a large part of the time of a substantial number of the field offices are concerned with assistance, either in the form of substantial programmes involving camps and shelter etc., or as provision of assistance to individual refugees (*Proposed Programme Budget for the Biennium 1984-85*, vol. III, UN General Assembly, Official Records: 38th Session, Supplement no. 6, pp. 18, 22).

18. UN Treaty Series no. 8791, vol. 606, p. 267, adopted by the General Assembly on 16 December 1966.

19. *Yearbook of the United Nations 1974* (UN Office of Public Information, New York, 1976), p. 361. The relevant resolution of the Security Council is 361 (1974), 30 August 1974. The General Assembly used the term 'refugees' in Resolution 3212 (XXIX).

20. A comprehensive account, based on close acquaintance with the documentation and on field experience, is Thomas W. Oliver, *United Nations in Bangladesh* (Princeton University Press, Princeton, 1978).

21. UN Treaty Series no. 14 691, adopted on 10 September 1969, came into force on 20 June 1974.

22. Universal Declaration cited in note 16, above. Article 13 (2) states: 'Everyone has the right to leave any country, including his own, and to return to his country.' Article 12 (2) of the International Covenant on Civil

and Political Rights, adopted as UN General Assembly Resolution 2200 A (XXI), 16 December 1966, and entered into force on March 223, 1976, says in Article 12: '(2) Everyone shall be free to leave any country, including his own . . . (4) No one shall be arbitrarily deprived of the right to enter his own country. [But (2)] . . . shall not be subject to any restriction except those which are provided by law, are necessary to protect national security, public order (*ordre public*), public health or morals or the rights and freedoms of others.'

23. For a brief account, see Guy Goodwin-Gill, *The Refugee in International Politics*, (Clarendon Press, Oxford, 1983); pp. 109-11. An extended treatment is Atle Grahl-Madsen, *Territorial Asylum* (Uppsala, Swedish Institute of International Affairs, 1979).

24. Leon Gordenker, 'The United Nations and Refugees', unpublished paper prepared for the annual meeting of the International Studies Association, 1985.

25. See Elizabeth Winkler, 'Voluntary Agencies and Government Policy', *International Migration Review*, XV, 1-2 (spring-summer 1981), pp. 95-9; and Robert G. Wright, 'Voluntary Agencies and the Resettlement of Refugees', ibid., pp. 157-74.

3

The Novel Nature of Recent
Refugee Incidents

Recent forced migrations can be assessed against the standards developed for the establishment and use of international machinery and the parallel definition of refugees. This chapter will present arguments showing that, set against the expectations implicit in international practice since the end of the Second World War, recent forced migrations have characteristics that are unique. They represent a striking departure from the perception of refugee problems in recent history and a contrast with earlier migrations.[1] This argument is only enhanced when it is put into a broader context of social, political and historical trends. Identifying the novel characteristics of recent refugee incidents will provide a coherent framework for the subsequent analysis.

The definition of refugees in the UN Convention centres on the sort of political decisions by governments that directly produce refugees. It emphasises the fear of persecution by governments or their agents as a cause of flight and refusal to return. Though world history records scores of incidents of persecution, convincing explanations are still needed as to why suddenly in the last part of the twentieth century hundreds of thousands of men, women and children should flee their homes in places that had previously never or rarely known such mass movements. Nor does historical review lead to an indisputable retrospective prediction of the notorious refugee incidents in places once so effectively excluded from the consciousness of the rest of the world as to be mysterious. It does not tell us anything about the sudden appearance of planeloads of asylum-seekers in airports far from their homes. And it says nothing at all about the clearly sharpened awareness of refugees in publics around the world. Such explanations can be better approached by examining some recent political, administrative and social developments in the relations among contemporary nation states.

New technology and new nationalism

The rapid improvement in transportation and communications which have taken place in the technically advanced parts of the world during the last two centuries has increasingly facilitated the extension of governmental administration to every corner of national territories. The invention of the telegraph, telephone, radio, steamship, railway, motor car and aircraft have all helped governments to strengthen their grip on territory and human behaviour. At the same time, improvements in communications have made possible the rapid movement of people seeking to change their place of residence either for short periods or for ever. The most obvious effects of such ease of communications and its relationship with government are to be seen in Western Europe and North America. It has probably been of least influence in those areas of Africa that were the last to be colonised. In other parts of the world, less affected by the technological advances of Europe and North America, the old isolation, local autonomy and difficulties of movement until recently remained dominant, if distantly challenged.

The disintegration of colonial empires and increasing demands for economic development for rapidly growing populations — all partly an outcome of the spread of modern technology — converted what till then had been comparatively stable regions into areas of social and political turmoil. Everywhere in the former colonial world by the late 1970s, the relatively light hand of administration in outlying territories — especially where doctrines of indirect rule framed colonial policies — was replaced with the centralised formal structures of modern nationalistic government. As the colonies came to independence, the new governments took over and expanded the existing administrative structures in order to extend their actual control to every part of their domains. This extension of administration was frequently linked with the promotion of nationalism as a means of bolstering governments ruling accidentally defined territories that included a mixture of societies. In the older independent states, the existing administrations tightened their grip with the use of aircraft, better ground vehicles, and above all telecommunications that became cheaper and more accessible each year. Moreover, training schools and universities soon began churning out administrators to replace the departing colonial officers. In many countries the new administrative corps surpassed its predecessor in number of staff, number of functions undertaken and territory brought under supervision within a decade. The new politicians and civil servants frequently held passionately nationalistic views and, needless to say, bound their own futures to the success of the new regimes.

Such projection of the administrative reach of government more often than not went hand in hand with the spread of comprehensive programming for society and economy. Such policies were aimed primarily at economic development but also at integrating states which included peoples that had previously been largely isolated from each other. Economic development necessarily involves social change. The central governing required for development also implies changing relationships. Such changes often inspired resistance, especially where governments adopted what were perceived as alien practices, which might include, for instance, the replacement of herding by agriculture, the control of population movements in rural areas, the forced delivery of crops to government, taxation, census and compulsory schooling or military training.

Governments faced with resistance to the extension of their control often responded with coercion, now easier to employ than ever before because of the more elaborate structure of the state and the spreading use of more modern technology. In addition, sovereign governments everywhere, whether new or old, take great pains to protect their security. Security, moreover, was in many instances defined by governments as loyalty to their nationalistic or other ideology. Whatever difficulties development, nationalistic promotion and social change may entail, the creation and use of a military and police force seems relatively easy. The clarity of military organisation, the universal acquaintance with violence, the earlier resort of colonial regimes to arms in the face of resistance and their training of indigenous units all contributed to the construction of military or paramilitary forces. In the former colonial territories, recruits were often available from the ranks of the liberation forces. Elsewhere, military traditions frequently formed an important part of the historical heritage or, as in some Latin American states, were integral to government.

The same technological changes that made possible the extension of administrative control contributed heavily to the creation of military forces intended to serve governments, whether new or old. Basic weapons became ever cheaper, simpler to use and more deadly. The means of transportation and of communication also bore cheaper price tags and more efficient specifications. Within a short period and for a relatively small price, any government was able to acquire a staggering destructive capacity. It was therefore capable of exerting significant and unavoidable threats or forceful coercion against sizeable populations, either within its boundaries or outside them.

Thus, more governments than ever before had the means to root out intractable elements in their societies. These governments could bring coercive violence to broader territories than ever before in history and could affect more people than ever. Furthermore, population growth continued in most parts of the world, usually the most rapidly in the new or developing countries. Given its new capacities, any government was likely to find the flight of a considerable number of its subjects relatively simple to arrange. This could be done either deliberately or incidentally for the purpose of executing a specific programme.

Remarkable aspects of contemporary refugee incidents

Reflecting the widely distributed modern means of control available to governments, refugee incidents since 1945 have included five remarkable characteristics.

Numbers

The numbers of people commonly identified as refugees has reached unparalleled levels, both in the aggregate and in terms of the numbers of individual incidents.[2]

In the aggregate, at almost any time since about 1960, the totals of refugees have varied between 10 and 15 million. The people involved are, of course, not always the same ones, for repatriation and resettlement causes ebbs and flows. Nevertheless, such high absolute totals over a period of several years are historically unprecedented. Individual incidents, moreover, have included striking mass exoduses, such as the flood of over 700,000 *émigrés* from Palestine, or the collapse of Pakistani rule and the creation of Bangladesh that caused some 10 million of the poorest people in the world to spill into India.

Mass exoduses of this magnitude and in such conditions of

urgency were new to the sad history of refugees. Knowledge of their plight was rapidly communicated to every part of the world by government message and the mass media. In the rich countries where voluntary action was permitted, it resulted in waves of sympathy and private initiatives to offer aid. The magnitude of the responses in terms of cash, supplies and voluntary work at home and in the field was also remarkable.

Location and development

With the exception of the Hungarian episode, every one of the mass exoduses took place in developing countries, some of them with probably irrevocable membership of the least developed category used by UN development agencies.[3] Some of these regions, such as the Indian province where the Bangladeshis arrived, have practically no means of coping with additional people. The same holds true for Somalia. This area had the additional handicap of being relatively ill-served by modern communications, a difficulty inspired partly by the deliberate isolation enforced by the government during years of close co-operation with the Soviet Union. For the most part, the Indo-Chinese who fled to Thailand arrived in some of the least flourishing sections of the country; this was especially the case for the Khmer. Most of the Afghan refugees sought asylum in the North-West Frontier Province of Pakistan, parts of which have long been treated as practically unreachable for administrative and developmental purposes; even when the refugees left the backward Tribal Areas, the local hospitality, however warm, could not overcome the endemic poverty. The situation in Baluchistan Province was even grimmer.

The influx of large numbers of people, most of them destitute and many weakened by hard trekking, hunger and disease, in these poor areas constitutes an immediate disruption of local development plans. In order to keep the hordes of refugees from overrunning the land, as well as to bring them some immediate material relief, the host government is forced, willy-nilly, to devote significant administrative and financial resources to them. Apart from the human sympathies that are common to people everywhere, to do otherwise would result in a scandalous degree of misery and loss of life that would soon be known of everywhere in the world.[4]

Moreover, the costs in development terms to the refugees' country of origin can also be substantial. Mass exoduses often include individuals from every branch of society, including those with skills required for developing the economy. Such skills not only have academic origins but also derive from administrative and commercial experience. When governments single out a particular group, such as shopkeepers, civil servants of a particular ethnic origin or employees of foreign banks, for hostile treatment, they may cause the departure of key operatives needed for economic development. Furthermore, the departure of a substantial part of the population from one section of the countryside will reduce land use and production. This will cause the waste of, or a decline in the return from, earlier investment, including agricultural land and buildings.

Assistance from abroad may save the lives of the refugees, and may keep their presence from further impoverishing their surprised hosts. It will not, however, prevent the distortion of ongoing development programmes. Nor will it guarantee the newcomers a productive share in the society of the country of asylum. It is more likely at first to encourage the mere preservation of the newcomers, granting them physical safety and food, shelter and basic medical care but no productive work or much concrete reason to hope for the immediate future. In addition, especially in the poorest countries, the influx of supplies from outside will almost necessarily be seen by some local people as a tempting opportunity for a quick profit. A weak economic infrastrucutre — a feature that is part of the definition of underdevelopment — will prove incapable of close management of the supplies. The leaks into the local markets can damage earlier, reasonably reliable, arrangements for the production of food and other necessities. These can also be disturbed by sudden demands for water and transport and sometimes for services and labour from the local economy. Widespread corruption can also follow the importing of such valuable goods as medicines and shelter materials, not to mention food. Finally, some in the local population will almost certainly begin to regard as undeserved rewards the benefits that refugees receive without working. Where ethnic identities do not prevent it, others among the local inhabitants may even seek to join camp-dwellers or refugees receiving supplementary assistance in order to obtain a standard of certain living without the gruelling work this generally involves.

Such friction and disturbances to life would affect any government, but for weak regimes in developing countries the results can be well-nigh disastrous. Settled development policies must be reviewed. Whatever the level of outside assistance, some of the local costs will involve the security of the state; for refugees often bring with them a determination to root out the regime that caused their plight. This could encourage political activities and guerrilla movements among the refugees, thereby attracting threats and enmity from the government responsible for driving out the asylum-seekers. In addition, the entry of a mass of people implies the need to strengthen the means for keeping local law and order. This can cause resentment on all sides. Over a longer period, the host government has to find some means of coping with the refugees' demands. They can be returned to their country of origins, which may involve delicate and potentially dangerous political discussion. In some situations they can be resettled locally, but this too requires policy changes, financing and new programming. Refugees can be sent on to third-country resettlement should the opportunity for this arise. But among the most recent incidents only in the case of Indo-China have refugees from developing countries had much of a chance to proceed to third-country resettlement. What a government can hardly do — as testified by the situation in Lebanon during the summer of 1982 — is leave the refugees as they are with their current status: the result will almost certainly be turbulence and violence. In any case, most of the governments affected by recent large-scale exoduses are among the least well-equipped in the world to cope with such problems.

Large-scale migration

Some contemporary refugee incidents involve large-scale migration. This may induce permanent immigration. Such a possibility may be inferred from experience with post-war displaced persons and refugees who either declined to return to their original homes or were forbidden to do so. Where they received asylum at once — even if this was grudging or partial, as in the case of the Palestinians, or willing and organised as in the case of the Mozambicans in Tanzania or the ethnic Chinese from Vietnam, who made their way overland to China — this constituted immigration. In the more dramatic case of the Indo-Chinese who made their way to countries of South-East Asia or Hong Kong, resettlement in a distant, alien world became the means of dealing with the situation. This too constituted a large-scale migration and subsequent permanent immigration. The long-standing presence of Eritreans in Sudan could likewise be seen as a sizeable completed migration. The recent movement of individuals, most of them Jewish, from the Soviet

Union also involves considerable numbers, none of whom expect to return.

These migrations differ from typical earlier movements in a number of striking ways. They all involve some — and usually a great deal of — co-operative international planning after the exodus has begun. With the possible exception of the Soviet *émigrés*, the migrations require government decisions or the operation of special programmes rather than primarily personal decisions. All imply substantial socialised costs in terms of initial care, preparation for resettlement and resettlement itself.

Not every refugee incident results in a high level of one-way migration, although a certain amount undoubtedly follows each outflow. Nevertheless, the fact that resettlement in distant places has been of an organised nature and employed repeatedly since 1945 remains remarkable. Moreover, it is a fact which highlights the junction point between the establishment of a generally recognised legal status for refugees and their conversion into immigrants with legal status in the country of reception. Large-scale migration in an orderly fashion calls for adjustments in immigration policy. As intergovernmental agencies have usually undertaken part of the necessary operations and, in some cases, have actively negotiated with governments of countries of immigration, that jealously reserved subject of immigration is opened to some slight degree to extra-national influence. Thus, the interconnectedness characteristic of the contemporary world frames the outcomes of some major refugee situations.

Organised transnational programmes

The emergence of unprecedented numbers of refugees in some of the world's poorest countries gave a strong impetus to the rapid growth of transnational networks[5] to assist these people. In part, the networks represent the expansion of the originally modest UNHCR and the continued operation of ICEM at varying levels. It also found renewed use for the skills developed immediately after the Second World War in the handling of refugees and displaced persons. These networks have intergovernmental components, the participation of voluntary organisations, co-operation from the relevant sections of national administrations and a generally broadening scope. They include individuals who join and leave as well as those permanently employed. For the most part the networks include elements only from a non-Communist world, but in a few instances the Eastern European governments have worked parallel to the main refugee networks.

Networks dealing with refugees can be understood as functional ordering devices that link organisations and individuals working for the relief and termination of refugee incidents. Seen in this light, the creation of transnational efforts to cope with refugee incidents results in a chain of relationships that begins in the field where refugees first seek asylum. It extends to national government level, moves out to intergovernmental organisations and transnational private groups, loops back to the field, extends arms to the national governments involved in financing the effort and resettling some of the people, reaches out to the local communities and their governmental and non-governmental leaders involved in resettlement or repatriation. Such networks probably constitute some of the longest chains of international co-operation ever assembled. Furthermore, such networks represent novel organisational forms, appearing within formal structures that depend on nation-states rather than private or mixed public-private efforts. It seems likely that transnational networks will prove increasingly useful in an interconnected world, even when ideological doctrines suggest that they have no social utility or legal standing.

Because large-scale forced movements of population tend to create so much social and political disturbance, the networks tend to widen to include functions which, strictly speaking, have nothing directly to do with refugees. The presence of extreme hunger among refugees in areas where not enough food can be obtained invariably suggests the involvement of the World Food Program, the Food and Agriculture Organization of the UN (FAO) and the UN Children's Fund (UNICEF). Bilateral donors — especially the United States as a food surplus country — will almost surely be approached by intergovernmental organisations and by the country of asylum. So will the European Communities. Any regional organisations to which the host country belongs are also likely to come into contact with the incident. Such voluntary organisations as the Red Cross Societies will be engaged, either on their own initiative as the news of the incident filters out or by an involved government or other organisation. From then on, the list of voluntary organisations engaged is likely to grow, and to include church groups, *ad hoc* organisations and volunteers.

Matters concerning repatriation call for diplomatic negotiations, as do certain resettlement issues. If refugees have taken asylum in the territory of a government that has a difficult relationship with their country of origin, approaches with regard to repatriation may be delicate and troublesome. In any case, if UNHCR forms part of the relevant network, it is likely to make such approaches. If the situation is tense, as in Indo-China or the Horn of Africa, the diplomatic aspects are likely to be handled at a distance from UNHCR and other organisations professing primarily humanitarian goals. The case can move into the broader political jurisdiction of the United Nations. In recent years, the UN Secretary-General has taken a direct interest in such negotiations.

In a hardened situation like that of the Palestinians, the negotiations involve refugees only as a subsidiary matter and the networks concentrated on them generally remain at some distance from the high politics of the issue. In some instances, as was the case with the Khmer refugees seeking asylum in Thailand, the treatment given the asylum-seekers has a direct bearing on the regional political relationships. If the Pnom Penh government or its Vietnamese protector concludes that those granted asylum really are capable of becoming an anti-government guerrilla force, then the relationship of Thailand and other ASEAN countries with Vietnam will reflect that perception.[6] This in turn will affect the activities of the refugee network.

Furthermore, the refugee networks develop information of significance to international political relationships. For example, if refugees result from repressive governing practices, such as the unbridled use of official violence, the facts cannot long remain hidden. They can form the basis for complaints about the violations of human rights to which both the UN and regional organisations have become increasingly sensitive. Such information will also stimulate public reactions in influential countries, especially the Western democracies, and thus feed back to the operations of the refugee networks.

The extended networks for handling refugees thus have a dual character. On the one hand, their very extension and the involvement of so many diverse components mean that they can claim a neutral specialisation in humanitarian affairs. Their claim of non-partiality often protects their efforts on behalf of asylum-seekers. On the other hand, the manner in which they conduct their operations and the information they develop can have a direct bearing on wider and potentially dangerous political relationships among governments. Furthermore, as refugees result from political decisions, the networks always feel a tension between assisting those in need and the implications of their positions for wider relationships among states.

Definitional insufficiencies

The size and complexity of refugee incidents has both tested and expanded the capacity of transnational networks to cope with the mass outflow of asylum-seekers. The work of these networks continues to be based explicitly on the narrow definitions of the late 1940s, when the hope of governments was strictly to limit their attention and commitment to refugees. Yet the very expansion and general success of the networks in handling exoduses raises doubts about the viability of the underlying conceptual basis founded on the immediate post-war experience.

To begin with, the transnational system for handling refugees rests on the assumption that any new asylum-seekers would most likely emerge in fairly developed societies with capable administrative and legal structures. This is the implication of the emphasis on legal protection contained in the original UNHCR Statute and of the formal emphasis given to this aspect of the work of his Office. Furthermore, the definition of refugees in the 1951 Convention assumed deliberate persecution on the part of a government as a cause for refugee status. It can be argued that the specificity of this line of reasoning excludes the effects of those governmental actions which threaten the existence of individuals and groups without taking on the form of specific punishment or harassment directed to them alone. The definition therefore does not include many of the results of social policies that have been involved in the larger exoduses.

In addition, the definitions of the Convention have no provisions for the results of international violence. Civilians are supposedly protected, in the event of inter-state fighting, by the Geneva and Hague Conventions and by the International Committee of the Red Cross. Yet UNHCR has become involved in refugee-like situations that violence produced in Cyprus and in Bangladesh. The UN General Assembly has encouraged such involvement, and UNHCR has usually shown little reluctance to take part. In the case of the Khmer, however, UNHCR deliberately held back from assisting the people stranded along the Thai-Cambodian border, where at first ICRC and UNICEF carried the main burden. Such cases illustrate the ambiguous fit of the leading definition of refugees to some apparently common contemporary events.

In general, efforts to construct an international system of protection for human rights have been kept separate from the handling of refugee affairs. Both governments and international bureaucracies have generally favoured this separation on the grounds that humanitarian actions should not be confused with the highly political issues of human rights. Yet refugees result from the denial of human rights. Their legal status in asylum involves undertakings by governments to protect human rights, including such rights as life, work, education, equality before the law and due process and freedom of movement and of speech. In addition, humanitarian activities have political implications. The very act of keeping fugitives alive, however humanitarian the intent, may result in the ultimate formation of a guerrilla movement. The assistance given to an elite fleeing from a revolutionary regime — as in Cuba or in Pinochet's Chile — keeps alive the dissident view. Seeking repatriation of refugees implies an adjustment of a governmental policy or set of actions that could have far-reaching importance.

Finally, questions can be raised about the conception that an office such as UNHCR, endowed with a massive budget and large bureaucracy as the result of instructions approved by the UN General Assembly, can remain non-operational. Exactly where the boundaries between operational and non-operational can be found is less than clear. When large-scale camp installations or resettlement projects have to be created quickly, even leadership constitutes a kind of operation. So does the application of standards of performance as the prerequisite for financing a project or a programme. As long as UNHCR is forced to involve itself closely with such enterprises, its role as a non-operational agency can be questioned. These questions relate to the very concept of non-operationality.

Such definitional and conceptual issues arise from a consideration of the recent masses of refugees, the means developed for handling them and the conceptual basis of these efforts. Additional steps towards a clear, logical and perhaps partly predictive analysis can be made. The following sections of this study undertake to sketch such analytical schemes.

Notes

1. Cf. Aristide Zolberg, 'The Formation of New States as a Refugee-Generating Process', *The Annals of the American Academy of Political and Social*

Science, 467 (May 1983), pp. 24-38. Theoretical arguments include emphases on 'push' and 'pull' factors and structural causes. See Charles H. Wood, 'Equilibrium and Historical Structural Perspectives on Migration', *International Migration Review*, XVI, 2 (summer 1982), pp. 298-319, and Robert L. Bach and Lisa A. Schraml, 'Migration, Crisis and Theoretical Conflict', ibid., pp. 320-342. An interesting analysis from an economic standpoint is Norman Carruthers and Aidan R. Vining, 'International Migration: an Application of the Urban Location Choice Model', *World Politics*, XXV, 1 (October 1982), pp. 106-20.

2. For a discussion of refugee numbers and directions of flow, relevant to this and the next section of this chapter, see Earl E. Huyck and Leon F. Bouvier, 'The Demography of Refugees', *The Annals*, 467 (May 1983), pp. 39-61. This treatment makes the point that forced migrations are also caused by environmental factors, not exclusively by political decisions aimed at precise human targets.

3. For additional discussion, see Gordenker, 'Refugees in Developing Countries and Transnational Organization', ibid., pp. 62-77.

4. Not every incident taking place at any one time gets uniform treatment. For example, American television devoted far more time to dramatic film of the 'boat people' from Vietnam than to the 'foot people' who were then entering China. Nor does every mass communication system, each based on national jurisdiction, spread the news with equal zeal.

5. Interlocking organisations and individuals who set policy or administer programmes that have to do with services for networks. These networks wax and wane, but some kernel of organisation tends to remain, especially around UNHCR and ICM. The networks may be characterised by active communication, by having certain tasks in common and by the mutual concern of coping with one or more situations posed by the presence of refugees. All extend beyond national borders. Their components may include organisations formed on the basis of intergovernmental, national, non-governmental or personal membership. No comprehensive description of the refugee network exists, and data is available now only to trace parts of some of them. Yet field observation leaves no doubt of the existence of such networks.

6. Thus took place a series of armed incidents in 1984 and 1985 between Thai and Vietnamese troops on the border where Cambodian resistance movements are located.

4

Causal Elements in Contemporary Refugee Incidents

Refugee flows in the modern world stem from a variety of causes, some of them isolated and others interconnected, some deeply rooted in history, others of more recent origin. These causes may be intermingled and be responsible in varying degrees for particular refugee flows. In any specific incident, different elements may wax and wane. Possibly the only generalisation which comes close to covering every refugee incident is one that points to actions undertaken by governments as the most likely source of causal factors.[1]

Yet such a generalisation remains far too abstract to be of much use when it comes to analysing the historical data on refugees. It may well give a first clue as to where to seek an explanation, but it provides little basis for making any but the roughest forecasts of refugee incidents. Whether accurate forecasts could ever be made at all, or developed with the aid of techniques simple enough to be of use in making a rapid response, remains an unanswered question. Nevertheless, without a careful analytical scheme neither the complexity of past incidents nor the possibility of future flows can be fully understood. This chapter attempts to set out such an analytical structure. The intention is to separate out from one another those elements that contribute to refugee incidents and thereby to make a step towards the eventual development of a capacity to forecast such events.

The propositions set out in this chapter stem from the implications of the foregoing historical sketch and the discussion of conceptual assumptions regarding refugees. Where it seems advantageous in this chapter, the historical illustrations will be given additional detail; other examples will be added.[2] At the same time, it would be misleading to claim that the analysis here was of an indisputable, comprehensive nature. The unsystematic nature of accumulated research on forced migration nourishes uncertainty. Relatively few incidents have been studied in depth, and even these were approached from differing angles.[3] In much of the research, such as that concerned with Cubans and Haitians landing on American beaches, policy issues took precedence over explanation. In some instances, scant factual knowledge has been adduced. Far too often, fragmentary reports and tendentious claims predominate, as was the case with studies of the Cambodian and Vietnamese refugee situations. The building-up of factual reports has, moreover, been held back by the location of some of the most important refugee incidents — such as those in Afghanistan and Somalia — well outside the mainstream of journalistic resort and inadequately covered by the library material available for scholarly study.[4] The actual siting of many recent incidents of forced migration — such as those in northern Ethiopia or from Chad — have proved beyond the reach of researchers with an interest in refugee phenomena, notwithstanding a few fleeting observations. Finally, by their very nature, refugees invite controversy. The authorities concerned with them have often preferred caution to frankness, paucity of detail to full description. The normal concerns about the safety of persons, whether they are camp inmates or visitors from outside, become magnified and may be used as a justification for restricting observation. This comment applies in some measure to both national governments and various transnational agencies.[5]

The discussion that follows assumes the concept 'refugee' to include persons who have left their customary homes under the pressure of fear for their present or future lives, because of immediate, overt threats or — more comprehensively — clear denials of basic human rights whose enjoyment is required for continued life over a short or longer period. Even if it is not accepted that such conditions are rights, they remain necessary for life with a minimum of dignity. These rights include some of the obvious forms of civil protection, such as freedom from arbitrary punishment, imprisonment or execution; and from damaging interference from governmental administration, such as arbitrary arrest or physical displacement. They also include the right to life itself, to minimum security within society, to food, shelter and health protection. Without such rights, or conditions, people will, it is assumed, tend to flee if they are able to, or else, will seek a means of making flight possible. Such movements can be distinguished from migrations in general by the fact that the denial of rights is manifest and immediately present.

To define 'refugees' in this manner does extend the concept into the more general rubric of migration. Such an extension, which violates the narrow boundaries enclosing the notion that emerged from intergovernmental negotiations, can be justified on two grounds. First, the definition used in the 1951 United Nations Convention, as we have seen, emerged in a particular set of conditions and is deliberately narrow and exclusionary. The definition used in the African refugee convention only emphasises the narrowness of the concept defined earlier by the UN General Assembly. Either approach excludes some contemporary situations in which those affected believe their existence to be threatened and consequently take flight, even though the standard elements of persecution for political, racial or cultural reasons are hardly visible or are minor ingredients of the context. Second, while refugees in the sense of United Nations definitions result mainly from programmed actions deliberately undertaken by governments, the simultaneous or subsequent movement by broader categories of people who differ from refugees only in legal theory rather than in their actual circumstances, may be excluded from international concern. Forced movement may also result from governmental or other social activity that was not deliberately aimed at defined groups. Some of these latter migrations are covered by the definition adopted by the Organization for African Unity and as yet applied — whether deliberately or coincidentally — only in certain African incidents.

The categories set out below should be understood as having an analytical purpose. They are separable from one another for the purpose of analysis. No single category is likely to cover any particular refugee incident completely; in any given incident, factors that fall into several categories are likely to be involved. Each of these factors would have a varying degree of influence, depending on the particular circumstances of the refugee movement.

International war

War, armed conflict between the military forces of one state (or even a tribe or clan from beyond customary boundaries) with another, has always caused human beings to flee their homes in order to avoid immediate danger. Sometimes this departure has resulted in long absences, sometimes only in shorter displacements. Perhaps the most usual pattern is one that involves a fairly rapid return of the forced migrants to their homes. Their return depends initially on the transfer of active fighting among armed forces to other sites;

alternatively, it may require a cessation of violence, such as an end to aerial bombardment or infantry patrols, in the neighbourhood of civilian populations.

Fighting phase

Just before a war actually enters the phase of active campaigning by one armed force against another, or in advance of predictable battles within defined areas, civilians are likely to seek shelter from injury incidental to the hostilities. Sometimes civilian administrators, or military authorities, or both, try to prevent injury to civilians by arranging for them to be moved. Sometimes civilians act on their own initiative. Military authorities may regard the movement of civilians as a handicap for forces in the neighbourhood.

Ground fighting

Those living in areas where ground fighting is either likely or possible may, using their own methods, anticipate the forthcoming violence and, acting on their own initiative, attempt to get out of the way; or else local authorities may originate or encourage such anticipation. Alternatively, this may take place without official sanction. Such a desire may be stronger in border areas than elsewhere, at least in the opening phase of a conflict, because of the obvious expectation that armies will be ordered to win territory. Thus, an outpouring of people from the border areas occurred in Europe at the beginning of the Second World War; once the strong, largely successful, German attacks were actually under way, the volume of shelter-seekers from the surrounding areas increased. Fighting in locations where several national boundaries converge may lead to a great deal of confusion in which nationals of different jurisdictions are scattered helter-skelter amongst one another. This took place in Indo-China following the success of the North Vietnamese military forces in their drive southwards. It also could be seen in Western Europe during the final weeks of the Second World War, when fast-moving military columns pursued the collapsing German forces. Soldiers detached from their units and deserters may also join civilians on the move. Artillery and automatic weapon fire accompanies the presence of modern military forces, and increases the understandable alarm of those who find themselves in the firing zone. Amidst the confusion, those fleeing may either leave their homelands deliberately or do so heedlessly or unintentionally.

Aerial bombardment

Potential victims of attacks from the air can less easily anticipate danger than is the case with other forms of bombardment — such as that from artillery or mortars — which accompany ground forces. Once aerial or other bombardment begins, especially if it has a systematic form with regard to targets, at least parts of the affected population will try or be directed to move to shelter. The nearest safe areas may well be within the jurisdiction of another national government. Those among the departing population who have a choice may well attempt to go to such shelter. Polish nationals who in 1939 tried to escape from German attack, for instance, in many cases chose to move eastwards into the Soviet Union or Czechoslovakia rather than to the rear of the invading army. In contrast, others tried to escape from the Soviet invaders by crossing into German-held territory. Movements of refugees and others in such circumstances sometimes come under aerial attack, as was the case early on in the Second World War on the western front and at various times in Eastern Europe. Such attacks on displaced persons may be made in a deliberate attempt to spread terror and produce the kind of confusion that interferes with military operations. The violence may also be aimed at forestalling the entry of asylum-seekers into particular areas, as has happened along the Thai-Cambodian border.

Propaganda and political warfare

During the fighting phase of a war and frequently before it, radio (and occasionally television) broadcasts and loudspeakers may be used to encourage people of the enemy state to flee. Propaganda of this sort was used frequently by both sides in the Iran-Iraq war of 1982-1985 and also during various periods of the fighting that took place between Israel and surrounding countries. These communications, which are frequently designed by sophisticated experts, may be aimed at causing confusion, at ridding territory to be conquered of unwelcome inhabitants, at lowering the morale of enemy military forces and of the civilian home front, and even at the humanitarian protection of the civilian population in the spirit of the laws of war. During the fighting phase, broadcasts may be supplemented with leaflets dropped from aircraft or exploded from artillery shells. Such propaganda generally promises good treatment to those who surrender to the invading forces or who cross into the territory of the attacker. In a sense, the invader promises asylum to anyone who defects.

Liquidation phase

The cessation of hostilities between military forces may give rise to a movement of population. Those wanting to escape from a particular political system or its social or personal consequences may try to leave their homes and go over to the side of an enemy state, especially when the latter seems to have victory in its grasp. Such movements may take place despite substantial material cost to the individuals concerned, who fear they will be plundered in any case. In other instances, those who leave may already have suffered material despoliation. Movements of this sort took place in Indo-China following the unification of the country under the North Vietnamese regime. Large-scale population movements took place in Korea after the defeat of Japan and the subsequent occupation of the north by Soviet troops.

Many variations on this pattern form part of the long record of forced migration. An important example is the movement of members of ethnic groups to join their fellows abroad, where a greater degree of security from violations of human rights as well as material well-being is available. This was characteristic of Jewish emigration from Germany and Eastern Europe after the Second World War and from the Soviet Union and other Eastern European countries in the mid-1970s. In both these instances it was conceivable (but eventually proven untrue) that the migrants concerned could have remained where they were without being under much threat. For most of the individuals involved, however, a manifest conviction of danger was the reason for departure. Similar movements in several locations occurred during the closing phases of decolonisation. The expulsion of Asians from Uganda and the frightened exodus of Portuguese settlers from Angola and Mozambique furnish apt examples.

Furthermore, some liquidations of armed incidents include formal exchanges of population. The justification given for these is that they reduce the threat to or from dissident groups or give expression to the fraternal feelings of the individuals concerned. Thus, Greeks and Turks were exchanged following the Greco-Turkish fighting in the early stages of Ataturk's establishment of modern Turkey. So, too, were ethnic Germans driven out of the Soviet Union and other Eastern European countries after the Second World War; in this instance, those involved showed evidence of a high degree of fear as well as of active pressure.

When labour, whether paid or forced, has been recruited from occupied territories for employment in home industries of either side during a war, the likelihood of some people wishing to remain with the victors, in spite of offers to return home, is high. The reasons may comprise personal liaisons, such as marriage, which involve no active element of force. But in other instances, political, religious and social factors may loom large. Those declining repatriation may believe not merely that their material or personal situations would be harmed by their return; they may also argue that their human rights would be denied, that they would be subjected to reprisal or revenge, that they would be punished for deeds that had been forced on them or that they had now changed their minds about loyalty to their state of origin due to having a better knowledge of the reality they had left behind. Their resistance to returning may spur a considerable number of them to move towards a place of safety. Such a movement of population occurring as part of the liquidation of hostilities may affect large numbers. An obvious example can be seen in the fate of the hundreds of thousands of East Europeans and nationals of the defunct Baltic states who had been forced by Germany to work in factories and construction projects in Western Europe. Even prisoners of war may try to remain, as was the case with some of the Chinese soldiers captured during the Korean War. Such migration takes place in two stages: forced removal, followed by refusal to return to the place of origin.

Internal turbulence

Turbulence within a state that is not involved in external hostilities or armed attack may cause its inhabitants to flee to safer areas, either within the national boundaries or in other countries. Such turbulence may result from long-term changes in a society or from short-term failures in the governmental or administrative processes. It may be differentiated analytically from the tension that is attendant on deliberately undertaken, planned social change; this latter cause will be dealt with separately below.

Violent governmental change

Revolutions and *coups d'état* cause a highly familiar type of refugee movement. In both cases, leading governmental personnel and those who work closely with the state apparatus or identify their immediate and long-term interests with the fallen regime face a violent change in their position. Both revolutions and *coups* usually constitute immediate, visible threats to the physical security of existing elites and those associated with them. Revolutions aim at the displacement of a current elite by a different one and at fundamental changes in the construction of a society. *Coups* seek the replacement of one ruling faction by another of the same elite, some of whose members are dissatisfied.

Revolution[6]

A government that resists a revolutionary movement may fight on for a lengthy period before eventually being brought down. Even if it is not brought down, the fighting will oppress the population in much the same way that international hostilities do. Either a revolutionary movement or a resisting government, or both, may receive outside support. Such support lends an international colouring to the conduct of the revolutionary struggle and to its human victims. As each revolution has its own specific characteristics, the precise results in terms of refugees tend to differ, but examples can be given. Considerable numbers of refugees entered other European countries during the Spanish Civil War; their situation was often extremely perilous, in part because of the fears stirred up in other governments by the involvement of the Fascist powers on the side of Franco and of the Soviet Union on the side of the Republican government. The revolutions in Russia in 1917 and in Nicaragua in 1979, regardless of the differences between their circumstances, were both the cause of a great deal of movement of human beings in proportion to the population as a whole at the time fighting was taking place. In both these cases the sympathies of foreign powers ensured that some transnational attention was given to those affected.

During a period of revolutionary upheaval, even when little fighting takes place, people may leave for shelter abroad, some of them in a state of destitution. However, whatever their fears, it may be quite unclear whether their return would place them in a particularly threatening situation or one that would leave them open to persecution. The realisation of such threats would depend on the way in which the revolution had developed, its aims and sometimes the nature of outside involvement. After a revolutionary group has seized power, its conduct determines whether the feared threats can reasonably be deemed by third-party observers to have materialised. The anti-colonial revolution in Zimbabwe resulted in the departure of many thousands of Europeans whose economic contribution — as all those involved admit — was of great value. That they feared harsh treatment also cannot be denied. Yet in retrospect, their fears did not in fact materialise, and their fellows who remained suffered no persecution, whatever other complaints they may have. In contrast, during the Iranian revolution of the late 1970s, many thousands of well-to-do people left the country with as much of their wealth as they could assemble. Their departure was treated by at least some outside governmental authorities as culpable or evidence of wrongdoing. Others, such as certain members of the Baha'i faith, correctly anticipated religious persecution and departed ahead of it. Furthermore, the revolutionary government insisted that its political opponents who fled abroad were criminals because of political activities carried out during the Shah's rule in addition to their later stances.

Coups d'état

Because a *coup d'état* involves only a relatively small part of the society and involves the exchange of one elite for another, any resulting exodus is likely to include senior political figures and military officers who formed part of the replaced regime. Junior civil servants and officers usually form a relatively smaller part of the emigration than their numbers at home would suggest. In some cases, as when a group of military officers took over the government of Surinam in 1982, many displaced politicians simply found ways to go abroad. (Later repression and assassinations suggest that those who left could claim that they conformed to a narrow model of the political refugee.) This has been the case with many *coups* in the past in Latin America, where the notion that a political refugee is an exiled political leader is commonly understood.

Nevertheless, to generalise that *coups* do not create large numbers of forced migrants would be to mislead. Some of the new regimes that emerge from *coups* have old scores to settle. Such was the case in Chile when the Pinochet regime forcibly replaced the Allende government. Others have extremely ambitious plans for reform. Still others intend to resist reform by force if necessary. Any of these courses could impel forced migration. Thus, the aims of the new regime and its immediate repressiveness or violence would condition the initial flow of refugees following a *coup d'état*.

Insurrectionary social structures

In some societies, inherent elements cause conflicts of an insurrectionary nature. These result in a persistent outflow of people who have strong formal claims to refugee status and believe themselves to be forced into migration.

A clear example of such a society is South Africa, where extreme social stratification is enforced on the basis of racial separation. The black majority face a life of assured lack of equal political, economic and social opportunity. They are excluded from all important social decisions and expect to remain so as long as the existing structure endures. The scanty turnout of Coloured and Indian voters for the 1984 elections to the new parliamentary chambers set up to represent them by the (white) National Party government is evidence that even these favoured groups expect their exclusion from important social decisions to stand. The much larger number of African voters (to use the South African government's designation) have no representation whatever. There can hardly be any doubt that all but the whites in South Africa believe themselves deprived of basic human rights and political participation.

Enforcement of rules to maintain such a society ensures violent responses. When the repression of human rights is carried out efficiently, as it is in South Africa, the responses are necessarily limited to inchoate turbulence. The leaders of such sporadic outbursts who survive repression form a continuous stream of refugees. The numbers grow rapidly whenever a severely violent period ensues.

As the expectation of violence on the part of the ruling group of such a society is constant, so is repressive action. The resulting atmosphere tends to encourage departure among some parts of the population that do not directly suffer repression or who are only relatively little molested by the authorities. Some incidents of flight from Eastern Europe have the same cause as these from South Africa. Individuals among the population channel a sense of hopelessness arising from a separation between well-rewarded governors and the masses into deliberate flight, as can be seen in the case of many refugees from East Germany to the Federal Republic.

71

National loyalties

Two distinct issues of nationalism arise from the extension of state control to almost every part of the earth. The first of these relates to the use of colonial boundaries to mark off most of the new states that were established after the Second World War. These boundaries divided existing culturally distinct nations among two or more states. At the same time, the European idea of nationalism, which remained popular in older states, proved highly attractive in the new one as a means of mobilising the population and ensuring that governmental plans would meet with favourable responses or at least would not be treated as alien and undeserving of loyal reactions. The consequences of nationalism in either of these forms can be read in part in forced migration.

Divided nations

Cutting national groups apart by allotting their territory to different states often stimulates irredentism. If a government responds by trying to reunite the pieces, this can lead to tension with that country's neighbours and ultimately to violence. Refugees soon appear, as is almost inevitably the case with military activity.

Even if violence is not used in the effort to reunite a nation, the people on one side of a border may consider themselves poorly treated by a majority and take flight to join their cousins. Such movement may take on a particular intensity when incompatible religions or social practices are responsible for defining national differences or when the political aims of the groups concerned in essence rule out reconciliation. Such causes operated in Palestine in the late 1940s, in Somalia following the creation of the state, and in India and Pakistan at various times but with particularly dramatic effect during the Bangladesh conflict of 1970-71. Similarly, differences in economic and social conditions may result in the movement of ethnic cousins across national boundaries but without visible elements of force.

Minorities

The persecution of minorities, ranging from minor harassment to genocide, is a time-honoured way of promoting or cementing the solidarity of national groups. It functions to distinguish the dominant nationality from the subordinate. In so doing it also offers a psychological legitimacy for nationalism of a sometimes extreme sort. Even without the efficiency of modern administrative techniques, it was a prominent producer of refugees. The persecution of national minorities can be either overt or obscure and indirect.

Overt persecution includes restricting the rights of minorities by a deliberate decision on the part of the government or dominant group. It ensures that the minority will be separated from the main body of the state's inhabitants. It opens the way to dealing with the minority in an unpredictable and arbitrary way, although it is conceivable that authorities would systematically apply discriminatory legislation in a predictable manner. Sometimes persecution of a minority takes the form of expulsion without the right to export property or wealth. In such instances, refugee status can hardly be questioned. Those affected are clearly being deprived of what are basic human rights. The expulsion of the Asian residents of Uganda during the early seventies was an obvious example of persecution of a minority in order to stir up national feeling. The government doubtless assured them of an even worse fate should they have tried to remain or to return. In this instance, some of the Asians in question found new homes rather quickly as a result of certain individuals having dual nationality or of the representation of several nationalities (in the legal sense of having status as a subject of a sovereign) within a family. This fortunate solution in no wise diminishes the fact that a minority was persecuted for the purpose of promoting nationalism.

Indirect persecution takes place when a national group encounters no formally organised punitive measures, whether from state authorities or other social groups. It results in the virtual exclusion, by the use of informal methods, of the group concerned from modes of participation in the society so that essential rights are either called into question or denied. From the point of view of the affected group, other parts of the society appear more highly favoured. The present and future of the group — especially if it is a minority — seem to have become mean, threatening and generally unacceptable, if not directly threatening to life. This has recently been the case, for example, for Jews in the Soviet Union, for many of those who left Cuba after the Castro regime took hold and for some of the refugees from Vietnam. It also appears to be the situation for some of the Indians who fled Guatemala for Mexico.

Direct persecution, initiated by government policies or the decisions of dominant groups, can encourage indirect persecution and unofficial actions against the subordinate nation. Acting as individuals, or through social factions, members of the dominant nation are able to attack, rob or humiliate other groups. This activity can soon convince a national group that the surrounding society has become so hostile and uncertain that the search for asylum is a better risk. Such was the case in Rwanda and Burundi during the late 1960s when a great deal of strife affected both the dominant WaTutsi minority and the subordinate BaHutu majority. In Rwanda, the Tutsi rulers were replaced by Hutus, while the dominant group stayed in power in Burundi. Whatever the situation at top government level, uneasiness and violence continued at that of the peasantry. The result was a substantial flow of refugees from both countries to surrounding areas where they were given temporary or long-term asylum and opportunities for resettlement. Unofficial pressure also tends to build up during revolutionary situations. It seems to have produced, for instance, a good many refugees from Iran.

Brutal government

Apart from punishing national groups, many governments have on occasion and sometimes repeatedly or for long periods treated all or part of their subjects with brutality, insensitivity and arbitrariness. Even the most poverty-stricken governments seem easily able to acquire the material capacity and organisational skill needed to cause pain to those under their control. Moreover, certain results of repressive policies ruthlessly carried out are immediate: supposed enemies can quickly be brought to heel. Also, certain desired patterns of behaviour on the part of the population may necessitate the use of psychological and physical pressure. Such activities may be classed as positive brutality. This involves an obvious denial of human rights, sometimes indeed in methodical form. It can be distinguished from the harsh treatment that is regarded by its perpetrators as consonant with an explicit, integrated plan for social reform, which is discussed below. It can also be differentiated from the heedless brutality of incompetence, where neglect and disregard have damaging effects on all or part of a population.

Positive brutality

The use of a wholesale denial of human rights simply as a means of keeping a group of governors in power or in the belief on their part that gentler handling of the population would lead to national disorder or chaos forms an all-too-familiar aspect of human history. It is an approach to political mastery and social control which has repeatedly led to forced migration.

Where official repression is directed at individuals or well-defined political groups that are deemed to be enemies of the state, refugees of the classic sort will soon emerge. If the government attempts to close the frontier, to concentrate target groups or to interfere in other ways with communications, refugees will appear in limited numbers compared to the potential migration, but eventually some may be expected to find a way out. If the frontier is deliberately or otherwise rather open, or if there is a tradition of allowing political dissidents to seek asylum, then signals that refugees are on the move will soon become obvious. When little selectivity steers the use of repression, then migrants will be produced from many parts of the society. The whole social atmosphere can be infected by growing feelings of insecurity and negative economic effects.

Selective repressiveness can conveniently be illustrated by the refugee exoduses during the 1970s and 1980s from Argentina and Chile, when right-wing governments were in power. Examples of a more general effect could be seen in Guatemala and El Salvador during the early 1980s when the hunt for anti-government guerrillas took precedence over a decent reserve on the part of the said governments. Major sections of the population were disturbed by this, and many thousands sought asylum abroad. Other examples can be seen in the Bahutu-led government's treatment of the WaTutsi in Rwanda and the handling of the insurrectionary BaHutu by the WaTutsi in the government of Burundi. The large-scale migration from Cuba also involves at least some positive brutality.

Positive brutality can take many specific forms according to the fecundity of the imaginations of its directors, but it invariably includes the deliberate, large-scale denial of human rights to leaders or to populations as a whole. It appears tied neither to time nor place, nor even to particular political constellations. Although it seems clear as an analytical category, in actuality it merges with self-serving repressive dictatorship and incompetent government, as discussed immediately below.

Self-serving, repressive dictatorship

Dictators who attempt at all costs to hang on to personal power against all comers have terrorised whole populations, especially in some of the poorer countries whose inhabitants have little defence against modern weapons and rudimentary but unfamiliar administrative techniques on the national plane. Such a dictatorship can cause extraordinary breakdowns in the everyday life of a society and can spew out waves of frightened people. Moreover, as if such unpredictable behaviour on the part of a tyrant did not cause misery enough, it usually also involves the persecution of minorities and military violence, sometimes beyond the control of the central authorities. An outstanding example of this was the dictatorship in Uganda of Idi Amin, who commanded and otherwise encouraged the use of unbridled force against any who were suspected of failing to conform to arbitrary and incomprehensible policies. Personal vendettas and tribal vengeance sheltered behind force on behalf of the central regime. The surrounding countries became hosts to thousands of forced migrants. A less well-known example of similar ferocity can be seen in the rule of Maçias in Equatorial Guinea, which led perhaps as many as half the population to leave that country during the late 1970s.

Incompetent government

A government that is quite incapable of making or implementing decisions or of controlling its administrative apparatus, with the result that civil life becomes uncertain and threatening, may be deemed incompetent. Such incompetence may affect either only certain districts of a state or all of it. As life becomes more disorderly, those governmental units still capable of taking action, such as the military, the police force or certain economic establishments, will probably attempt to operate to the advantage of their own members rather than in accordance with a general policy. Personal and political rebuffs will be repaid, often to an excessive degree. Property will be seized and families disrupted. Secessionist movements may develop, especially where ethnic or national differences figure prominently in the society. Refugees, sometimes in very large numbers, will result from this sort of breakdown. Even if it does not involve a great deal of violence, such a situation will impel people to leave in order to escape the predictable decline in the quality of life and — in poor countries — famine.

Such breakdowns caused by governmental incompetence affected Uganda under Amin and Zaïre many times in the decade that followed independence in 1960. In many respects, the situation in Lebanon in 1983 after the withdrawal of the Israeli forces that pursued Palestine Liberation Organization units to Beirut may be characterised as governmental incompetence. The flows of refugees to the surrounding countries provide ample evidence of the effects of such a situation. Furthermore, the very instability caused by governmental incompetence invites incursions from irredentist movements, dissidents, exiled political movements and advantage-seeking neighbouring states. Such incursions will cause even more people to seek asylum. As much by omission as by commission, a government which either breaks down or proves itself unable to cope with day-to-day short-term problems subjects those under its jurisdiction to brutality or harsh conditions. The results resemble those of positive brutality.

Deliberately undertaken change of social structures

Deliberate attempts on the part of governments to alter existing societies to planned new forms or to undertake substantial changes in fundamental social arrangements have also induced substantial flows of migrants. Since the Russian Revolution of 1917, these flows have received international attention and treatment. They have followed both turbulent international situations and revolutionary changes brought about from within by leaders using their newly gained power to execute large-scale social change. Such changes can also follow a *coup d'état* or a peaceful election which gives a government a mandate to execute social plans.

In the new developing countries, deliberate revisions of society usually aim at the ultimate consolidation of an unintegrated polity and modernisation of the economy and society. During the last 40 years, perhaps most such undertakings have been based on some notion of socialism, a strong role for government, an eventual classless society and comprehensive national planning. This pattern fits the situation in Cuba and Ethiopia, to give two prominent examples. In some more highly developed countries, such as Germany and Italy between the two World Wars or Argentina under the hand of Juan Domingo Perón, a radical corporatism was projected to replace a more relaxed social order.

Deliberate social change can also proceed along ethnic or religious lines. The former can be illustrated by the installation of the *apartheid* system in South Africa following the 1948 elections. This social change relied on years of study by the leaders of the National Party, a grandiose statement of doctrine and comprehensive legislation. As for a planned change along religious lines, examples can be found in the creation of Pakistan in 1948, the aftermath of the Iranian revolution and the reconstruction of Libya under Colonel Khaddafi.

The number of conceivable variations to be seen among attempts made at altering the social order either along doctrinal lines or in accordance with plans of one kind or another is perhaps infinite. Yet the declared aim in all cases invariably entails some kind of far-reaching change. Such change seriously disturbs social institutions and the expectations that previously prevailed. These disturbances have the capacity to produce migrants, many of whom will feel that they have been forced to move and some of whom will conform to the formal specifications of refugees.

Violent or repressive liquidation of elites

Revolutions and the execution of certain ideological programmes, such as Communism, involve the replacement of governing groups by quite different individuals. Because the projected change is of a comprehensive nature the definition of the elite to be replaced may be broad indeed, for instance the *bourgeoisie* or the capitalists. In a revolution, the old elite will usually have resisted change and taken part in any programme of violent repression against the movement. The new regime will not hesitate to use heavily repressive measures against such persons in order to hasten the enactment of its social programme. If the successful revolutionaries believe that the old elites will for ideological reasons promote implacable resistance to the new course, the likelihood of repression is high.

Once a revolutionary government begins to employ violence or heavily repressive measures against the members of the former elite, there is an increased likelihood that its members will flee in order to avoid destruction or punishment. Such flights resulted from the Russian and Chinese revolutions and to some extent from the Castro victory in Cuba. At the same time, governments with broad aims may find themselves in a situation of unexpected complexity; they will then sometimes choose contradictory policies. These, or the poor administration of a revolutionary programme, may tend to reduce or inhibit the outflow. The skills of the old elite can often be put to use by the new regime, which offers incentives to the defeated group to stay on. This occurred in Zimbabwe after the fall of the Ian Smith government and its replacement by the Mugabe government. Alternatively, a new government may find itself unable to manage without the skills of the old elite and try to prevent some emigration by either overt or covert methods. It may also attempt to 're-educate' those whose skills are in demand or to 'rehabilitate' those undergoing punishment. People treated in this way may well view such treatment as repressive, threatening and an excellent reason to depart, even if the government intends to retain them for their work. The use of 're-education' — which is frequently almost lethally heavy-handed — combined with a policy of retaining those individuals and groups perceived as potentially useful to the new regime practically guarantees that asylum-seekers who evade obstacles will have a strong claim to protection under the 1951 definition of refugees. In any case, when they emerge in a country of presumed asylum, they are likely to be without financial resources and to require immediate material help. Some refugees from Vietnam and Laos during the early 1980s fit this pattern.

However, a new government intent on broad social change does not necessarily define the elite that it intends to replace in broad terms. If it chooses a narrow definition, for whatever reason, it may produce only a few asylum-seekers. These may be viewed by other governments as classic political refugees from the top of the political pyramid. Under the traditional rules, particularly as these have been applied in Latin America, such refugees soon receive asylum in neighbouring states or in a handful of countries — such as France — that support the notion of political asylum. Thus, most political leaders who fled Chile after the assassination of Salvador Allende and the installation of the right-wing Pinochet regime found shelter easily. Their numbers, though perhaps substantial, did not approach the proportions of a mass exodus. In other instances, the elite to be rooted out may be defined in racial or ethnic terms which narrowly limit the number of those affected. This was the case, in part, in Poland during the late 1950s when Communists of Jewish extraction were deprived of leading positions and in known cases urged to emigrate. The outpourings of white settlers from some of the newly-established African states, such as Kenya in the early 1960s and Angola and Mozambique, in the 1970s, were of a similar nature. Thousands of individuals were involved in such departures, which they attributed to fear and pressure. These instances suggest that extremely bitter struggles for self-determination on the part of majorities against dominant elites identified on the basis of race may result in an outflow of people who believe themselves confronted with ruin or worse.

Legitimate replacement of elites

The replacement of one elite by another or changes of leadership connected with broad changes in society need not be violent or repressive. They may be planned and executed as part of a legitimate public policy and without involving repressive or inhumane intentions. The effects will obviously be visible in the form of a reduction in privileges — which may have been unearned — and a withdrawal of the honoured status that such groups once enjoyed. Such policies, though they can deprive the affected elites of their livelihood, do not involve punitive actions on the part of the government administration or the law-enforcing institutions. For instance, in India, Zambia and Zimbabwe, remaining members of the European elite — even those asked to remain in their civil service and military posts — could no longer automatically enjoy privileges on the basis of colour. As the government deliberately embarked on policies of localisation (that is, racial equality) in the civil service, politics, the military and society generally, members of the former elite were obliged to compete with those they once dominated. However much some of the affected persons may have contributed to the society, they could no longer count on unearned prestige. Similar effects flowed from reforms of land ownership in some former colonies. The privileges once enjoyed by colonial settlers were drastically reduced in such places as Kenya, Zambia and Zimbabwe, although here those concerned were not simply deprived of land; rather, the farmers were brought down from commanding heights.

In general such policies may inspire migration, sometimes of substantial proportions of the privileged groups; yet such migrants cannot as a rule claim asylum as refugees in the sense of the 1951 UN Convention. Because the policies encouraging migration can be defended as legitimate and desired by the majority, no obvious violation of human rights is implied. Nevertheless, those affected may be so convinced that their livelihood and long-term security are under threat that they feel obliged to depart. When their exit is accompanied by measures to control the export of capital and goods, the emigrants may arrive in their expected places of asylum with their ability to fend for themselves much reduced and certainly unable to live in their former style. Moreover, their skills, especially if based on specialised technical or cultural factors such as legal practice or plantation agriculture, may not be transferable or relevant to the demand for employees in their new places of residence. Nor are their political views and social practices always adaptable. As a result, some of the migrants may be unacceptable to asylum countries as settlers. They would equally be a matter of indifference to the government of their former homeland, which they have rejected. In such circumstances, their practical situation may resemble that of refugees under the 1951 Convention who are obliged to find asylum and self-sufficiency.

Economic obsolescence

Just as members of the elite or of defined sections of a population can be treated as dispensable under new social plans, so can broader layers of the masses not identified as opposing a government by political means. For example, social planning to encourage industrialisation can lead to the exclusion of certain kinds of artisanal production or agricultural work from an effective role in the economy. Nomadic patterns can be prohibited, or the practice of 'slash and burn' agriculture suppressed. Private property, such as mills or retail shops, can be socialised and the former owners told to shift for themselves. Such policies have been applied in various developing countries. People affected by these policies, especially the followers of traditional patterns, may conceive of their situations as desperate and seek to leave their homelands, either openly or covertly. Such emigrants have included Syrian shopkeepers from some West African countries, Asians in parts of East Africa and businessmen in Nicaragua.

Social policies with broad effects may also be implicit in the conduct of a government over an extended period of time. The insistence by a ruling elite on maintaining patterns of production that support its members but impoverish the masses would affect the population just as seriously as forced nationalisation would affect economic enterprises. In the case of Haiti, for example, the failure to produce any substantial economic development (not to mention the incompetence and repressive character of the Duvalier government) has given those faced with inevitable hunger a strong impetus to leave the country. Useless in their homeland, they brave destitution and legal proceedings in alien surroundings in the hope of finding work and asylum.

Mass economic obsolescence of so serious a nature as to cause people to migrate occurs most often in the developing countries or in situations where doctrinaire socialism, based on the elimination of defined classes, is to be installed. In precisely such cases, the social welfare provisions needed to tide over those affected during the period of transition either simply do not exist or else are not extended to the afflicted groups. In developed countries, the government will generally take measures to ease the effects of economic obsolescence and prevent so much pressure from building up as to force people to depart or face starvation. Nor is it always possible for those suffering from the effects of economic obsolescence to leave their homelands without incurring costs higher than those they would have incurred had they remained there. Yet whatever the legitimacy of the economic programmes which induce departure, they raise a serious issue concerning the basic human right to live, for people who have no work or other source of support do not enjoy minimum rights.

International political tension

Internal turbulence and deliberate structural change within states may provoke international political tension. Governments may also deliberately adopt policies intended to influence neighbouring countries, either by affecting their populations or by in some way suggesting threats to national security or to the existence of other governments. Such threats may be empty of real content or they may constitute early signals of a programme of heavier real pressure, including military action. These actions, too, will raise international tension. A certain amount of political tension, sometimes in an extreme form, sometimes relatively mild, precedes international war. But not all tense situations are resolved by fighting, and some may continue for decades without erupting into armed strife.

The government actions and decisions discussed in the following paragraphs have a heterogeneous character but are none the less real. Though they are less likely to lead to mass flows of population than some of the situations referred to earlier, they may cause some departures and on occasion the exodus of well-known individuals. At the same time, many of those who leave their homelands because of the impetuses noted here may not fit the formal definitions of refugee or even the usual conception of forced migrant.

Ideological opposition

Sharply opposed ideological stances adopted by governments tend to encourage dissidents to leave their homelands. This clash of doctrine may accompany revolutionary or other kinds of far-reaching social change. The departing dissidents oppose the general political orientation of their governments. They may have suffered punishment and active persecution or may consider that they are living under unacceptable pressure or threats; or else they may anticipate a worsening situation and try to leave ahead of it.

Dissidents who escape through restricted borders usually claim formal refugee status. They are likely to be treated as such in their country of asylum should they make their way to a territory where the ideological or political persuasion opposed to that in their own country holds sway. Clear examples of this are the Poles who slipped into Austria during the Polish unrest of 1981-82. Czechs and East Germans have also left their native countries in appreciable numbers since the end of the Second World War to enter Western Europe. In the case of East Germans, they have assurances of asylum in West Germany.

Those dissidents who leave under arranged conditions and have promises of asylum do not fit the definition of the 1951 UN Convention on Refugees but are usually received in the land of asylum as refugees. The recent flow of Jews from the Soviet Union is one illustration of this, as is the exodus from Vietnam to the United States under the orderly departure programme arranged by UNHCR. The Vietnamese who depart might conceivably have become refugees — and some of them are in bad odour in Vietnam for being either capitalists or pro-American — but because they are not outside their own country or deprived of government protection they do not satisfy the basic legal requirements. The outflow of many tens of thousands of people from Cuba can be explained partly on the basis of ideological opposition between the governments in Havana and Washington. The Cuban government regarded the emigrants as unreliable, socially pernicious and favourable to the anti-Communism of the United States. Therefore it eventually allowed them to depart without much restriction. The United States claimed to offer political freedom to those who opposed totalitarian rule and that the Cuban outflow merely demonstrated the depth of democratic opposition to the Castro government. In South-East Asia, the United States used a similar rationale for offering asylum to Vietnamese who were connected with the American presence and who feared persecution from the victorious North Vietnamese.

When exclusionary religious ideas become the basis of a national ideology, as in the case of Iran, tension may build up with nearby governments. Along with social and administrative pressures, this may create an atmosphere which propels minority religious groups to depart, even in the absence of any direct persecution on the part of the government. When British colonial rule in India ended with the creation of Muslim Pakistan as well as India, a vast migration ensued. It was driven by fear and considerable unofficial violence, although this was clearly not intended by the two new governments.

Political warfare

When governments undertake positive, but not military, tactics to frustrate the aims of other governments and disturb their functioning, this may be understood as political warfare. Ideological opposition may be used to justify such political warfare. Tactical measures taken to reach strategic goals, whether stated in ideological or other terms, may induce flows of refugees. A great variety of instruments is available to fit a like variety of situations. This section will touch on some that seem most relevant to forced migration.

Propaganda

Radio broadcasts, printed matter, film and photography and, in some circumstances, television (whose use may soon be extended by earth satellite transmission) can be used by governments and sometimes by private groups to carry messages to wide sectors of populations in other countries. These messages aim at demonstrating the truth, justice and other attractions of an opposing regime. They may encourage a widespread belief among a population of the benefits to be gained from leaving their homeland. A flow of migrants may result, demonstrating a partly induced degree of dissatisfaction which approaches the intolerable. Propaganda had an important role in the outflow of Hungarians during the 1956 uprising, and it continues to encourage — indirectly if not deliberately — illegal emigration from Eastern Europe. Propaganda from the Soviet Union, Eastern Europe and Cuba occasionally encourages nationals of the United States and Western European countries to seek political asylum in the other camp.

Inadvertent, unfocused information that has a propaganda-like influence can emanate from the ordinary media operations of adjacent countries. The tightly controlled population of a repressive regime may hear on the radio and sometimes see on television that easier or more favourable conditions exist nearby. A number of people will be encouraged to escape in this way. This mechanism can be readily observed in East Germany where West German radio and television broadcasts are readily receivable, in Cuba where American radio can be heard, and in North Korea where radio broadcasts can be received from the south.

Support of opposition groups

Governments or private associations sometimes support organised opposition or dissident groups in other countries. Such support may be either clandestine or fairly open. It may be limited to verbal expression but may also include financing, material support in the form of, for instance, propaganda materials or medicine and in some cases military supplies. Outside support of opposition groups is intended to promote political change, either of the regime or of its policies. It therefore tends to encourage internal turbulence and may result in persecution or heavy pressure being put on those who favour the foreign-supported movement. Some of this pressure may be sanctioned by law. The resulting stresses may cause certain people to act as if they were deliberately forced to migrate or were indeed subject to persecution.

Foreign-supported opposition movements were important during the period of decolonisation which followed the Second World War. The Soviet Union, for instance, supported anti-colonial movements in Angola and Mozambique during the breakdown of the Portuguese colonial regime. The message that was understood by many settlers included threats to their livelihood and security, and most of them left. Central America in the early 1980s offers another example of foreign-supported opposition. Both Cuba and the United States had their governmental clients: the former in Nicaragua, the latter in El Salvador and Honduras. Along with military violence, a widespread awareness of danger stimulated a movement of these countries' inhabitants to places of presumed safety. It seems clear that when the encouragement of opposition groups is successful in developing or formulating opposition to a government, revolution or insurrection may soon follow, inducing further forced migration.

Economic pressure

Programmed interference by governments with foreign economic relationships — which may be intended as punitive sanctions or merely as irritants — can also be used in political warfare. When the more ambitious kinds of interference succeed, they tend to cause emigration from the target country, because people in affected industries lose their livelihoods. American sanctions against Cuba may have given more urgency to plans by Cubans to emigrate; for some, it may have been a matter of economic survival to leave. Some who leave their homeland under economic pressure are able to retain some of their resources and thus have little need of material aid in their new home. As some of those affected by economic sanctions or who foresee damage are likely to be leaders of industry and business, a proportion of those who leave will also have arranged for legal residence in other countries and have meagre grounds for a claim of asylum. Others may arrive seeking asylum who feel that they have been deprived of basic rights. However, the number of those who claim to have been forced to migrate because of economic sanctions is likely to be small if the history of this type of political warfare is any guide.

Organised international political action

While international tension can commonly be traced to autonomously decided policies of sovereign governments, such international institutions as the United Nations or the Organisation for African Unity may create generalised political pressure in certain situations. They can attempt to legitimise political warfare undertaken by national governments. Multilateral efforts can contribute to the tension surrounding a dispute; this will endure until efforts to settle it succeed or an armed struggle results. Organised activities that develop an international standard of behaviour by governments may become the basis of an ideology. Consequent promotion of such an ideology could increase international tension.

Dispute-handling

The engagement of a multilateral organisation in a dispute-settling process leads immediately to an increase in awareness of the international conflict in question. More governments necessarily become involved in it, as knowledgeable witnesses if nothing more. Ensuing discussions within the jurisdictions of the governments concerned may convince the countries' inhabitants that war or a painfully sharp crisis may ensue. They may wish to remove themselves from possible future danger and thus seek to leave. It is probable that the involvement of the United Nations and the Organization of African Unity in the Rhodesia/Zimbabwe dispute had this effect. Similarly, it is very likely that OAS pressure on Cuba at the time when Fidel Castro was consolidating his successful revolution was partly responsible for the departure of Cubans to asylum elsewhere.

Political attacks

International organisations, especially the United Nations, receive the power from their member-states to impose economic and political sanctions in circumstances where a threat or breach of the peace has occurred. While this power has rarely been exercised, it provided the basis for economic sanctions against the Ian Smith government of Rhodesia. The export of tobacco and certain minerals was sharply reduced as the result of a boycott imposed by the UN Security Council. At the same time, normal diplomatic intercourse and the ability of Rhodesians to travel was put under pressure; some white Rhodesians promptly departed to havens in South Africa, Britain and elsewhere. Although the case did not lend itself to claims of deprivation of human rights as a basis for material aid or asylum, it is conceivable that sanctions organised by an international institution could have such an outcome. In fact, at one stage Portugal claimed that so much damage had been done by the sanctions to the economies of its African colonies that it had a right to help from the UN in accordance with the provisions of the UN Charter.

Protection of human rights

International co-operation to establish and nurture regimes to protect human rights may result in pressure being placed on alleged violators — usually governments — of the general norms. Such pressure will most likely take the form of publicity or criticism by other governments. But it may go further — as with the strong criticism of Greece by the Council of Europe during the dictatorship of Colonel Papadopoulos — resulting in the political isolation of the regime in question and the strengthening of its internal opposition. Allegations and investigations of violations of human rights have the effect of sensitising those who have been deprived in their own situation. They may feel encouraged to seek better conditions elsewhere or to raise protests which will result in their persecution and, thus, additional reasons for departure.

Complaints under the Helsinki Agreement against Soviet and Polish government actions, and Polish adherence to the convention on freedom of association supervised by the International Labour Organisation were probably responsible for stimulating the departure of some who felt their conditions had become intolerable or who became politically active in ways that accorded with international instruments. In an indirect way, the Polish government acknowledged the force of the human rights situation as a reason for exile when it offered activists a chance to emigrate without obstruction. Complaints against South Africa as a violator of human rights also tend to enforce claims for asylum on the part of political activists who make their way abroad in order to avoid punishment. Others may be encouraged to leave surreptitiously in order to join liberation movements. A number of South African whites have defected so as to avoid service in that country's military force which they claim violates international law and human rights.

Notes

1. For some theoretical treatments, see footnote 1, Chapter III, and Egon F. Kunz, 'Exile and Resettlement: Refugee Theory', *International Migration Review*, XV, 1-2 (spring-summer 1981) pp. 42-51.

2. Most of the incidents referred to in this chapter are common knowledge. As the intention here is to use this common knowledge as illustration, the reader is referred to the Bibliography for references to material that may elaborate on the incidents mentioned.

3. Cf. William Shawcross's treatment of the Cambodian refugee situation, *The Quality of Mercy* (Simon and Schuster, New York, 1984) and the much more chronological and factual report by Barry Wain, *The Refused* (Simon and Schuster, New York, 1981) on the flight from Vietnam. However valuable such reports may be, based in part on eye-witness accounts, they suffer from a lack, for instance, of real access to the authorities in the countries of departure, rely little on documentation and certainly have few pretensions to scholarship. At the time of writing they are, none the less, main sources and unlikely to be supplemented in the very near future, though complementary material will gradually emerge.

4. Comparability of data remains very difficult because of differences in approach, in depth of accounts and variations in normative intentions. As a rule, also, the less developed the country of origin or the receiving country, the less likely it is that refugee issues will have been dealt with thoroughly. Thus, histories and political studies of Ethiopia are available; they rarely deal with mass movement and have practically nothing to say about refugee issues. The public papers of governments vary as much as the issuers do and are often unconvincing without bureaucratic papers, to which there is no access. No one as yet seems to have persuaded the authorities in Hanoi to provide access to papers of the sort that automatically accompany, for instance, consideration of a proposed law in the United States Congress.

5. Bureaucratic defensiveness, sheer lack of time and resources, and efforts to manipulate opinion can all be added to the list of understandable concerns related to the protection of threatened individuals.

6. The term 'revolution' is used in the sense of a deliberate effort to produce a drastic change of social policies, along with the replacement of a ruling group. Violence may be employed in order to gain social control. The term implies a considerable level of popular support in contrast to, say, the circumstances surrounding a palace *coup d'état*.

5

Responses to Movements of Refugees

Once refugees begin to move, they must arrive in, or attempt to enter, the territory of some state other than their country of origin. Alternatively, in what the United Nations calls 'refugee-like' situations, they may be displaced within their homelands, moving later into the territory of other states. Their appearance, or the expectation that they will arrive, calls forth patterns of reaction that can be sketched from contemporary refugee incidents. This chapter undertakes to set out such reactions. It takes up where the previous chapter left off, shifting from causal factors to the way in which governmental and other social organisations react to the impact of asylum-seekers. It concentrates on the implications of important recent forced migrations, referring to certain incidents by way of illustration.

Governments, it is assumed here, will not as a rule simply drive people away, although they have been known to do so. Moreover, governments that do not adhere to the UN Convention on Refugees may claim to have no obligation to give asylum to anyone. Nevertheless the UN General Assembly has endorsed the principle of *non-refoulement*, and governments that do adhere to the Convention take on the legal obligation not to send refugees back to persecution or into danger. When incidents of *refoulement* occur, the refugees either fall into the hands of the very authorities from whose jurisdiction they sought to escape or else end up in the territory of a third government. In the latter case, they remain refugees and the patterns set out here will apply. A government that flatly refuses to do anything for those who are fleeing and sends them away may risk moral opprobrium but is not actually obliged to deal with the material effects of the direct presence of refugees.

Urgent assistance

Forced migrants, even those who may have had substantial financial resources and connections abroad, almost always require some
form of urgent assistance. Their need for shelter, food and medical
care may be so strong as to take precedence over any legal procedure
normally required for the granting or refusing of asylum: if the
individuals concerned are not given immediate help, they will die.
In other instances, the need for such assistance as will provide the
basic necessities of life may press for but not quite demand emergency action. Later, if asylum has been granted, assistance in the
form of information and orientation also takes on an urgent
character. Those granted asylum need to have a clear sense of their
rights as far as work, the various kinds of welfare services available
and movement within the host country are concerned.

The massive refugee movements that have recently taken place
in some of the least developed parts of the world have called for
urgent reactions on an unprecedented scale. Bangladesh, Somalia
and Indo-China have provided concrete examples of this. At the
rate of hundreds per day, refugees arrive from across a border; they
soon number thousands. They suffer from hunger, disease, wounds,
exhaustion and psychological confusion. Along the way, in some
cases, they have been beaten, robbed and raped after having bribed
their way to an escape route. In other instances, they may have
moved under the cover of a darkness that failed to shield them from
attacks by military and police. They may enter areas where the local
authorities have little capacity to be of help, or even to ensure decent
lives for the local residents. It may take weeks before national,
regional and global reactions are able to summon aid.

Responses within a state

Only broad generalisations, taking in a boundless variety of specific
actions, seem possible with regard to the responses of national
governments to an influx of refugees. Each country's government
and population tend to treat specific emergencies according to its
own social practices. The standards that a government applies may
be influenced by the urging and programmes of transnational agencies, such as the Red Cross movement. In most cases, however, local
cultural and ethical practices are likely to dominate. Though in
theory international legal obligations to respond in a manner

consistent with humane practice or human rights standards should control the behaviour of a government, in reality these obligations are limited in scope and by the interpretations that governments give — or omit to give — them in the course of application.

Modest numbers

Faced with a modest number of asylum-seekers, the people and authorities of most societies are likely to react in a compassionate way. In almost any emergency situation, certain individuals come forward to assist those who are threatened. Their example often resonates throughout the surrounding society. The authorities and social groups, such as the churches, either echo this compassion or invoke it at once: for example, Muslim precepts regarding guests and fellow believers appear to have had an important influence on the initial reception of refugees in the Horn of Africa and in Pakistan. As a rule, African governments claim that their subjects react hospitably to forced migrants. Some American church members insist on defying the authorities to give refuge to those claiming to have fled threatening conditions in El Salvador. In certain other situations, nevertheless, family, clan and religion set the boundaries of assistance: refugees who do not belong to the acceptable categories receive little or no help from local residents.

A general definition of 'modest numbers' appears impossible. As long as parochial, social and cultural perceptions regard the numbers as unthreatening, it may be supposed that the term 'modest' applies. When a superior authority — particularly national governments — begin to treat the presence of refugees as an issue calling for a general decision, then the numbers in question may be deemed to have exceeded the level of 'modest'. Local social and cultural perceptions of the appropriate handling of a few refugees will relate to the economic capacity of the locality and its inhabitants. Some refugees from Cuba to the United States were absorbed locally, with only the slightest glance from the national government. Somali families appear to have absorbed considerable numbers of relatives, however distant, from Ogaden. Yet refugees from Palestine, arriving in far richer areas, found no easy access to local absorption, perhaps because the authorities in asylum areas usually intervened at once. Groups of Tamil-speaking asylum-seekers from Sri Lanka began arriving in Western Europe in groups of approximately three to 20 people during the last months of 1984. Especially in the Netherlands and England, they were treated by the authorities as possible illegal immigrants, and some were returned to Sri Lanka. Others were housed in temporary status amidst public controversy involving the authorities, political leaders and voluntary agencies, but very few quickly received refugee status.

Large numbers

What is decided locally determines or has a strong bearing on whether an inflow of refugees is considered modest and dealt with at local level or whether broader decisions are needed and a higher authority is called on to assume responsibility. While no general rule can be given, in a situation where local markets display very rapid price increases and food and shelter become scarce, or when those already living in the host district view the newcomers as a threat to normal security, or to social stability, the national authorities are almost certain to intervene.

If, however, the national authorities decide for whatever reason, including local information or on the basis of estimates made in the capital, that the refugees represent a threat to national security, they will almost invariably take over the management of the influx. Political activity among the newcomers or threats from their country of origin has an effect on the national authorities: in Thailand, for example, the entry of both Vietnamese and Cambodians provoked a reaction from the authorities in Bangkok, who were alert to friction along the border with Vietnam.

When provincial or national authorities intervene in a situation that begins to overpower local sympathy, they may not necessarily treat the new arrivals as legitimate refugees. A process of this kind took place in the United States during the early arrival in Florida of those fleeing through Mariel. At first, the problem was treated as one of local assistance in which the national government avoided giving the asylum-seekers formal status as refugees. As the numbers mounted, material assistance inevitably became a burden too great to be borne by families and local organisations and engaged the attention of state and local government. A great deal of uncertainty remained as to whether the Cubans were to be treated as refugees under the United States Refugee Act of 1980. In fact they were not, even though the Federal government began to reimburse local authorities for expenses along the lines provided for in the 1980 act. Haitians who arrived at the same time by independent means were, however, not granted asylum, despite the fact that their numbers were fewer and that the local authorities seem not to have made an issue of their arrival.

These incidents in Florida, however, differ sharply from the situation in a very poor country, where the low level of international communication may be of great importance in determining when an influx of refugees is deemed an issue for the national agenda. In the case of Florida, the newcomers soon came into contact with the field officers of the national government who sought to exclude illegal immigrants. Whatever the formal position of the asylum-seekers was, their presence rapidly became known in the capital and the mass media; no policy of turning a blind eye would be tenable for long. The same applied to Polish *émigrés* who left as a result of the tension that arose in the wake of the Solidarity movement, and to the Tamils who arrived in Western Europe, usually via East Berlin, during the last few months of 1984 and the first half of 1985. To the degree that a national policy of alert policing of borders is executed, it may become generalised; thus the chance increases that an influx of forced migrants will become an issue beyond the capacity of the local authorities.

Voluntary agencies provide another channel of communication that may result in a refugee issue being raised from the local to the national level. If voluntary agencies with general humanitarian goals or programmes focused on immigrants exist in the area of a modern inflow, they will almost certainly attempt to provide emergency aid. Should they be overwhelmed or seriously engaged, their national headquarters will soon come to know of the incident. National voluntary organisations without local branches will become engaged as the sheer weight of numbers bring an incident to the attention of the national authorities. In many countries, the Red Cross society is practically an official government agency; its employment or otherwise will therefore depend on a governmental decision. Alternatively, its officials, acting on the basis of local information, may seek a governmental request in order to mount a broader programme.

The patterns suggested here vary almost infinitely in different places at different times. Even where considerable experience with refugees is in the immediate past — as in Zaïre or Sudan — precedent does not always make for accurate forecasts as to the treatment of a new group. In the latter two countries, shifting foreign policies complicate responses; so, in the Sudan, do the levels of agricultural production in areas that are often short of food. Thus, the reception of refugees can even be influenced by the failure of monsoon rains.

Obligations of states

Whether any specific legal obligation to give emergency assistance to asylum-seekers applies to a given state remains doubtful; its own laws as well as international agreements would presumably guide a government. Yet even the widely applied UN Convention on Refugees remains silent on this point, for it requires that welfare begins once asylum has been granted. The Red Cross promotes standards of governmental conduct that may bring emergency succour to asylum-seekers in time of war.[1] While the practice of governments in the case of mass influxes has been to give entire groups temporary, exceptional asylum and emergency aid,[2] in smaller incidents individual examination can take place and an immediate decision by authorities on the spot can deny entry. These practices, however, do not establish a legal obligation. Nor is it clear how many governments would accept that they have a general moral obligation to decide quickly on asylum. This point has caused a good deal of legal controversy with regard to Haitians seeking asylum in the United States, where some have claimed refugee status. The decisional process has in some cases been a lengthy one and in others has given rise to formal complaints about faulty procedures.

The UN General Assembly has made numerous recommendations to its member-states and other intergovernmental organisations to aid refugees in general and in particular those in such countries as Somalia, Sudan and the Arab neighbours of Israel. These entail no legal obligation even if they are sometimes used by international officials to argue the existence of a moral obligation or a course of conduct which accords with customary international rules. But it is extremely doubtful whether they can be enforced in a national court unless congruent domestic legislation exists.

Similarly, the UN General Assembly has asked UNHCR to care for the emergency needs of refugees generally and in some particular instances. Such instructions do not place a legal obligation on governments, which can, moreover, resist the attentions of UNHCR with little difficulty if they so wish. Both the Pol Pot and the Heng Samrin regimes in Cambodia, for example, refused to give UNHCR and other international agencies anything approaching easy access to the country and its people or even to its government.

The obligations of the more than 80 governments that have adhered to the UN Convention on Economic and Social Rights, which provide for decent standards of food, shelter and health for all within their jurisdiction, are conceptually firmer than mere recommendations. Even this list of rights, however, is treated by the adherents to the convention as a standard of aspiration rather than as a set of immediately applicable rules.[3] If governments offer aid to newcomers which conforms to the standards of the convention or to levels recommended through other international actions, they usually do so on the basis of local practices and laws rather than by giving effect to generalised international rules and practices.

Transnational responses

In forced migrations of any notoriety, a transnational response to the need for emergency assistance is likely. A transnational response engages persons or organisations — including governments and intergovernmental agencies — from countries other than those entered directly by asylum-seekers with emergency needs. A wide variety of responses in terms of organisations and forms of aid may follow an appeal for help or other warning of the need for humanitarian assistance.

The government that allows outside assistance for asylum-seekers on its territories retains formal control over the actual execution of transnationally supported programmes; in fact, the supervision by the government may be rudimentary or hardly undertaken. This may be the case even when elaborate agreements are reached between the government and aid donors. Variations in this regard ultimately depend on what the affected government decides. As some emergency situations overwhelm local and even national authorities, the host government may in fact give way to programming by out-side organisations or persons. Thus, a transnational response to emergencies involving forced migrants can sometimes supersede the ability of the host government to make effective decisions.

Bilateral governmental responses

Any government may, either on its own initiative or at the request of the beleaguered authorities, offer material aid. Bilateral arrangements based on such offers may be encouraged by a close existing relationship among the giving and receiving countries before the emergency took place, or the relations may grow closer as a result of the response. Bilateral aid may also signal a hope on the part of the donor to dominate the reactions of the receiving governments towards the asylum-seekers or to exclude the influence of other organisations.

The Soviet Union and its close allies customarily refuse to assist intergovernmental agencies or to co-operate with non-governmental groups offering aid to refugees. If members of the Soviet group offer any assistance at all, they do so on a bilateral basis, as they did in Cambodia following the Vietnamese intervention. The United States sometimes supports intergovernmental agencies and non-governmental collaborators while simultaneously providing bilateral aid to a government. Governments also occasionally offer aid to migrants whose character does not fit easily with the programmes of intergovernmental bodies. The outflow of Jews from the Soviet Union, for example, does not involve UNHCR, in part because the asylum-seekers migrate in an orderly fashion and have the assurance of a place of asylum, either in Israel or the United States.

Intergovernmental responses

Almost all refugee incidents involving more than a few asylum-seekers imply some involvement on the part of intergovernmental organisations. These responses range from informal discussion through diplomatic representation of the appearance of asylum-seekers to ensure that a few refugees get proper care to the mounting of large-scale programmes based on extensive networks of agencies and individuals who actually administer the assistance. While the nucleus of a network has a permanent existence within an established institution, or set of institutions, large-scale emergencies may stimulate vast *ad hoc* organisational constructions, tying several networks together. An impressive total of human and financial resources may be assembled.

A government that receives asylum-seekers on its territory can usually take an initiative that will trigger a transnational response to help with material assistance in an emergency. It can choose to stimulate organisations specialising in coping with disasters, those specialised in handling refugee situations, those dealing with tasks that may involve refugees or with a combination of these.

A few intergovernmental organisations have developed some capacity to react to disasters, but not a comprehensive basis or one that relies solely on their own initiative. The UN Disaster Relief Organisation, which has had considerable difficulty in creating a useful role, supposedly concentrates on co-ordinating information. It has no facilities to assemble and move supplies or personnel to the points of need. It is able to provide only very modest financial support; other organisations will, presumably, react to its warnings. Some of these organisations do in fact respond to man-made disasters, especially when the UN system or regional grouping offers a basis for action. Yet even here, intervention is unlikely without encouragement from the relevant governments and positive permission from the government of any country where a field programme is to be undertaken. Thus, the World Food Program can often furnish supplies in emergencies, sometimes very rapidly by diverting them from other programmed developmental users; it supplied substantial quantities of foodstuffs, for example, for use in Somalia and for the Cambodian refugees. UNICEF and the World Health Organisation have furnished both supplies and expert personnel. Small numbers of experts can be despatched for short terms by other organisations, such as the Food and Agriculture Organisation of the UN or the UN Educational, Scientific and Cultural Organisation. Regional organisations, such as the Organization for African Unity, or the [British] Commonwealth of Nations, also sometimes offer personnel.

UNHCR has the greatest capacity and experience of all the intergovernmental organisations to respond to emergencies involving the forcible displacement of human beings, especially of those belonging to the formally defined category of refugees. As a virtually permanent organisation with definite assignments that have been repeatedly approved by the UN General Assembly, UNHCR can claim to act with the backing of an international constituency. It is able to react to requests from governments in need on the basis of executive decisions. It does not need first to refer requests to legislative organs. The High Commissioner has an emergency fund of $10 million on which to draw, and a great deal of successful experience at raising contributions from governments., Many of the UNHCR staff have worked on earlier emergencies and taken part in the rapid expansion of field facilities. UNHCR also organised an emergency unit in 1981 and has set out programmed responses to requests for immediate assistance.[4] In recent years, UNHCR has — as, for example, in the Sa Kaeo holding centre for Cambodians in Thailand — managed a considerable number of enterprises designed to assist forced migrants in emergency conditions, even though its mandate formally prohibits it from taking an operational role.

A response by UNHCR to an emergency usually includes legal protection of refugees in addition to material assistance; in fact, from a historical standpoint, legal protection remains its primary task with material aid developing as an essential precondition in some situations. Legal protection can also be of an emergency nature, as for example when the government of Thailand forcibly expelled thousands of Cambodians at Preah Vihar in 1979.[5] *Non-refoulement* of refugees is a fundamental principle of UNHCR's existence, as well as of that of asylum-seekers. Moreover, expelled refugees who fall into the hands of those they are fleeing are by definition beyond emergency material aid from an intergovernmental organisation.

As a rule attempts to promote legal protection of refugees against such threats as *refoulement* or expulsion, whether in an emergency situation or otherwise, remain cloaked in diplomatic discretion. Little is known about UNHCR activities in particular situations where legal protection fails, though occasionally it becomes publicly known — as, for example with the case of the treatment of Haitian entrants in the United States — that UNHCR has actively tried to promote treatment that accords with its standards. Sometimes UNHCR deliberately makes a public statement on a situation which involves the refusal of asylum and the endangering of human life. It did so more than once during the tense situation caused by the 'boat people' leaving Vietnam and also with regard to the Moskito Indians from Nicaragua who sought asylum in Honduras.

Incidents such as these involve political decisions on the part of national governments. In contrast, UNHCR emphasises its humanitarian interest. Consequently, its emergency interventions to preserve the rights of refugees are given an air of public restraint, however much private activity is undertaken. This activity may in fact have a considerable effect when it takes place at field level in rapid reaction to a threat. The effect, however, depends on the attitude of the government concerned, not merely on whether UNHCR makes a plea for the rights of refugees. As UNHCR has offices in some 90 countries, it has in any case more capacity and skill than any other organisation to react to an emergency in which the rights of refugees to be free from the threat of *refoulement* are threatened.

The UNHCR chain of field offices can stimulate governments to request material assistance from international agencies. UNHCR personnel may suggest directly to governments, or to other diplomatic representatives who may approach the government concerned, that broader material support may be available through the international community. Such initiatives can be supported from UNHCR headquarters with additional suggestions regarding the availability of assistance coming via other channels. This possibility gains credence as a result of UNHCR's recent experience with material assistance and from the fact that it has some financial resources for immediate use. Yet whatever the tone of UNHCR suggestions, the formal right of the government faced with asylum-

seekers to decide on its policies remains. It must in the end consent
to the involvement of intergovernmental agencies.

UNHCR responses to requests for material assistance either
immediately or in the very near future involve the appointment of
an 'operating partner'. More often than not, this partner is the
government affected by a refugee inflow. This has invariably been
the case in very large-scale refugee inflows, such as those in Somalia
or Pakistan, although the international agency may have an influential role in setting up the programme and in the selection and use
of other offers of assistance. As a rule the terms of the 'partnership'
are explicitly set out in a formal agreement — generally treated as
confidential and kept from public view — between UNHCR and
the recipient government. UNHCR provides at least supplementary, and sometimes complete, financing for the refugees. It attempts
to verify that relevant budgets are prepared and that expenditures
actually produce the intended results. It does not, however, render
highly detailed accounts of the results of this supervision. Responsibility for the camps and settlements almost always rests on the
operating partner, while UNHCR provides counsel, specialised skills
and services and a channel of communication to wider networks.
Other organisations are usually involved, depending on the attitude
of the recipient government, especially when it comes to delivering
ameliorative services to the asylum-seekers or administering camps
and other enterprises that consume or distribute the material
assistance. This group of assisting organisations generally signs
tripartite agreements with UNHCR and the government. These
agreements, like those between UNHCR and a recipient government tend to be secluded from examination by outsiders.

Most emergencies imply little activity for the Intergovernmental
Committee on Migration. Its skills in selecting and transporting
refugees and other migrants to lands of permanent settlement have
more relevance to the liquidation of refugee incidents than to
immediate responses. Nevertheless, when Cuban nationals overran
the Peruvian embassy in Havana at the beginning of the events
leading to the Mariel exodus, ICM offered and, within a few days
supplied, the emigrants with transportation from Cuba to asylum
abroad. This service was soon brought to an end by the Cuban
government.

Regional organisations of governments may conceivably have
several roles in emergencies. The European Communities have
established a substantial emergency fund; its officials have the power
to make disbursements from it. The OAU has little financial

capacity, but it can sometimes make useful policy recommendations, encourage the granting of asylum and in a modest way offer technical advice. The OAS has on occasion appealed for both places of asylum and financing to meet emergencies. Its interest in human rights supports the general policy of granting asylum. Still other organisations — such as the Council of Europe or the Nordic Council — can be instrumental in spreading awareness of refugee incidents, supporting the protection of rights and appealing for support.

Although intergovernmental organisations may assemble and dispose of important resources for use in an emergency situation, their capacities remain rather narrow compared with the number and variety of possible appeals to them. Furthermore, their permanent officials work within close limits when contemplating initiatives. This is no self-starting system that spouts money and goods whenever it senses an emergency humanitarian situation.

The tightness of these limitations can easily be seen from the fact that a fund of $10 million, at the discretion of the UN High Commissioner for Refugees, is set against needs. In 1984, the programmes it then had in progress cost more than 20 times that much. A large-scale emergency can easily wipe out $10 million. The World Food Program provides substantial shipments of food for developmental purposes in the developing countries. It does not explicitly plan for emergency service, and in some circumstances is not able quickly to divert foodstuffs for rapid material assistance to forced migrants. It does not keep vast stores in various convenient locations under its own control. It oversees the shipments of stores provided by governments within their own jurisdictions. UNICEF and WHO operate under similar restrictions as far as their programmes are concerned, which are specific and of a nature limited with regard to supplies, although UNICEF does maintain a warehouse for emergencies. In the case of other organisations with skills of possible relevance to refugee situations, it may be necessary to make policy decisions in a somewhat laborious manner through bodies made up of government representatives. This is the situation generally in such developmental agencies as the UN Development Programme, even though its resident directors serve as the senior officials of the UN system in many locations.

In any intergovernmental organisation, action depends on a request from a concerned government. This formal limitation translates into quite real policy issues. Even if a government requests urgent material assistance of a sort that seems possible and permissible, the directors of intergovernmental agencies have far from *carte blanche* to move supplies and personnel to the field. Such a government request must correspond to the legal capacity of the international agency in question. For example, UNHCR may well respond to a request from a government for material and legal aid for refugees, but it simply cannot undertake to remove a group of refugees unless it is clear that they have safe asylum prepared elsewhere. Furthermore, the host government has a direct interest in and responsibility for the way an international agency executes its programmes. It may maintain a surveillance that is so close as to resemble control, as was the case in Cambodia; or alternatively, as in certain instances, it may try to tie the intergovernmental programme to specific guidelines which can affect the local economic situation. The Thai government, for instance, insists that rice and other food for the holding centres financed by UNHCR be purchased locally. That government claims that this fosters efficiency.

Merely engaging an intergovernmental agency in a refugee situation may stimulate an awareness of discordant aims within the requesting government with regard to the work of the outside organisation. To begin with, emergency aid is the aim, but the quality of the assistance and the way it is administered may have a long-term effect. It is axiomatic among field officials that the manner in which an effort to assist refugees begins will probably determine a great deal about the way it ends. For instance, UNHCR routinely asks governments to provide first asylum to refugees as a condition of its participation. But some of the South-East Asian governments point to their lack of adherence to international treaties regarding refugees and do not envisage even a distant possibility of asylum for those who fled Indo-China. A stiff attitude on the part of an international agency in such circumstances could result in the deaths of innocent people.

This dissonance of policy and programme was illustrated graphically in Thailand. By the creation of several categories of assistance and shelter, the Thai government and UNHCR dealt in different ways with Vietnamese refugees who had a high probability of resettlement and with Cambodians who had a low one. UNHCR was able to operate holding centres — not refugee camps with implied protected status — for some Cambodians. Others were confined to the dangerous border areas, where UNICEF and the ICRC came to the rescue during 1979-80. This did nothing to soften the opposition of the government in Pnom Penh to the whole effort on the border where it correctly observed that its armed enemies were encamped. Nor did it make it easier for donors to convince the Heng Samrin government to allow its personnel to check on the distribution of internationally provided supplies within Cambodia. Thus, the engagement of the intergovernmental organisations in emergency assistance posed the question of whether services to refugees or national policies should guide activities on the ground. A stubborn government can in the end usually go a long way to set the conditions.

Within this legal and political framework, intergovernmental organisations — including UNHCR — usually avoid appearing publicly to offer assistance to a government which has not yet requested it. Even when a request has been made, there can be difficulty enough in working out adequate conditions for the rendering of emergency assistance. At the same time, the intergovernmental agencies can often discreetly stimulate a request, especially when clearly capable of offering practical help in meeting a difficult local situation. These formal requests have great significance for the organisations, which are then able to fulfil their mandates, satisfy desires on the part of their staffs to serve, justify and expand their organisational existence and demonstrate that refugees in need actually benefit. Accordingly, UNHCR staff members consulted repeatedly with the Somali government before it asked for assistance in late 1979. Some would judge that the request nevertheless came too late to prevent a disaster. Whatever the case, UNHCR had little time to prepare plans as the flood of people rapidly grew. As usual, UNHCR made no open predictions about the wave of refugees from Ethiopia. Thus, it is not clear what anyone expected. The discretion surrounding the UNHCR initiatives reflects an organisational policy that forbids public anticipation of refugee situations.[6] This prohibition derives from the belief by senior officials that anticipation of specific refugee flows would be an affront to the governments concerned and thereby prevent the organisation from serving its unfortunate clients.

The demands of very large waves of refugees — such as those occurring in South-East Asia and the Horn of Africa — induced marked alterations in the usual style of initiatives by intergovernmental agencies. Increasingly, the UN Secretary-General has appeared as the focal point for appeals and negotiations. Thus, at the 1979 Conference on the South-East Asian Refugees,[7] Secretary-General Kurt Waldheim presided over a gathering which ostensibly had a purely humanitarian colouring. It made no recommendations, but did dramatise the possibilities of international community actions and put the attending governments under a certain moral obligation to react. It would be naïve to imagine such a meeting without diplomatic initiatives to persuade governments not only to help but to halt the actions which cause refugees. Vietnam was represented; its hard-bitten statement gave no quarter to its critics. Secretary-General Waldheim nevertheless negotiated an agreement — suggested by France — under which Vietnam stated its willingness to limit the outflow of refugees. Waldheim himself made it public at a press conference. The Secretary-General appointed Sir Robert Jackson, perhaps the most experienced international administrator in humanitarian emergencies, as a co-ordinator for material assistance to Cambodians. The clear expectation — which took effect almost immediately — was that this official would undertake initiatives. The General Assembly, moreover, has repeatedly called attention to the need for help in specific refugee situations, especially in Africa, while the UN Secretariat mounted special surveys of needs. This series of actions suggests that both new opportunities and new complexities may develop for organisational initiatives.

Some governments — such as that of Ethiopia — have treated the extension of intergovernmental activity as an opportunity to put their own cases for assistance more strongly. They call attention to their own needs, and see to it that there is an echo in the General Assembly. They can point to a large number of displaced persons in refugee-like situations on their own territories or they are giving asylum to groups of refugees that the rest of the world little notices. They claim a right to international aid at a level provided refugees elsewhere. UNHCR and some other agencies have responded to these claims; their programmes are intended to discourage more outflows of refugees and increase the likelihood of return. Thus, the result of emergency assistance programmes has generally been to educate governments about additional possibilities of support and to stimulate additional requests for the involvement of intergovernmental agencies.

Voluntary organisations

The provision of emergency aid to refugees has increasingly involved voluntary agencies in all their variety and specialisation. Several among them will almost certainly react to any emergency situation, but it is impossible to predict accurately which and to what extent. Nevertheless, a few generalisations may be set out with some degree of certainty.

Voluntary organisations acting in refugee emergencies almost always have their main support in highly developed countries and seek financial contributions from a public wider than the government. Generally speaking, they reflect relative economic affluence and rely on public appeals for both moral support and finances. Very few of these organisations — for instance — the US-based International Rescue Committee — come into action in an emergency because of their special interest in refugees. Still fewer are prepared to leap into action in an emergency with a full roster of personnel and warehouses of supplies. Among the organisations that have taken a special interest in refugees, some are connected with larger, religious bodies. Lutheran World Services which helped Tanzania with the long term asylum given refugees from Mozambique during the anti-colonial uprising may serve as an example. So could Catholic Migration Services, which assisted with the repatriation of Zimbabwean refugees in a very rapid operation. Other agencies dealing with refugees based their interest on the place of resettlement; this applies to some of the Jewish organisations that deal with refugees going to Israel. Other agencies help in disasters of any kind. The League of Red Cross Societies and its national member organisations provide the clearest example of an agency with broad aims that is able to help in cases of man-made disaster that lead to forced migration. Others provide highly specialised aid, sometimes connected with development programmes. OXFAM and Médicins Sans Frontières are among such groups. A number of relatively new organisations, such as the evangelical World Vision, have taken a recent interest in refugee affairs and offer help in emergencies.

Both the general humanitarian agencies and those with narrower aims have increasingly joined in large-scale programmes for emergency aid to forced migrants led by intergovernmental organisations. Such voluntary agencies typically function in one of three modes of relationship to each other: they can operate under contracts with UNHCR or sometimes another intergovernmental agency; they can join in a governmental programme supervised by UNHCR; or they can make an independent arrangement for their operations with a government that undertakes its own direction of the relief effort. These arrangements vary from situation to situation and may also lack internal consistency, depending on the aims and persuasiveness of the voluntary agency in question and its reception by a host government. To give some examples, the International Rescue Committee has provided medical care to certain Afghan refugees in Pakistan and Thailand. In both these cases, the government and the agency developed their plans, which were fitted to UNHCR programmes. In Somalia, where UNHCR had formal sanction as the co-ordinating agency for the government, Médicins sans Frontières sent teams during the heaviest influx of people from Ogaden.

The specific organisational patterns, however, vary widely. For instance, in 1979 ICRC worked as a full partner with UNICEF during the emergency presented by the starving Cambodians on the Thai border, but it had no role in the official refugee camps or holding centres in Thailand. The World Food Program delivered food to the Thai government for use in sectors on the border where ICRC and UNICEF had no entry. General governmental practices with regard to voluntary agencies in emergencies usually give most shape to these arrangements. In Thailand, the government admitted voluntary agencies to refugee relief projects on its territory; these efforts did not need always to be connected to the major intergovernmental programmes. In contrast, the Somali government insisted that UNHCR approve the entry to voluntary agencies. Other governments, such as those of Pakistan and Sudan, strictly controlled the entry of voluntary agencies and did not as a rule offer them much encouragement to bring their personnel to the field, even when such programmes would have fitted into the work of the intergovernmental agencies.

Voluntary agencies on their own are able to provide only a small fraction of the financing required to cope with a large-scale influx of migrants requiring emergency care. Inevitably, governments must make the decisions on large contributions. These are often aggregated through intergovernmental agencies, but sometimes governments insist on making all or part of their donations to the host authorities. Nevertheless, the despatch by a voluntary agency of specialised personnel or key relief items may have an important effect. At the same time, the effectiveness of such contributions may depend heavily on the degree to which governments and intergovernmental organisational partners are able to co-ordinate their work.

Continuing assistance

Once the need for urgent assistance has been met, at least in some form, care for refugees enters a continuing phase. This ends only with the final disposition of the incident, a function which is dealt with in the next chapter. Once the continuing phase begins to get more attention from local authorities and outside helping agencies, the tone of the activities changes. Now the refugees increasingly begin, implicitly or explicitly, to make demands that are commonplace in a normal society. They need social services of every kind and the use of a social infrastructure, whether created especially for them or borrowed from the surrounding community. At the same time, because of their uncertain legal and social circumstances, refugees necessarily pose social issues in a special form. But now, less pressure tends to surround the furnishing of assistance and the abundant experience of the past can be applied more routinely.

The kind of interaction that takes place between national governments, local governments, intergovernmental agencies and voluntary agencies does not differ in principle from what can be observed in an emergency phase; but it now becomes easier to set limits to activities, establish responsibility, abandon unnecessary reactions and stabilise organisational relationships. The need for policy decisions does not change; the accent does. Maintenance of the refugees over many weeks or months occupies the attention of the authorities. Administrative niceties can once more be given attention. The supervisory role of UNHCR or other providers of material assistance from outside the polity now loses the bite of urgency but gains salience through the exercise of expertness. More attention can be given to individual cases among the masses, and decisions can be made about demands for longer-term legal asylum.

Although very large refugee movements inevitably result in the establishing of camps, these represent by no means the only form of continuing assistance. Moreover, camps should be understood as a forced response to the presence of refugees. From the experience of UNRRA onwards, the avoiding of the creation of camps and the emptying of those that did exist has been a constant aim of the international agencies dealing with refugees. The long-established camps administered by UNRWA in the Middle East are usually cited by officials as glaring examples of what should not be allowed to develop. At the same time, the setting up of camps may be unavoidable, depending on local circumstances, the numbers of forced migrants involved and government policies in operation where the refugees originated and are received.

As the continuing phase of care for refugees is able to rely on steady experience dating from the end of the Second World War, it soon begins to take on a settled appearance. The bureaucratic organisation which functioned earlier provides examples for each new situation. The camps disappear from the mass media. In a sense, the aftermath of flight and displacement becomes a normal situation for the authorities in charge. The refugees themselves find a place in the social structure, however temporary it is intended to be.

Shelter and food

Small numbers of asylum-seekers can be assigned to existing housing, or to social hostels. For example, asylum applicants from Sri Lanka arriving in the Netherlands and the German Federal Republic in late 1984 and early 1985 were put up in pensions, hotels and hostels at the cost of the said governments and in some cases with allowances from UNHCR or a voluntary agency. In the case of large-scale refugee incidents, such as those occurring in Eastern Sudan, Somalia, Pakistan and South-East Asia, camps have to be constructed.[8] Governments usually insist that these be of temporary character, although some in Thailand have served for five years or more. The construction of such camps, it is fair to say, always poses the same issues: the technical difficulties can be overcome, if the policies are clear. The policy issues include such questions as how close to the border or to towns the camps should be, how secure from outside contact, how permanent and how large. Furthermore, land must be provided through the decision of the host government. Refugees in the poorer countries usually begin at once to use any available materials to construct temporary shelters and can be counted on to upgrade the initial, flimsy camp facilities if materials are provided. But if a planned and orderly camp is foreseen by local authorities, building contractors may be paid to undertake almost all the work. The building of camps can easily lead to local shortages of labour and materials as unexpected demands are made on the market. In some cases, expensive materials have to be imported from abroad, including in many cases tents and temporary shelters.

Refugees who have legal permission to live in the society of asylum — which is the clear aim of the UN Convention on Refugees — are able to purchase their own food supplies. In cases of spontaneous settlement, such as have occurred in Africa in such places as Tanzania and Eastern Sudan, the forced migrants soon come to grow their own food. In such instances, supplementary food for those in special need (for example, children and pregnant women) as well as seeds and tools may sometimes be furnished by the local authorities or supplied by international agencies. Large camps, however, call for the doling out of food, especially in the early stages; later, some food may be grown. Much of the required food may be purchased on the local market in some cases — as in Thailand — or may be imported. The patterns vary greatly according to the local potentials for farming or for purchasing food and even according to what herds or other supplies the migrants bring with them. Camps also usually involve the necessity to supply water. If they are sited near potable water, the difficulty may be minor; but if, as with some of the Thai camps and most of those in Eastern Sudan and Somalia, or on the Chad border, the area is arid and rains are seasonal, great hardship and suffering can result. In some cases, the highly inefficient practice of trucking potable water from distant wells to the camps has to be undertaken. Yet such technical difficulties involving camps are on the whole manageable, providing that policy decisions on the part of the host government and assisting agencies are made in time and are based on the best available technical knowledge.

Medical and social care

Refugees who enter the society of the asylum country are usually able to count on the medical services that are available to the local population. Their demands can easily overtax the local facilities — as the Sudanese government claims was the case with Eritrean refugees in the Kassala area, for example. But for Chilean refugees in Spain or France, for instance, there is no real problem in this area.

Camp populations pose heavy and quite specific medical problems.[9] As they are a dense group from a different geographical location, they may be susceptible to epidemics or else bring unusual disease with them. Moreover, the very living conditions of a crude camp may increase the danger of disease. These dangers may be further intensified by insufficient or inappropriate sanitary arrangements and water supplies. A further set of issues involves the health of certain groups among the camp population, such as the elderly, young children, those who have come to asylum from famine areas and those wounded in fighting. Thus, the camp situation involves public health services for the protection of both the surrounding population and the refugees. It also in effect demands the creation of a health service where there was none. In addition, that service will require specialised skills for the treatment of particularly threatened sectors of the population and for advising other camp services, such as food preparation, on the medical implications of diet.

Psychiatric and psychological care for refugees may loom unexpectedly large in continuing situations.[10] Stress, disorientation, separation from family members and social groups and the absence of customary social occasions such as prayers in a temple or church can all take their toll. When the reason for forced migration involved pressure of a severely destructive kind, as happened in Cambodia, the psychological effects can be especially marked. Moreover, lengthy periods of idle residence in camps gives rise to a well-known attitude of dependency and passivity described as 'camp psychosis'. The psychological pressure of refugee life sometimes leads to aggressive behaviour, particularly among the young, which camp authorities are called on to deal with as part of their role in maintaining security.

Voluntary agencies working in camps and UNHCR have developed programmes for counselling. Social workers and individuals with psychological training try to reduce the danger of psychiatric reactions and to prevent the forming of camp psychosis. They help to organise in the camps positive forms of activity such as study groups, library services, music, handicrafts, games and other forms of recreation. Given the inherent psychological pressures of refugee status, such programmes are anything but wasteful luxuries; they take measures to prevent the destruction of the personality and the resultant costs incurred by mental illness or institutional care.

Schools

For the young, some form of schooling is a necessity — as it is in almost all human societies — whether the refugees are housed in camps or located in an established community.[11] In camps, where numbers of refugees are substantial, there is some likelihood that teachers will be found among the population. In some groups, schools make up part of the religious institution and priests among the migrants may be available as instructors. Both lay and religious teachers may organise schools spontaneously.

Schooling also provides a means of occupying free time and preparing refugees for the future. Without schools, children would suffer later from a lack of skills essential for taking part in their future society, whether in the country of origin or elsewhere. Furthermore, adults can be prepared for new occupations or can upgrade their skills. They can also be taught skills useful to camp life, such as assisting in clinics or helping with the administration.

The authorities in charge of camps generally take prompt steps to create schools. They invariably receive support from voluntary agencies and UNHCR and sometimes from other intergovernmental agencies if they so wish. UNHCR is able to furnish specialists in education to help in organising schools. When it is known that the possibility of third-country resettlement exists, schools may embark on the orientation of those likely to emigrate.

School supplies and books may pose a considerable problem. Normal requirements, such as paper and pencils, may be expensive and in short supply. Not without reason, such goods are given lower priority in shipping than foodstuffs and medicine. As a result, the establishment of schools and the pace of instruction may be retarded. Moreover, books have to be obtained in the appropriate languages and at the appropriate level for the classes offered. In addition, locales for classes must be found or constructed.

In contrast to the camp situation, where schooling has to be constructed from the ground up, refugees with formal legal status who are given asylum are often able to make use of the local schools. In some instances, schools using their native languages will be available. In other cases, refugee children and adults receiving training will need to develop sufficient skill in the local language in order to profit from the opportunity for training. The refugee care network has sometimes been able to create special classes for refugees with asylum in order to teach them local languages more rapidly, but more often than not the responsibility rests on the refugees. As people differ in their adaptability, the mere availability of schooling is no guarantee that its offering will effectively be absorbed by the asylees. When it is not, the considerable problems of adjustment will be intensified. At this point, counselling by social workers and psychologists may be useful but not necessarily available.

In general, the international network caring for refugees has had vast experience in the social aspects of asylum. Within the network, those with the skill to organise educational facilities and provide social counselling constitute something of a subgroup that can be involved at the appropriate time. But as with all such assistance, the government giving asylum has the ability to prevent or support the provision to these services.

Limitations and inhibitions

Several kinds of limitation, some of them mentioned earlier, affect the provision of immediate relief and subsequent care to forced migrants. These limitations tend to interact with each other. The nature of the limitations and their interaction lends uncertainty to forecasts of what responses an emergency and the later situation will call forth. Moreover, these limitations continue to apply in the later phases of coping with refugees, discussed below.

Structural

A principal set of limitations grows out of the structure of aid-delivering arrangements. Intergovernmental institutions have a limited capacity to act and even less if required to act quickly. The only relevant institution with a predominant interest in refugees is UNHCR. The quasi-governmental ICRC also has a strong, though not exclusive, interest in forced migrants who have suffered inhumane treatment. The resources of both seem to be permanently under pressure. UNHCR can expand its capacities only after appealing to governments for more support on the basis of an after-the-fact appraisal of a refugee emergency, and ICRC actually operates under similar conditions. While UNHCR has recently strengthened its ability to act swiftly in an emergency, it has only limited and informal abilities to forecast and prepare in advance for the provision of specific assistance. Its creation of an emergency planning unit and the publication of a handbook for responses represents a distinct improvement. Yet it is noteworthy that this effort, resulting mainly from internal initiatives, was undertaken only after three decades of experience. Even so, UNHCR still has to await positive requests from a government. ICRC policy demands protection of its neutrality, which may translate into equal access to victims who are still in their own country and those who have escaped inhumane conditions. Other intergovernmental agencies have both limited capacities and multiple competing demands, many of which result in continuing programmes.

The intergovernmental organisational system as a whole remains, even after decades of experience, poorly co-ordinated when it comes to delivering immediate aid for refugees. UNHCR can sometimes provide co-ordinative leadership, and now and then such an initiative may either be encouraged by the UN Secretary-General or provided by him and his staff. On other occasions, a national government will either provide a co-ordinative impulse or undertake the analytical staff work required to improve co-ordination. Nevertheless, intergovernmental organisations of substantial importance — such as the European Communities — generally operate outside the UN framework and may not necessarily be attracted to it for the giving of emergency aid.

Bilateral arrangements between donors and governments involved in relieving an emergency can usually be made only on the basis of *ad hoc* arrangements. Such devices can, in principle, be drawn up through the UN system or other intergovernmental facilities. Nevertheless, bilateral patterns generally signify that a donor government intends to maintain control, or at least close surveillance, over the uses of its contributions. Political aims may be linked to humanitarian goals. Sometimes, moreover, such contributions must conform to national law, or to religious practices, which may make the engaging of multilateral organisation difficult or impossible. Finally, the recipient government must also agree if the various bilateral donors are to co-ordinate their programmes effectively. Host governments may find advantages in avoiding multilateral oversight in favour of unco-ordinated bilateral arrangements.

Thus, the weakness of intergovernmental arrangements, the responsiveness of bilateral schemes to given situations and the effects of national policies may all delay or limit relief and other immediate aid to refugees. The overcoming of structural shortcomings may call for exceptional leadership on the part of either national or international figures or agencies. Even so, the difficulties remain substantial and expectations that the full available capacity will be brought to bear in any particular emergency can only be restrained.

Legal

The dominant legal inhibition on relief is the requirement that the government of the territory where the refugees are located must give its consent to any operations. The only exception can be found on the high seas, where ships' masters are legally obliged to offer help to those in distress,[12] whether or not they are refugees. Here there is no question of consent. This obligation came into play with the incidents concerning the Indo-Chinese boat people, which remains an unusual case.

On land, governments have the power, whatever the legal

obligations, to turn a blind eye to the presence of a refugee emergency. They may cause a scandal or damage themselves, but the decisions remain theirs; outside organisations can do nothing more than plead to be allowed to extend assistance. This has occurred, alas, in not a few incidents, such as during the outflow of people from Equatorial Guinea during the Maçias dictatorship, at the beginning of the forced migration of Rwandese from Uganda in 1982 and at various times on the Thai-Cambodian border. Moreover, governments can usually prevent domestic voluntary agencies from reacting very much. Even in a situation of belligerence, the consent of the invading force is required before aid can be brought to refugees in occupied territory. ICRC reacts to this requirement by insisting that both belligerents allow it equal access. During the Second World War, UNRRA was specifically empowered to work in occupied territories to assist displaced persons but needed the permission of the occupying armies before beginning operations. A similar pattern was followed by the UN Korean Reconstruction Agency;[13] in Korea, the civil affairs units of the American military began relief work as part of the army command. Only later was UNKRA admitted, and then on a restricted scale.

Furthermore, legal restraints apply with regard to the character of the asylum-seekers. UNHCR works primarily with people outside their own country unless the UN General Assembly authorises a special exception to assist those who are in a 'refugee-like' situation. The definition of 'refugee-like' depends on earlier General Assembly resolutions and practice, but its application is regarded by UNHCR as different from its usual approach. ICRC offers assistance to refugees as part of a general class of civilians affected by warfare. As a rule it does not bring aid to refugees outside a situation of belligerence. Voluntary organisations determine for themselves their areas of interest, but such decisions generally conform to earlier organisation experience. Whatever their wishes may be, they proceed within national legal systems.

Financial and administrative

Structural and legal constraints on immediate aid to refugees merely reflect more general financial and administrative issues involving refugees. All refugee incidents have organisational consequences. These vary from the initial perceptions and signals preceding decisions through the entire gamut of responses discussed in this chapter and the next. Some of these consequences, moreover, involve the routine internal processes of the acting organisations. They are spelt out in concrete form in terms of financing, administration and deliberations over decisions.

In principle, the organisational issues created by refugees differ little from those invariably associated with public sector activities intended to foster the welfare of social groups. As programmes on behalf of refugees are incapable of returning profits or any significant income, they depend entirely on exogenous sources of financing. The level of financing now required far exceeds anything ever raised from private sources; financing therefore depends on governmental decisions. These decisions must take place, whether at the national or international level, in a competitive arena, where multiple demands for the funds raised by taxes come forth ceaselessly. The amounts set aside for refugees ultimately depend on the familiar political processes of budgeting and allocation of finances. However familiar such processes may seem, they involve the sensitivities of national taxpayers who through a system of levies become obliged to hand over a portion of their income to refugees. The governments that do the taxing deliver a portion of their subjects' incomes after international processes that are limited to persuasion. Moreover, because it is difficult to foresee the need for financing refugee activities, the requests for contributions are often of an urgent nature and may call for the making of decisions at national level that lie beyond the normal budgetary process.

The large scale of recent refugee flows would in itself be sufficient to raise organisational issues to a new prominence. Moreover, the acceptance of resettlement in distant countries as a routine method of liquidating refugee incidents calls for large expenditures and organisational complexity. Recent demands on the administrative capacities of organisations dealing with refugee affairs pose difficulties of scale, direction and accountability at both domestic and transnational levels. Older, simpler administrative structures have been profoundly shaken and their basic patterns brought into question. New relationships among co-operating organisations have had to be improvised. The pattern of connections among governments, international institutions and voluntary organisations displays a high degree of variation, as it is adapted to local circumstances, sometimes in great haste. Notions of accountability and supervision have also changed. A persistent question, especially in the case of fast-developing emergencies, poses the issue of whether it is more important to keep tidy accounts than it is to act at once to save lives. The questions by governments and outside observers concerning the appropriateness of expenditures tend to come after the emergency. It would be hard to claim, however, that a settled design has been adopted or even that it would be possible.[14]

Several kinds of criticism of administrative structures and procedures in connection with refugees can be distinguished. The first of these concerns mismanagement and inefficiency. The second has to do with complexity of structures and the difficulties in producing timely, appropriate decisions. A third relates to forward planning and leadership.

Accusations of mismanagement and inefficiency emerge often enough in the press and other mass media in connection with refugee movements as to seem virtually predictable. Supplies delivered for refugees can often be found on the open market, either inside or outside camps, which leads to colourful articles about 'black marketing'. The fact that camp administrations now usually encourage the creation of markets in order to achieve the distribution of supplies to those who need them in the quantities that are required tends to be overlooked. Furthermore, given the necessarily divided organisational responsibilities, arising from the complexity analysed above, leak-proof distribution may be an idle hope. What remains are the issues of how much waste can be permitted and who should decide. This, too, is not simple and often depends more on local politics than on management.

Another criticism of management has to do with timeliness of delivery of assistance and of its distribution in such tangible forms as the establishment of camps or shelters and the provision of food. Such criticism comes frequently from sources sympathetic to refugees and from the mass media. Whether such criticism is tenable depends on the nature of the incident, reactions by governments concerned and by the international agencies. All the factors that contribute to the complexity of decision-making where the national and international functions intersect come into play here. It may take weeks before a government is prepared to allow international assistance and many weeks after that before substantial help can be mobilised. Whether it can then actually reach refugees without long delays depends in part on the geographical location and the infrastructure. The difficulties of achieving the smooth management of supplies, for instance, can be illustrated by the slow movement of goods to refugees from the docks in Port Sudan to camps in both eastern and western Sudan in early 1985. The roads and railroads simply were not in a condition to handle the imports rapidly, nor were there enough railroad cars or trucks. The same applied to grain and other food sent to Ethiopia to cope with widespread famine at the same time. While some assistance with the infrastructure can often be arranged through intergovernmental and voluntary agencies, governments generally resist seeing their own administrations replaced or dominated by foreign organisations. In such a case, mismanagement of the assistance — in the sense that it is not flow-ing rapidly and smoothly to those who need it — may be easily demonstrated to those who put the assisting of refugees before all else. Few governments will simply abandon their normal pro-grammes in order to give refugees absolute priority. From their point of view, management also includes unbroken services to their own constituents. International arrangements cannot easily or quickly overcome such resistance. Threats from international agencies to shut down their programmes, for instance, may neither result in more help reaching those in need nor in a reversal of policy by a reluctant government.

Criticism based on concepts of efficiency also involves much uncertainty and vagueness. No conceptual standard of efficiency that has general agreement exists. Presumably it would be possible to measure cost-effectiveness, using ratios of expenditures and the movement of commodities or people as a tool. But difficulties of comparison arise at once. Moreover, it is far from clear that such ratios are relevant to a particular situation which could involve very high-cost logistics but still save lives. Criticisms about efficiency frequently mask more general comments about organisational behaviour and are sometimes merely a demand for harder work, Such criticisms are commonplace in national legislatures when their members want to attack bureaucracies; they have also been used in commercial and industrial contexts. In any case, where matters affecting refugees are concerned the experience of efficiency studies is probably not sufficiently extensive for a general standard to be set and may be too slim even for the development of broad con-cepts. The UN system is equipped with at least three means of exploring efficiency. These are its Joint Inspection Unit, its internal audit mechanism and its external board of auditors. Years of experience on the part of these offices have as yet failed to provide an agreed standard of efficiency. This is not to say that such a stan-dard can be conclusively ruled out, but it does suggest that the con-cept of efficiency should not be used as if it were universally understood. When it is employed by national governments, it tends either to inhibit organisational operations or else to increase pressure to carry out reforms favoured by the governments taking the initiative.

Management and organisation nevertheless pose very real difficulties in refugee affairs. To begin with, the decentralised network obviates the setting up of any central hierarchical organisation, even if one were sought. Then the political overtones of refugee affairs inevitably introduces elements of danger and caution. Therefore diplomatic negotiations among governments, intergovernmental agencies and voluntary ones necessarily become part of the organising process for an individual incident. As professional diplomats generally assume, such negotiations do not fall into any regular pattern. Moreover, each of the negotiating agencies has its own style of decision-making.

With the expansion of their tasks, the intergovernmental agencies have had to adapt their administrative patterns. An index of the need to adapt can be seen in UNHCR, which has grown from 50 or so officials at its creation to more than 1,600. With such expansion and with the establishment of many field offices, easy internal communication by word of mouth becomes impossible: a bureaucracy needs to be created. In the case of UNHCR, it followed partly functional lines, with bureaus for protection, assistance, administration and external relations. But it also followed geographical lines, with country offices within the assistance bureau. A general staff function was reserved for the Office of the High Commissioner. Since the appointment of Jean-Pierre Hocké, who in 1986 succeeded Poul Hartling as High Commissioner, a geographical pattern has been favoured. ICM, a much smaller organisation, has a largely functional organisational pattern. Such organisational structures might have proved entirely unexceptionable were it not for the fact that activities on behalf of refugees wax and wane. To man an organisation sufficiently densely to cope with any conceivable emergency would promptly stoke up criticisms relating to costs, management and efficiency. But to expand and contract with need also causes difficulties, because it involves the entry of untrained personnel who may lack the organisational discipline to work in accordance with the standards of the organisation. Field personnel in particular may escape from the discipline, either intentionally or otherwise. Later come the hard decisions to reduce personnel after peak periods have passed. Donor governments tend to watch such proceedings with an anxious eye, while senior officials feel themselves under constant pressure to cope with higher work-loads without raising operating costs. Because some governments —

usually the major donors — demand a high standard of accountability for the programmes they support, the expansion and contraction of the agency may lead to further difficulties and perhaps
to an inherent caution.

Forward planning and leadership, as has been noted earlier, pose
real difficulties at the international level. Governments generally
seem to prefer not to have reminders that refugees have become an
all too permanent part of their landscape. By organising internationally, governments share responsibility for refugees, but they
also create an opportunity to push the matter out of domestic sight.
A High Commissioner for Refugees, an ICM or a group of zealous
voluntary agencies can count on a reasonable welcome from many
governments, so long as their work remains physically distant.
Moreover, the highly defensive treatment of the political implications of refugee issues on the part of governments inherently limits
the ability to carry out effective forward planning, either in the public
or private sector. The lack of a reliable early warning mechanism
is particularly striking.[15] In these circumstances, leadership tends
to be exerted, if at all, during crises in which the lives of thousands
of asylum-seekers come under direct threat. This quality of leadership in fact stimulates existing bureaucracies and employs existing
policies far more than it stimulates new thinking. On the whole,
it seems fair to conclude, the organisation for refugees at the international level has a reactive character. Furthermore, those who must
be led have an abstract quality: the followers in the first instance
comprise governments. The implication is that only very severe
refugee issues impinge on the consciousness of broad publics. It
follows that sustained popular support for institutions and policies
to help refugees may be non-existent or very meagre and of short
duration.

Whether an appropriate structure for managing refugee activities
could ever be designed and established for perpetual functioning
remains doubtful. Certainly experience from UNRRA onwards has
not been one of smooth organisational fit and function; rather the
historical developments suggest a great deal of *ad hoc* adaptation and
expediency, always limited by the inherent tension of international
arrangements.

Financial provisions for coping with refugees reflect limitations
that accord with those in management. When a national government has to deal with a refugee flow of any consequence, the new
local costs will usually incline it to seek assistance through co-
operative measures. Intergovernmental organisations, especially

UNHCR, and other United Nations agencies that have reacted in narrower ways to refugee flows, offer a ready-made means of spreading financial costs, gathering resources and engaging a large administrative network to meet the needs. The necessary funds are assembled primarily by persuading governments to make voluntary contributions.

Voluntary contributions to intergovernmental agencies normally emerge from an elaborate deliberative process. The executive head of an agency proposes a budget, which almost always requires approval by a supervisory body of governmental representatives or by a full-membership organ, such as the UN General Assembly. It follows that governments can keep a watchful eye on projected programmes or review past programmes if they care to do so. But adoption of a budget does not ensure financing: it is merely a plan. Budgets for agencies requiring voluntary contributions, such as UNHCR or UNRWA, in no sense entail obligations on any government. The actual obligation is undertaken by governments either in a pledging conference, of which several per year are held under United Nations auspices, or following a direct appeal to governments. Officials of the relevant secretariats prepare the ground for the pledging conferences by giving their governmental counterparts some notion of what magnitude of pledge might be expected from other governments or by the organisation which is being financed. However, the final word rests with the governments. Some principal donors, such as the United States, have frequently conditioned the amounts of their pledges on the donations of others. The final pledge by such a government may be expressed as a proportion of the total. Moreover, the scale of obligatory contributions used by the United Nations for the administrative budget, or by the counterpart from another agency, may also serve as a guide to the expected level of contribution. It is, moreover, generally understood that the main burden of donations will fall on the rich countries, rather than equally on all governments.

UNHCR depends primarily on voluntary contributions, although an annual item of about $7 million is included in the obligatory budget of the United Nations. This item has remained stable for a decade or more and covers a diminishing proportion of UNHCR outlays. At the same time, it provides a basis for a continuing scrutiny of UNHCR personnel actions and expenditures within the normal UN rules. Continuing programmes can be budgeted and financial demands distributed among governments on the basis of their agreement. But new programmes, representing the recognition of a new refugee incident of any considerable scale, cannot be forecast under UNHCR practice. As a result the High Commissioner has to appeal to governments when such cases arise, which may number between eight and ten, or more, a year. UNHCR officials generally have some idea as to what governments are prepared to give in each case. Moreover, they use the familiar device of voluntary agencies — such as the churches — of using large donations as examples for others to follow. They keep a close watch on the budgetary processes of the principal donors and use this information to time requests whenever possible. In ICM and UNRWA a similar process takes place, although these agencies usually have less need for emergency appeals than UNHCR.

The relative handful of governments that contribute substantially to intergovernmental organisations assisting refugees comprise the highly developed countries represented in the Organization for Economic Co-operation and Development and some of the oil-producing states. Independently of national contributions, the European Communities have also been the source of large funding for specific refugee programmes. By a factor of nearly four to one on a scale of absolute dollar values, the United States is the largest contributor; but in 1984 it ranked sixth and in 1985, fifth on a *per capita* basis.[16] Similar proportions apply in other agencies.

The financing of assistance to refugees goes beyond mere maintenance either in camps or in the situation of relative independence provided by a community of asylum. It usually includes social services of various kinds, including medical care, schooling and other training, counselling, work projects and possibly also preparation for departure, a subject which will be given more attention in the next chapter. As has been noted, these services cause national, international and private organisations to become enmeshed with each other in complex, often improvised ways. Moreover, the larger the refugee population, the more complicated the programmes are likely to become and the more financing will be required.

An ever-present element in decisions to finance assistance for forced migrants derives from national political values. Governments seem to find it much easier to recognise a humanitarian task when the victims concerned embarrass an unfriendly government which caused them to flee. It is equally encouraging when the asylum-seekers hold political views that are acceptable to the government on whose territory they are seeking shelter or when they are or are likely to become active enemies of a hostile government. The legal

Table 5.1: Top 20 National contributions to international refugee aid agencies

	1983		1985			
Country	US $ Contribution per capita	Country	Population (in millions)	GNP per capita	Contribution (in millions of $)	Contribution per capita
Norway	$3.82	Norway	4.2	$13,820	$18.6	$4.43
Denmark	3.04	Denmark	5.1	11,490	15.2	2.98
Sweden	3.02	Sweden	8.3	12,400	19.7	2.37
Qatar	2.12	Switzerland	6.5	16,390	13.6	2.09
Switzerland	1.54	United States	238.9	14,090	193.4	0.80
Kuwait	1.49	Netherlands	14.5	9,910	11.1	0.76
Canada	1.14	Canada	25.4	12,000	18.7	0.73
U.S.	1.05	Saudi Arabia	11.2	12,180	7.3	0.65
Liechtenstein	0.79	Kuwait	1.9	18,180	1.1	0.57
Netherlands	0.77	Finland	4.9	10,440	2.7	0.54
Australia	0.76	Germany	61.0	11,420	32.9	0.54
United Arab Emirates	0.67	Japan	120.8	10,100	56.9	0.47
Saudi Arabia	0.56	Australia	15.8	10,780	6.8	0.43
Japan	0.48	United Kingdom	56.4	9,050	23.9	0.42
Finland	0.44	Belgium	9.9	9,160	4.0	0.40
Belgium	0.43	Luxembourg	.4	12,190	.1	0.35
Germany (FRG)	0.42	Libya	4.0	7,500	.9	0.22
Libya	0.39	Iceland	.2	10,270	.03	0.15
Iceland	0.31	Ireland	3.6	4,810	.5	0.14
United Kingdom	0.28	Italy	57.4	6,350	7.5	0.13
Luxembourg	0.26					

Note: Contributions by governments to the European Communities for refugee services are not included. Bilateral assistance also does not appear in these tables. The contributions made to ICM, UNHCR and UNRWA are included.

Source: United States Committee for Refugees, *World Refugee Survey 1983* (American Council Nationalities Service, Washington, 1984) and *World Refugee Survey 1985* (Washington, 1986).

and ideological foundations of the transnational system for dealing with refugees obviously oppose such considerations. Governments acceding to the Geneva Conventions and the UN Refugee Convention formally undertake the obligation to give aid and protection to those who need help, not those who claim it on the basis of political significance. It would, nevertheless, be blindness to overlook the way in which political bias affects the speed and scope of refugee aid. The Soviet Union and its allies for the most part decline any share in helping refugees of any sort and avoid legal obligations. The United States strongly supported efforts to assist Afghan refugees in Pakistan and those in the Horn of Africa who fled from Ethiopia. It was ready with emergency reactions and supported the programmes of intergovernmental and private bodies. It shows far less sympathy for those who are in flight from danger and oppression in Haiti or El Salvador and in urgent need of help.

Political values of varying hues colour government attitudes to the work of UNHCR and other international agencies dealing with refugees. Government representatives seek to influence these agencies to operate in such a way as to accord with domestic political demands.

Ideological and geopolitical factors, domestic policy interests and bureaucratic process all have some share in what is done to meet the immediate needs of refugees. As these interests interact in a complex manner and little long-term consensus exists beyond abstract guidelines, they condition and limit reactions to pressing refugee situations.

Notes

1. Sections I and II of the Geneva Convention Relative to the Protection of Civilian Persons in Time of War, of 12 August 1949, has particular relevance to persons caught up in a war and provides for, among other things, the collection and care of wounded and sick civilians. Section V establishes a central information service, which helps locate missing persons and with family reunification. The text of the Convention is to be found in *International Red Cross Handbook* 11th Ed. (International Committee of the Red Cross and League of Red Cross Societies, Geneva, 1971), pp. 157-225. The ICRC and the League of Red Cross Societies actively support the study of this and other conventions.

2. Goodwin-Gill, *The Refugee in International Law*, pp. 17-18, summarises current practice and suggests that states seek to broaden their freedom to act by avoiding the use of formal terminology associated with legal rights of refugees.

3. The text is in the Annex to UN General Assembly Resolution 2200 (XXI), 19 December 1966; it came into force on 3 January 1976. 'The type of obligation is programmatic and promotional.' — Ian Brownlie, *Principles of Public International Law* 3rd edn (Clarendon Press, Oxford, 1982), p. 572.

4. UNHCR *Handbook for Emergencies*.

5. This incident was well documented by reports in the press. A summary account is to be found in Shawcross, *The Quality of Mercy*, pp. 85-92 and includes details of the way that the emergency reaction developed.

6. Nicholas Morris, a senior UNCHR official who was then in charge of the programme in Sudan, forecast in December 1984 that as many as 300,000 new refugees could be expected in eastern Sudan. This very rare statement, perhaps the first of its sort from UNHCR, gave rise to protest from Ethiopia. His forecast was also incorporated in an appeal for additional funds, sent to governments by UNHCR. Morris is quoted by a Dutch journalist as saying (my translation): 'We certainly made a political declaration, but it was also objective. You surely know that if there is a growing lack of food in Ethiopia, the people will come here to get something to eat.' Koert Lindijer, 'UNHCR faalde bij hulp in Soedan', *NRC-Handelsblad*, 11 February 1985, p. 4. See also Gary Putka, 'The tragedy of Sudan's spreading starvation is that it's caused by man's errors, not nature's', *Wall Street Journal*, 22 January 1985, p. 1.

7. Wain, *The Refused*, pp. 216-225, gives a useful brief account of the conference against a background of South-East Asian politics. I conducted interviews at the conference which confirm Wain's account.

8. For a glimpse of the lengthy series of questions regarding the establishment of camps, see UNHCR *Handbook for Emergencies*, chapters 3 and 6. A useful bibliography follows the latter chapter.

9. Ibid., chapters 7-10, give a sharp, clear outline of this complex of demands.

10. On the subject of the psychological difficulties encountered by refugees, see J. Donal Cohon, jun., 'Psychological Adaptation and Dysfunction Among Refugees', *International Migration Review*, 15, 53/54 (spring-summer 1981), pp. 255-75. This article concentrates on the effects of refugee life at the phase of resettlement in a third country after asylum but refers to the experiences in camps. *The UNHCR Handbook for Emergencies* (p. 57) remarks that 'The shock of having to leave home and circumstances of life in the early stages of an emergency, create major emotional and social problems and exacerbate existing problems . . . Social work is in the broadest sense the vital bridge between the refugee and the goods and services of the new settlement. Without help in adjusting to this new environment the sense of loss and isolation can deepen even in circumstances of relative material well-being.'

11. Ibid., pp. 165-7. The organisation of schooling in the refugee camps in Thailand reached a high level as third-country resettlement programmes developed. The countries of immigration wanted prepared refugees. See the brief account in 'Educational Programs in Refugee Camps — Providing a Headstart on New Lives', US Committee on Refugees, *World Refugee Survey 1984* (Washington, 1984), pp. 34-5. Visitors to refugee camps often encounter makeshift schools, set up by teachers or religious leaders, sometimes with help from the camp authorities, sometimes spontaneously.

These not only provide some training but also help maintain some feeling of solidarity among the refugees.

12. 'The duty to rescue those in distress at sea is firmly established in both general and conventional international law.' Goodwin-Gill, *The Refugee in International Law*, p. 87. This author sums up the state of the law and the implications in the subsequent five pages. Though not every captain or every government follows this law, it is an established practice. What happens to the floating fugitives after they have been picked up is another matter, with difficult implications.

13. The only extensive account of UNKRA is Gene M. Lyons, *Military Policy and Economic Aid: The Korean Case, 1950-1953* (Ohio State University Press, Columbus, Ohio, 1961).

14. During 1980, as large-scale refugee flows took place in South-East Asia, in the Horn of Africa and in Pakistan and Iran from Afghanistan, the Executive Committee of the Office of the High Commissioner for Refugees saw to it that for the first time it had a sub-committee to deal with administrative matters. In the Executive Committee, the Belgian representative expressed the hope that a large number of meetings would be devoted to the assistance programme and called the new sub-committee 'an excellent initiative' (UN Doc. A/AC.96/SR.330, p. 14). My interviews at the time confirmed that the donor countries were taking an unusually lively interest in the management of the relatively huge assistance programme, where the largest expenditures had to be made. Yet UNHCR was not the only channel. The US representative told the Executive Committee that his country had contributed some $2 billion to assist refugees of which $130 million was being channelled through UNHCR (UN Doc. A/AC.96/SR.330, p. 10).

15. Gordenker, 'Early Warning of Disastrous Population Movement', paper prepared for the Independent Commission on International Humanitarian Issues, The Hague, December 1984, and article with the same title in *International Migration Review*, XX, 2 (1986), pp. 170-89.

16. US Committee on Refugees, *World Refugee Survey 1984*, table 7, p. 41.

6

Resolving Forced Migrations

In a world that abhors the presence of unadministered space or people, the presence of forced migrants must be treated as abnormal. Government authorities invariably react to refugee situations by trying first to contain them and later to eliminate them. Yet the second reaction creates a certain paradox, especially where emergency assistance has been offered. The essence of protection for refugees lies in the implicit or explicit acceptance of their right to flee; if they can leave, they cannot be sent back to persecution. They receive assistance which enables them to stay alive at a crucial point in their odyssey. After that, their very survival calls forth efforts from governments and other agencies to shorten or terminate the uncertainty of their circumstances.

Efforts to eliminate refugee situations are a major result of any flow of refugees to a place of first asylum. Governments, intergovernmental agencies, voluntary groups and individuals all have a share in such responses. Yet the outcome of such efforts does not necessarily integrate all the migrants into a new society; nor is the way opened to their smooth return to their country of origin. The disorderliness inherent in the causes of refugees and their subsequent existence colours the ultimate outcome of their flight.

Three standard approaches to the liquidation of refugee situations will be dealt with in this chapter. These are repatriation, resettlement in the place of first asylum and resettlement in a third country.[1] It will also deal with a series of ancillary issues that have emerged in connection with ending refugee situations and consider the implications of failures to find ways to liquidate incidents of forced migration. In this analysis, it is assumed that refugees are spared physical or other forms of coercion in their movement from temporary asylum to normal status.

This assumption accords, of course, with the principles that have guided the development of a transnational system for protecting refugees. It also fits with the notion that human rights can and should be protected through international, as well as national, devices. Nevertheless, it is an assumption which cannot lightly be accepted as a description of reality. Attempts at securing the protection of the rights — including that to physical safety — of refugees and other forced migrants are matched by a sad history of violence, repression and brutality against those in flight. That, if carried far enough, will certainly liquidate refugee situations. Furthermore, some governments have insisted on the return, using force if necessary, of their nationals who either fled or were driven abroad. This was the case with the Soviet Union after the Second World War. In other instances, refugees have been put under heavy pressure, even if direct physical abuse of individuals was avoided. Confining them to idleness in camps shut off from contact with the surrounding society, delaying the administrative determinations necessary for integration or normal residence in a place of asylum, informal campaigns against them and other similar manifestations have been used.[2] These reactions could be represented as at least neglect of the notion that refugees should have as much voluntary choice as possible of their future.

Repatriation

If forced migrants would voluntarily choose to return to their countries of origin, the immediate difficulties caused them and their hosts would come to an end. The refugees would presumably be able to go back to their old homes, take up their lives in a society to which they were accustomed, avoid the pains of adjustment that all aliens encounter and incur the least possible expense for public authorities and other social groups. UNHCR and other agencies that deal with refugees almost always specify repatriation as the best outcome of a refugee situation. Repatriation, officials always emphasise, calls for voluntary decisions; thus those who choose it produce no further long-term burden on either countries of asylum or donor governments. Moreover, repatriation has in fact liquidated refugee situations, some of them of considerable scale.

The principle that repatriation must be voluntary presumably eliminates any political implications in the method. That principle has a legal foundation which supposedly overrides the political elements in any decision. Yet not all governments explicitly accept this legal standard. Furthermore, the inescapable political content of refugee flows does not simply disappear once repatriation is selected as the means of liquidating a particular refugee situation. If people flee their own homes, they do so for what they suppose are substantial reasons. Their flight represents a rejection of conditions at home and a protest against the authorities who cause or allow such conditions. Asylum-seekers who left for such reasons cannot simply take the next bus or train home; they will return willingly only if they have some assurance as to their future. While freedom from persecution will doubtless be the highest priority from the state authorities' point of view, asylum-seekers are likely to understand their security as also involving economic opportunity and will seek guarantees. Assurances of physical, economic and social security usually require negotiations with the government of the country of origin. Therefore, repatriation necessarily entails international politics.

Voluntary repatriation of some — and often sizeable fractions of — refugee groups sometimes takes place immediately after the original cause has been eliminated. Thus the replacement of an oppressive government, such as that of Idi Amin in Uganda, induces a flow of people back to their homes. The end of the Ian Smith government in Zimbabwe spurred the repatriation of some 250,000 people who were treated by international agencies as refugees. Similar repatriation could be observed following the collapse of the Maçias government in Equatorial Guinea and the replacement of the Somoza government in Nicaragua. Some of this flow is spontaneous. In the case of Zimbabwe, it was assisted in an organised fashion by UNHCR. A policy framework for this aid had been built up by the UN Security Council, whose somewhat primitive system of economic sanctions had helped to encourage emigration. In any case, voluntary repatriation, whether spontaneous or highly organised, will depend on whether the refugees are convinced that the causes of their flight have moderated sufficiently to promise a resumption of important aspects of their old lives. In that sense, voluntary repatriation has a subjective tone.

Repatriation and causes of flight

Those who left their homelands in the mass forced migrations of recent years almost always did so in response to deliberate governmental decisions which either affected them directly or were specifically aimed at them. Their flight was sometimes welcomed by leading political or social groups within the society. Consequently repatriation in the more notorious contemporary situations, as well as in many others, often encounters inherent, stubborn structural barriers.

In such cases as those of the middle-class refugees from Cuba or the ethnic Chinese from Indo-China, it seems unlikely that the present governments would allow repatriation even if the asylum-seekers wanted it. If they did, they would probably insist on applying the same measures that provoked the initial flight. Where the refugees have a pronounced ideological basis for leaving — as was the case in Afghanistan or Hungary — repatriation would involve renouncing their opposition and having the renunciation accepted as sincere by the presumably offended authorities.

In general, it may be expected that governments which oppress certain groups or individuals so heavily that they choose to leave the country will not readily take up initiatives leading to the return of emigrants. Thus, if repatriation is to be arranged in such cases — for example, those of the ethnic Chinese from Vietnam, or the Cambodians in Thai holding centres or along the borders — the heaviest burden of initiating any arrangements will probably have to be borne by foreign institutions.

Negotiating repatriation

Given the nature of flight-causing conditions and the subjective aspects of voluntary repatriation, whoever undertakes an initiative for the return of refugees may encounter a string of obstacles. To begin with, initiatives have to come from somewhere. The country of asylum, which may be most interested in winding up responsibilities for refugees, may frequently have a troubled relationship with the country of origin. Yet it has an unmistakeable interest in shedding the burden of refugees. A clear — if somewhat extreme — example is that of the Horn of Africa, where Ethiopia and Somalia generally treat each other as belligerents: each government seldom gives the other credit for acting in good faith. Furthermore, refugee populations include those whom the government of the country of origin may in many instances regard as disturbing elements. This raises the question of whether any circumstances can exist under which their return would be welcomed. If the refugees have a political colouration, or political movements appear among them, this question becomes all the more salient. This was the case with those along the Cambodian border, and with certain refugees in the Thai holding centres. The Heng Samrin government would probably have nothing to do with the repatriation of large numbers of these people unless they were prepared to enter detention or 're-education' centres immediately on their reappearance. This has been the practice of the Ethiopian government with returnees from Djibouti.[3] The country of asylum may thus have little incentive or ability to press for repatriation without abandoning its own aims or having to ask the migrants to accept impossible or hard conditions.

A government with no particular interests in the area could raise the question of repatriation. Should it do so in a matter involving large-scale or notorious deprivation, the source government may well treat any such initiative as suspicious indeed. Its response may be the usual denial that the matter has even the slightest relevance to those who undertake initiatives. A government taking such an initiative may also be faced with requests for financial assistance in order to carry out the repatriation. Demands for other assistance may also be attached.

Intergovernmental organisations can sometimes take initiatives for repatriation. They have the advantage over national governments of formal impartiality and of spreading risks among their members, so that no single government is obliged to assume full responsibility. UNHCR has far and away the most experience of such ventures, but its basic instruction to avoid political activity usually operates to keep its initiatives very discreet. Its successes in arranging for repatriation — as in the case of Zaïre's Shaba Province or that of refugees going from Sudan to Zaïre — become public knowledge. Much less is known about its failures, although, as in the case of Djibouti and Somalia in 1983, its hand became visible after many months of inconclusive discussion concerning arrangements for the return of refugees to Ethiopia. Eventually arrangements for repatriation were worked out, but no mass return resulted; several thousands did accept repatriation through formally established channels.[4]

Negotiations apparently often proceed through diplomatic contacts in Geneva and in the capital of the originating country when such access is possible. The asylum-granting government and others — such as large donors, or those which have a direct interest — also usually learn of or are advised about such initiatives and their results. Because of the organisation's discretion, it remains difficult to judge the effectiveness of the totality of initiatives by UNHCR. Nevertheless, it is equally evident that repatriation under UNHCR auspices can never become a universally successful formula.

The UN Secretary-General, the regional organisations of governments and voluntary agencies are sometimes involved, directly or indirectly, in attempts to use repatriation. Thus, in Thailand, the UN Secretary-General's co-ordinator for relief to Cambodia, the UNHCR regional office and the Association of South-East Asian Nations have been connected with attempts to repatriate Cambodians of varying status. These efforts also involved UNICEF, WFP and ICRC to a greater or lesser degree. Voluntary organisations were an important channel of information.

In certain efforts to secure the repatriation of refugees, the existing international machinery, including the United Nations, may never become involved should governments prefer a bilateral approach. Even if a large majority of the governments of the world insist on the return of refugees — as they have done in the case of Afghanistan — no reliable mechanism exists either to initiate negotiations or to force them.[5] Governments a good deal less self-sufficient than that of the USSR have also resisted the ministrations of the United Nations not to mention customary diplomacy.

Attention to the central issues of human rights, either in the General Assembly or in more specialised bodies such as the Commission on Human Rights — one of the places where repeated and extended discussions of alleged mistreatment of Palestinians has taken place — guarantees nothing. In the case of the Palestinians, publicity has probably hardened Israeli attitudes on repatriation. Furthermore, there is no reliable incentive either to governments or to refugees to induce repatriation. UNHCR and organisations relevant to its work do not dispose of the funding required to provide, for instance, development programmes which would include refugees in a wider effort, although some tottering steps have been made in that direction. Even if greater abilities to offer incentives were available, that too would guarantee nothing in a particular case.

No greater incentive to return home could be offered refugees than the elimination of the conditions which had caused their flight. Even this incentive carries time limits, for eventually even life in a refugee camp may seem normal while opportunities to move away arouse fear. A drastic change in the government policies of the country of origin tends to precede the elimination of flight-inducing conditions. A change of such magnitude could probably emerge only from the replacement of a government. This could be carried out by legal means. Policies of the sort that cause significant refugee movements are, however, hardly likely to emanate from a repressive government which employs denials of human rights as a means of ensuring its grip on power. Such governments generally give way only to revolution, insurrection, *coups d'état* or military defeat. Drastic actions of this kind are probably unlikely to be undertaken primarily for the benefit of refugees. The historical record appears to provide no example of this, even if political movements among refugees — as in certain Central American situations of the 1980s — have had some bearing on changes of government policies.[6] To encourage formally designated refugees to organise political or guerrilla movements violates the legal terms of their status. It invites international conflict. That sort of violation would probably lead to an end to asylum or at least isolation from the surrounding society. The host government might well apply strict controls to the refugees in order to avoid the wrath of the originating country. If refugees and less well-defined forced migrants have an incentive to secure the changes in governmental policies necessary to allow their repatriation, they are scarcely in a position to become very active without the permission, acquiescence or supply of their host government.

Repatriation falls within the interstices of the organised international system, parts of which in certain circumstances can function to promote it. But this function depends on *ad hoc* leadership from any available source. Neither a government that grants asylum nor the refugees themselves would be a likely source of leadership. International officials, acting discretely, and disinterested governments stand a better chance of imposing leadership; they can, at least to some extent, secure support from voluntary organisations and pressure groups. None of this, however, promises much certainty. Success in repatriation has been and probably will remain patchy. As a method, repatriation retains its attractiveness to authorities dealing with refugees but will not easily become more reliable.

Resettlement in first-asylum locations

Before the formal and factual extension of government to every part of the world and the massive growth of population, the easiest way for forced migrants to cope with an inability to repatriate was simply to settle where they found safety. This constituted spontaneous resettlement. It required only acquiescence from any near neighbours and from the weak authorities, if any. Contemporary asylum-seekers are clearly unable to count on this way out, although such a situation does exist in some parts of Africa and Central America for considerable numbers of forced migrants and elsewhere for a few people who quietly become immersed in a new society. Not only does the administrative apparatus in sites of possible settlement tend to restrict such a possibility but also the massive numbers of recent forced migrations overload the settlement areas, such as they are. Furthermore, the situation of forced migrants may be made notorious through the mass media, thereby reducing the chances of a quiet absorption.

Asylum and the causes of flight

The grim backgrounds of those seeking asylum may seriously reduce their chances of on-the-spot settlement. A host government which strives to avoid identifying itself with the refugees' beliefs in order to obviate friction with the state of origin may not offer easy asylum; this could be interpreted on the other side of the border as either an unfriendly act or support for what could become an exile movement. Even if permanent asylum were not interpreted as threatening, allowing settlement close to the border that refugees crossed into exile may imply a threat to the security of the originating government. This has been the case in the Horn of Africa, where refugees in eastern Sudan have been moved from spontaneous settlements in order to reduce friction between Sudan and Ethiopia. Furthermore, a settlement close to the border can be viewed as a magnet drawing away valuable manpower from a place where it is needed. This 'pull' effect would be welcomed by a government that wanted to rid itself of individuals thus attracted or one that deliberately encouraged people to leave in order to embarrass the host, as was the case with the Cuban government during the latter part of the Mariel migration. If a host government perceives that local settlement encourages the dumping of human beings, it might then hesitate to offer asylum under the same conditions.[7]

In other situations, such as that of the quarter million ethnic Chinese who in the late 1970s fled North Vietnam for the People's Republic of China, the host government has a clear political rationale for accepting the refugees as settlers. This large flow of migrants followed the PRC military attack on Vietnam of 1979. Moreover, the PRC used the incident to distinguish its treatment of refugees from the denial of human rights in Vietnam. Nevertheless, some of the refugees found conditions on the state farms where they were placed more difficult and less promising than their earlier lives in cities and towns. Some of them fled again to Hong Kong, from where they were returned as illegal immigrants who already had permanent asylum elsewhere.

Limiting effects of on-the-spot settlement

Attempts to settle refugees in areas of first asylum sometimes lead to limiting local reactions. The effects, of varying character and intensity in accordance with local conditions, may be felt only in the immediate surroundings of refugee shelters. They can, however, easily become national issues, especially when large numbers are involved. Some of the limiting local effects begin during the emergency phase of assistance to refugees — when there is one — and continue throughout the effort to provide new homes.

To the host population, the cultural practices of refugee groups often represent a distinctly alien, irritating mode of conduct. For example, Vietnamese evoke little sympathetic reaction among the nearby Thai population. Similarly, refugee Blacks from South Africa, conditioned by a different sort of society and economy, sometimes appear to host communities in Africa as demanding interlopers. The highland Hmong people clearly cause themselves and others discomfort in their reaction to the warm, lowland conditions of north-eastern Thailand where they have sought refuge. Even were a will and resources to exist for the local resettlement of such refugees, the frictions that arise from cultural differences would impose restraints on planning for permanent accommodation.

Where open land can be found and the government has an interest in developing it — as was the case with some of the places where refugees from Rwanda and Burundi appeared in Tanzania — permanent resettlement may prove possible. In conditions of unemployment — as in Florida during the influx of Haitian asylum-seekers — cultural differences can assume a reinforcing role in dissuading the authorities from any interest in settlement. When social facilities already bear a heavy burden in a shaky economy — as in Sudan — the government may attempt to limit spontaneous settlement around native cities where schools, hospitals and other services are concentrated. In such circumstances, cultural differences may underscore the social costs of resettlement.

Jealousy

Resettlement in countries of first asylum can give rise to jealousy on the part of those living nearby. Even if refugees receive only a minimum of help to establish themselves in remote rural areas, local inhabitants can view the assistance programmes as an unwarranted favour to strangers. This is especially true when more advanced technical facilities are provided by outside agencies or when the refugees' skills exceed those of local people. Both these complaints were heard, for example, in eastern Sudan and in Pakistan where some spontaneous resettlement took place and attracted subsequent outside help. Voluntary agencies sometimes dispose of limited means of advanced assistance which can be put to the service of the refugees but not the surrounding community. Medical care on a personal basis, as contrasted with a concentration on public health, typifies such services.

Refugee populations also tend to include a high proportion of active, motivated individuals whose very presence betokens their above-average energy. Their working tempo may cause resentment among the surrounding population, as has been the case with some Eritreans in eastern Sudan. Resettlement schemes involving the provision of food and tools for initial phases of development may also stimulate hostile local reactions. The creation of an unwelcoming atmosphere bodes little good, either for the refugees or the surrounding community.

Approach of receiving government

A government with highly directive policies towards its population, or an authoritarian government with little respect for the rights of its subjects, may hold back from considering resettlement on its territory for any but those whose cultures or social practices make integration practically free of friction; or alternatively such a government may attempt to force local practices or tight supervision on the newcomers. In either case, the degree of adjustment required of the local population would be slight. Such close supervision tends to cause resentment among refugees used to different practices and can substantially reduce the chances of success. The unceremonious departure of Vietnamese settlers from Chinese collective farms can partly be explained in this fashion. Similarly, a vacillating or arbitrarily changing policy can either undo settlement work or obviate it before it has begun. Given the enormous variations between one government and another, it is difficult to forecast specifically how the behaviour of a hard-handed government will influence resettlement, except to say that it tends to constrain the possibilities of success even when beginnings are made spontaneously or with the unannounced acquiescence of the authorities.

Costs

Resettlement, inevitably involves costs. Local expenses cannot be avoided, no matter how much outside assistance comes into play. Such costs can mount geometrically if large-scale development schemes — like those proposed for eastern Sudan — become a vehicle for refugee resettlement. Even when costs are relatively modest, additional policing, general health controls, water supplies, transportation and general supervision must be provided. These can eventually be made to pay for themselves if resettlement, as is usual, entails economic development as a by-product. Refugee resettlement implies work, integration into the economy and self-support. This results in a broader tax base and an increase in the gross economic product of the country in question. Nevertheless, the start-up costs can be substantial and last over a considerable period. In such cases as that of Somalia, very modest schemes could be expanded only at really quite forbidding costs. Spontaneous resettlement may involve less obvious costs but nevertheless requires some expenditure.

Conceptual issues

Resettlement of refugees in countries of first asylum is generally based on a number of relatively simple concepts, especially in developing countries. As a rule these include self-support, integration, low costs and, not infrequently, the opportunity for eventual return. Although the expectation of repatriation is logically excluded by settlement, the spontaneous establishment of self-supporting communities may still be viewed by the local authorities as a lengthy prelude to return. This was the attitude of the Sudanese government towards Eritreans, for instance. The aim in all cases, however, is to place the refugees in the kind of employment which will allow their capacity for self-support to emerge, to protect their well-being and that of their neighbours and to promote the development of their children into useful adulthood.

All this implies the help of some social services and a degree of institutionalisation, even when the formal pretence of the government is that the refugees will one day depart. The conceptual pattern of resettlement thus depends heavily on the surrounding community. Governments probably hesitate to experiment in such situations. Where they have to accommodate large numbers, the financial and administrative costs, the strain on supervisory mechanisms and political constraints inhibit experimentation. Where small numbers need to be cared for, these can conveniently be eased into the existing community or even supported on the raw edge of integration. As a result potentially promising opportunities for refugees to make use of their own particular skills may be forgone.

Furthermore, only rarely have refugee communities found a role in larger national development schemes. The Sudan government has proposed precisely such schemes for its eastern province, where at least some 400,000 refugees from Ethiopia are sheltered. But costs there are likely to be high, and the Sudan government has necessarily sought outside support, with dubious results. The African countries as a whole drew up development plans for use in connection with refugees during the two International Conferences on African Refugees in 1981 and 1984.[8] These are aimed largely at self-sufficiency and the protection of existing development programmes, but not generally at explicit resettlement. Opportunities for economic development to promote resettlement of the Palestinian refugees were sought on several occasions, but the political attitudes of the host governments prevented their application.

In addition, the institutional basis for exploring and promoting new conceptual approaches to resettlement in places of first asylum falls short of what would be required. The national governments of developing countries flooded with refugees have little capacity to try new leads; milder conditions offer national governments little incentive for experimenting with novelties. The intergovernmental agencies give priority to pressing short-term demands for aid to refugees. The long-term development agencies — such as UNDP or the World Bank — have almost never sought to build refugee programmes into schemes which they approve together with national authorities. During 1983, however, UNHCR and the World Bank drew up schemes for refugee self-sufficiency in Pakistan; this was both exceptional and not immediately financed.[9] UNHCR and the World Bank have since then modestly extended to Sudan their co-operation on the identification of projects which could serve both refugees and local development.

UNHCR has generally sought the least disruptive and therefore the most conventional routes to integration, although it has tried to pioneer some rural settlements in Africa. It has also promoted the use of counselling to ease the integration of refugees into new communities where this is permitted. In addition, UNHCR has long provided financial support to reduce the burden on host governments of refugees unable to adapt to resettlement; these people include the aged, the infirm and the psychologically incapacitated. Despite these individual leads, the conceptual approaches to resettlement adopted by places of first asylum tend to lean towards the conventional.

In the United States, public discussion of refugee affairs frequently involves conceptual confusion. As that country has recently allowed more refugees to enter for permanent resettlement than any other country, this confusion sometimes casts its influence beyond the approach of American public authorities. In fact, only since the Cuban revolution has the United States faced any sizeable issue of refugees requiring first asylum and on-the-spot resettlement.

The previous experience of the United States was confined mainly to refugees who had first received temporary asylum elsewhere and subsequently arrived in American ports as immigrants. The American authorities' experience of immigrants is, needless to say, long and deep. While such groups face difficulties akin to those of refugees granted the rights of settlement, since before the First World War they have been served by an extensive network of voluntary agencies. Nor have the usual immigrants had to undergo the trauma of clandestine landings on new shores or escape from zealous secret police. The arrival of the Cuban refugees and others — such as the Haitians and Chileans — who come directly to American ports from their countries of origin, challenged both American conceptions of refugees and the practices of public authorities and voluntary agencies.

With the adoption of the Refugee Act of 1980, the United States government sharpened the conceptual edges of its approach. It included in the act the definition of refugees contained in the 1951 UN Convention, to which it had earlier agreed by adhering to the 1967 protocol to the Convention. As a result, asylum-seekers have a legal right to protection. Because some of these claims are judged by the American authorities to be well-founded, the United States has for the first time a substantial number of first-asylum seekers. Most of those granted first asylum want to remain in the United States as settlers; they usually reject offers of resettlement in a third country. Nor can the United States easily make persuasive claims that refugees arriving directly ought to be resettled in some third country, as it accepts large numbers of refugees from temporary shelter in Indo-China as permanent settlers.

Third-country resettlement

Refugees move to third-country resettlement on the basis of previously drawn-up lines of international agreement or of national policy. This movement falls under close regulation and is either of a kind designed especially to apply to forced migrants or one that has a more general application and covers immigrants as a whole. Refugees are unable to move from a situation of first asylum to assured resettlement in a third country merely on the basis of their own initiatives. Once they obtain first asylum they are in a position to take advantage of legal and administrative structures for resettlement. They may indeed be forced out of a place of asylum to another area where they are once again required to seek first asylum; alternatively they may shift, with the permission of the new host government, from one place of first asylum to another. The expectation, nevertheless, is that they will some day return to their country of origin. The principle of third-country settlement, in contrast, implies a movement from first-asylum status to that of a secure, welcome immigrant. It formally implies abandoning any real hope of returning to the land of origin. Resettlement in a third country almost always comprehends a commitment on the part of the refugee to seek integration in a distant new society, where the government guarantees the immigrant a firm legal status and sometimes more. Therefore, third-country resettlement converts a refugee into an immigrant with at least the legal rights of other immigrants. Because of the cause of their searches for asylum, however, refugees may benefit from special arrangements for their settlement.

Refugees and immigration policies

Forced migrants can sometimes find loopholes in national immigration policies which lead them to a permanent home in a third country. A typical example is a national regulation permitting or encouraging family reunion. The United States and France, to give two examples, have such regulations. These have proven of great importance in opening up the possibilities for third-country resettlement. The relatives of a refugee can usually take action, either on their own or with the help of voluntary agencies, to support the request for immigration status from a forced migrant. In other instances, national regulations or policies promote immigration on humanitarian grounds, granting a permanent home to, for example, sick, infirm, crippled or aged refugees. The Scandinavian countries and Switzerland have offered resettlement to some belonging to these categories. On occasion refugees fit categories designed by national governments to encourage the immigration of those possessing wanted skills, such as engineering. In all these approaches to third-country resettlement it is the national authorities that make the binding decisions.

Organised third-country resettlement has offered the most important means of eliminating some of the largest refugee incidents since the end of the Second World War. It was the principal instrument used by the International Refugee Organisation between 1947 and 1950 for clearing the camps in Europe. The men, women and children in question proceeded as immigrants to countries of resettlement in the Americas and Oceania in a carefully co-ordinated fashion in which international supervision dovetailed with national decisions. Later, Hungarians and Indo-Chinese entered mainly the United States and to some extent countries of Western Europe. France and other European countries offered places to Indo-Chinese and to refugees from Czechoslovakia and Poland after political turbulence sometimes accompanied by Soviet military action. In these cases, the refugees came to their country of permanent settlement from first asylum or temporary residence elsewhere.

Third-country resettlement offers substantial benefits to those who qualify for it and want it. It assures them a permanent place. It is almost always accompanied by helpful actions on the part of voluntary agencies as well as the receiving government. UNHCR and other institutions are required to offer only limited help, while clearing their books of considerable numbers of dependents. ICM and voluntary organisations are often able to participate in the re-settling process, thus fulfilling their mandates.

At the same time, third-country resettlement can hardly be relied on as a reliable mechanism which can be switched on whenever on-the-spot resettlement or repatriation fail to work. Because third-country resettlement aims at permanence, it necessarily becomes an issue of immigration, not merely temporary shelter. Little can be done from the outside about the decisions of governments regarding who comes into their territories and who is excluded. Even asylum for refugees is narrowly framed and often contested. Governments that are deaf to humanitarian appeals can remain blind to the need for resettlement. Intergovernmental organisations can make generalised recommendations to governments urging them to consider setting policies of admitting refugees. UNHCR and other organisations may discretely argue for easier immigration conditions for their clients but are hardly able to put on much pressure or offer large incentives to governments to favour forced migrants as immigrants. Moreover, even such discreet appeals must be delicately handled because of the particular sensitivity surrounding immigration.

The sensitivity that surrounds immigration matters is the result perhaps more than anything else of nationalistic sentiments. These can be framed in many ways, ranging from the need to maintain cultural purity to the economic self-interest of particular groups. They can also be based mainly on old habit and prejudice. In the United States, for instance, immigration policy has long been affected by nativistic sentiments and by popular pressure in favour of immigrants from Europe as opposed to those from Asia and in support of some European groups as opposed to others. In Western Europe, some publics insist that their countries are overpopulated and unable to provide room for more inhabitants. Others in that area claim a prior obligation to people from former colonies or insist that settlers from particular parts of the world will encounter severe social opposition. Japanese society, according to that country's government, promises a difficult time to any foreigner seeking to settle in it permanently. Similar remarks can be made about many other communities in the world. In a number of them, arranged immigration from the ranks of forced migrants is simply regarded as out of the question. The Soviet Union and the countries of the Eastern bloc, for instance, have never adjusted their immigration laws so as to offer resettlement within their territories to forced migrants; nor have refugees often been known to seek resettlement in that direction.

Apart from the social and sentimental barriers to the resettlement of forced migrants, such an approach gains little encouragement anywhere at times of economic stress. The erroneous belief that newcomers necessarily take away jobs from native populations retains a strong grip on trade unions and other groups in the United States and elsewhere. Other opponents of immigration at times of stress insist that the extra social costs cannot be met.

Moreover, the control of immigration is generally linked to policies relating to internal security. Governments that feel threatened by their own subjects sometimes believe outsiders to be even more menacing. In any case, the control of people entering a country has an unshakeable place in the roster of practices devised to protect national security. This is perfectly consistent with strong nationalism.

When national immigration rules include in the same category both third-country resettlers and refugees seeking first asylum, the two groups are inevitably forced to compete for places. The Mariel exodus from Cuba to the United States provides a stark illustration of this kind of competition. Even with an annual quota of 50,000 available for refugee resettlement, the newcomers promptly overwhelmed the number of legal places at their disposal. Had those leaving Mariel been classed as refugees, the numbers accepted from Indo-China would have been reduced; yet if they were not called refugees, there was still no existing category for their entry. In this instance, the existing regulations were bent and adjusted until the Cubans were granted asylum without formally acquiring the legal status of refugee. Such improvisation is, obviously, not always possible, even with a great deal of durable popular goodwill.

Preparation for resettlement

By the time refugees have entered the process of resettlement in a third country they will have uprooted themselves from their own cultures, clans and families. They will have had to adjust to refugee conditions while bereft of familiar social support and uncertain about the future. They will often have spent many months in the subsistence life of camps. Resettlement in a third country calls for yet another adjustment, often the greatest of all: they have to make the transition between temporary uprooting and permanent arrangements, usually in an utterly alien atmosphere without even the ragged blanket of psychological comfort that other countrymen in similar circumstances in the next dormitory cubicle represent. As the countries of immigration have tended to be geographically and culturally remote from places of temporary asylum, the task of readjustment weighs heavily. As a result, third-country resettlement has generally called forth attempts to prepare the new immigrants. Such preparation reduces the difficulties experienced by the host authorities in settling the new arrivals. It helps to ensure a more rapid adjustment.

Furthermore, the new country of asylum will probably require meticulous legal preparation in order to establish identities and ensure support once the refugee arrives. Legal screening also attempts to eliminate possible threats to national security, such as could be introduced by political activists or espionage agents. In any case, visas or valid immigration permits must be issued to refugees destined for resettlement. The government that offered temporary shelter must also be in possession of detailed information on movements.

The question of appropriate documentation, as all refugee incidents make clear, poses particular difficulties. Applicants for asylum often leave their homes clandestinely and have no subsequent access to official papers such as birth certificates and passports. Even if they did have such documents initially, these may have disappeared or been stolen in the course of flight; by definition it can be assumed that the authorities of their homelands decline to co-operate in the furnishing of such materials. Yet immigration authorities everywhere require documentation, including health certification, and sometimes regard as doubtful the temporary documentation issued under UNHCR auspices. The function of the sketchy international regime for the protection of refugees thus takes on a particular importance at this stage.

The recent practice by the United States in the resettlement of large numbers of people — such as the Indo-Chinese — has been to send officials of the Immigration and Naturalization Service to the places of temporary asylum to make individual decisions on those who have prepared applications. At first carried out with such zeal as to build another barrier against immigration, their assignment was to explore the question of whether applicants for resettlement had 'a well-founded fear of persecution'. INS interpretations of this test were so strict as to arouse controversy over the trickle of people let through to resettlement.[10] Other national immigration services also send missions to camps in order to select appropriate settlers. They interview people for whom background documentation has been prepared and select those who conform to national standards. In these and other instances, organisations entrusted with the care of refugees help to arrange the required documentation and securing of materials necessary for legal entry into the countries of resettlement.

When the flow of resettlers continues over a considerable period or involves large numbers, an integrated process of preparation can be set up. Once migrants have had their applications for third-country resettlement approved, their documentation is assembled and reviewed. They can then be prepared for transportation. In Thailand, such an integrated process began operating soon after numbers of Vietnamese began to arrive during the late 1970s and has since become a closely managed routine. Migrants move from holding centres — as the camps of temporary shelter are known — to departure camps. There, ICM takes charge of preparing individuals for travel. It examines documents, conducts medical examinations, arranges for the chartering of local aircraft and sends off those concerned in what is an integrated, assembly-line process. Voluntary agencies assist in the departure camps with important human details, including social counselling and instruction in the language of the new country. Those bound for the United States usually proceed to special holding centres in the Philippines and Indonesia, where for a month or so they receive orientation courses in American customs and in the English language. The children's education continues. [11]

The educational and counselling programmes are intended to ease the transition to the new society and fill the psychological craters dug up by the experience of refugee life. The social aspects of departure take a real toll. Families are sometimes obliged to separate for a time just when new fears for the future mingle with hopes for a settled life. The enforced idleness of the camps and the arbitrary nature of the departure pattern — at least as perceived by the affected individuals — also take their psychic toll. Voluntary agencies have accepted contracts for services to assist the migrants. Their counselling and orientation work offers insights into the difficulties and frictions encountered by the refugees as they move to resettlement. It appears that this knowledge has been built into the programmes and can offer valuable assets for the societies receiving the former refugees. While it would be difficult to give a confident evaluation of such programmes, there seems little doubt that many individuals benefit from them.

143

Reception

Once the new settlers arrive in the country of permanent asylum, they undergo a final entrance examination. This is typically a matter of immigration process and almost entirely within the province of the national authorities who conduct it under national law. UNHCR and ICRC can sometimes intervene in individual cases, when these come to their attention. With rare exceptions, however, international officials have no fixed role in the decisional process; they may even lack useful information about it. When they do intervene, the mode is that of a consular or diplomatic official rather than of a functionary with decisional powers. Given the organised nature of third-country resettlement, it is likely that relatively few difficulties arise at the time of entry. Nevertheless, the treatment of such cases as delicate and requiring much discretion excludes the possibility of any confident generalisation. Furthermore, the variety of national regulations and procedures for appeal prevents any uniform approach being made by interested organisations.

Some national authorities, such as those in France and England, direct the newly arrived settlers to orientation programmes designed to ease them into their new lives. In other instances, as in the United States, the new arrivals immediately enter their new communities with support from local and national voluntary groups[12] and receive the benefits of orientation before departure. In either case, some of the newcomers will require extended help because of difficulties in adjustment or the breakdown of anticipated arrangements, such as regular employment or appropriate education. Nevertheless, such aspects of resettlement can be understood as only an aberration in a process that is generally familiar.

Planned migration to third-country resettlement can cause local reactions similar to those that occur with settlement in a country of first asylum. Alien values can induce local resentment, as was the case with the Vietnamese fishermen who were settled in a port on the Gulf of Mexico. Large numbers of foreign newcomers create a visible impact on local services, such as schools, hospitals and voluntary welfare services. Some of the newcomers will fail to integrate into the normal social life around them, either because of their own insufficiencies or because of structural reasons beyond their control, and come to depend on public welfare in order to survive. Nativist sentiment may be stirred up, especially in times of widespread economic difficulty.

Such reactions raise the questions of whether local governments can devise tactics to prevent difficulties from arising and whether designation of the newcomers as refugees serves any of the parties concerned very well. The effects on local communities could conceivably be handled with greater ease if the newcomers were approached as normal immigrants, not persons for whom elaborate special programmes were needed. Where voluntary agencies familiar with local conditions can be engaged and persons experienced in the care of refugees in camps or other places of temporary asylum are able to take part in the settlement work, other problems of adjustment may be avoided. Nevertheless, it remains hazardous to make suggestions of general policies, because so much depends on the local situation into which the refugees are expected to fit. The continuous compilation and comparison of experience in this regard may serve to inform those in charge of future incidents.

Finally, refugees involved in resettlement in places distant from their original homelands still bring with them political values. As they usually intend to stay permanently in their new homeland, they soon begin to take their rightful part in political activities. Because they cease to be refugees on receiving permanent status, the prohibitions against political activities that apply to persons given temporary ayslum have no relevance. The exercise of one's right to take part in social and political decisions — as a rule, integral to the protection of human rights — appears to be generally accepted as routine in countries of immigration, such as Australia or the United States. At the same time, if the former refugees undertake concerted organisation in favour of their compatriots in the country of origin or against the existing government there, they may soon come to represent a new element in the political life of their adopted country. They can also find themselves at odds with the government that gave them permanent asylum. Resettled refugees sometimes take a special interest in immigration policies, as certain Cuban and Hungarian settlers in the United States have done. Their voices on this set of issues can disturb existing relationships and also offer opportunities to political leaders to find new sources of support. At the same time, not all settlers take advantage of political opportunity, no doubt for a complex of reasons. As with other aspects of refugee behaviour, confident generalising about political activities would appear dangerous; yet certain experiences in the United States and Canada clearly suggest that resettled refugees are likely to have an active political role in their new societies.

Emerging issues

Attempts to liquidate recent refugee incidents have outlined — sometimes repeatedly — a set of emerging issues. Some of these inhere in any contemporary forced migration and may be expected to reappear. Others receive special emphasis in the context of specific political reactions. These issues include the demand on the part of governments for a fair share of assistance. They also comprise the use of economic and social development in refugee incidents and the financing of assistance, resettlement and repatriation.

Fair shares

Experience in recent years of very large-scale flows of refugees makes it clear that rather elaborate transnational organisation must be created and set to work in order to restore the asylum-seekers to normal society. The very scale of the organisation required gives rise to competition for scarce manpower and financing as well as for places for permanent resettlement when repatriation proves impossible. Although the fundamental requirements for caring for refugees and sending them on to a place of permanent residence remain the same in principle regardless of whether the numbers involved are small or large, the larger the mass the more strain there is on the permanent machinery set up for such a purpose. This strain invites errors and inefficiency and promotes a sense of crisis.

Even given common requirements and the similar effects of refugee situations, specific incidents differ from each other in subtle but significant ways. Compared with those in the Horn of Africa, for example, the Indo-Chinese refugee incidents inspired arrangements that were far more elaborate. With the exception of some of the shelters set up for the Lao in north-eastern Thailand, most camps and holding centres were deliberately separated from the local population and also from the border. A similar separation characterised the camps in Malaysia. While this isolation conformed to the policies of the receiving government, it was relatively costly. It required new construction and obviated the participation of refugees in the local economy, where some steps towards self-sufficiency might have been taken.

Furthermore, many of the Khmer, as well as the Vietnamese who had survived harrowing sea voyages, arrived in the camps in very poor physical condition. They required extended medical care, special nutritional supplements and at least temporary leave from any work. Moreover, the condition that Thailand and Malaysia, in particular, laid down for even temporary shelter was that no local resettlement would take place. This meant that any opportunity for third-country resettlement had to be visible and that its effects would be seen to limit the growth of camp populations. Thus, the initial material assistance that took place in new, hurriedly constructed special locations only began an extended process that included preparation for emigration. In order to reduce the numbers in the holding centres, moreover, the United States and UNHCR negotiated permission to construct temporary holding centres in the Philippines and Indonesia. In these holding centres, and even earlier, special orientation programmes were created to prepare the departing settlers for their new lives as permanent residents of the United States.

In the Horn of Africa, less sophisticated techniques were employed. The refugees from Ethiopia were accustomed to very hard conditions and no element of resettlement was included in any of the programmes. Nor were the Somali or Sudan governments in any position to insist on resettlement elsewhere as a condition of refraining from *refoulement*. In Sudan, from the time fighting broke out in Eritrea between separatists and the central government, a number of spontaneous settlements grew up near the border. Other refugees found their way to cities. Only much later, in the early 1980s, did the government conceive of camps linked to the economic development of eastern Sudan at considerable distances from the border. In Somalia, the government began to move refugees from camps close to the border to what were assumed to be more promising areas for self-sufficiency. The Somali government also hoped to make the camps more secure from Ethiopian armed attack; such attacks occurred from time to time on the border camps, because of the activity of anti-Ethiopian guerrillas in that area. In the mid-Somalia camps, too, as in Djibouti, self-sufficiency schemes took a long time to set up, partly because of the difficulty posed by the environment and partly because of limited financing and uncertainty over repatriation. Despite the very large numbers of people seeking asylum, the size of international staffs and the degree of interest on the part of voluntary agencies and communications media settled to a level dramatically below that seen in South-East Asia. If nothing else, it was simply much harder to get to the Somali-Ethiopian border or to the eastern Sudan than from Bangkok to the Cambodian border or to the Gulf of Siam.

By 1980, African governments were beginning to make a point of the vast difference in expenditure per head of refugees in Southeast Asia compared with the Horn of Africa and elsewhere in that continent.[13] They thus raised the issue of fair shares and urged that the expenditures on, and accordingly the services offered to, the refugees in Africa and South-East Asia be brought closer together. As these complaints emerged in organs of the United Nations, UNHCR had necessarily to respond, for the one-state, one-vote system of deciding on policies gave the numerous African countries a means of turning their criticism into instructions.

Four responses from UNHCR and voluntary agencies followed complaints about fair shares. The first of these explained why the costs per refugee of a process that ended in resettlement in North America, Europe or some other culturally and geographically distant part of the world exceeded those of basic material care in camps. A second type of response took the form of programmatic efforts to help the refugees in African camps attain some degree of self-sufficiency. For instance, in the inhospitable region of Djibouti which had never known cultivation, refugees received the necessary encouragement and technical help to embark on a vegetable-growing project using irrigation. In Sudan, UNHCR had earlier provided supplementary aid for spontaneous settlement and other schemes; there it tried to upgrade its efforts and to assist governmental plans for the opening of new facilities where refugees could take part in efforts to develop the agricultural potential of eastern Sudan. (It went largely unremarked outside expert circles that the Sudan government was busy removing Eritreans from urban areas where they had also spontaneously resettled.) The third response by UNHCR and certain voluntary agencies lay in the direction of repatriation to Ethiopia. In order to encourage repatriation, the Ethiopian government received assistance with reception centres for returnees; during the first two years of operation, several thousand people per year actually returned, but the growing shortage of food in Ethopia shattered any hope of large-scale return by this route. Finally, the developmental implications of a refugee presence, discussed in the following section, were given more attention. In the background was the unavoidable fact that the United States had decided for complex reasons — some of them largely domestic — that the Indo-Chinese refugees merited particular attention and that African refugee issues should get less prominent treatment.

While these responses helped to allay some government criticism, they did not really get to the heart of the matter. The question remains whether a generally applicable standard can be said to exist for the handling of refugee incidents which involve camp care and resettlement and whether it has been widely and fairly applied by the relevant authorities. Only minimum standards appear to have been spelt out. These apply mainly to emergency situations and the obtaining of first asylum. What happens after the provisions of such services remains a matter for determination on an incident-by-incident basis. It could therefore either be argued that an equal *per capita* standard of services should apply in all refugee incidents or alternatively that the standard should be adjusted in a way that is appropriate to the method used for liquidating the incident.

The two lines of argument lead to different outcomes as far as the administration of refugee incidents is concerned. It is clear that on the basis of expenditure per head in South-East Asia and Africa that if the two were made equal, substantially more services would go to the Africans.[14] At the same time, the process of resettlement and temporary care in South-East Asia would run down, assuming that governments were to maintain their present contributions. Once again, the spectre of wandering refugees unable to find asylum — even if under another name — would rear its head. On the other hand, if high *per capita* expenditures for the purpose of maintaining a third-country resettlement process are maintained, then the possibilities of self-sufficiency, repatriation and spontaneous settlement decline for Africans whose level of adaptability is high and who are suffering from a form of deprivation as poignant as that experienced by refugees in South-East Asia. An end to the steady haemorrhage of people from Vietnam and Laos would obviously reduce the pressure for fair shares simply by lowering the need for services.

Claims to fair shares are not likely to be decided in actuality along the clear-cut lines of this discussion; rather the issue has the typically political attributes of cogent demands that would obstruct each other if honoured fully. The outcome in the longer term is likely to be a series of negotiated patterns, each depending on the particular circumstances in which the incidents arose and the degree to which organised support for claims can be built up.

Economic and social development

The presence of refugees invariably affects economic and social development. How much depends on numbers and other factors present in the local environment. Their departure may upset the economies they leave behind, as did the expulsion of Asians from Uganda or the exodus of ethnic Chinese from South Vietnam. Even the departure of refugees from camps to places of resettlement may influence the economy in the neighbourhood of the camps.

When refugees enter a territory, they necessarily increase the demands made on the local economy and can sometimes disrupt existing development programmes. This was said to be the case when the presence of Zimbabweans reached large numbers in Mozambique. Even if no particularly disruptive results accompany the entry of refugees into an economy, their presence may be felt in the temporary distortion of customary patterns in local markets and on local services. The presence of Eritrean refugees in Port Sudan, for instance, is said by Sudan government officials to have driven the rent for housing to intolerable levels.

Not all the economic and social effects of the presence of refugees need be harmful to the local economy. In some cases, strong stimuli to development emanate from the newcomers. The Cubans in Florida, for example, have clearly stimulated economic development with a minimum of outside help. The settlement in Tanzania of refugees from Mozambique, Rwanda and Burundi led to the opening of new farms on lands that had been under-used. The spread of Vietnamese restaurants in the United States and Western Europe signifies the injection of a new element into the local culture.

The principal discussions of economic development in relation to refugees, however, have concentrated on the immediately deleterious effects and the potentials of longer-term novel programmes. The recent, heavy flows of refugees in developing countries, where the most clearly outlined development programmes with international support operate, have set off two important reactions. Governments and transnational agencies have adjusted certain existing development programmes to the new situations. At the same time, some transnational bodies, led by UNHCR, have attempted to link refugees to development programmes. This approach has found an echo in the search by some governments for additional, sometimes large-scale, support for national development programmes for the simultaneous purposes of improving the local economy and guiding refugees to self-sufficiency.

An influx of refugees, unexpected and unplanned, inherently contradicts the notion of planned economic and social development. Developing countries that receive assistance from such international agencies as the World Bank and the UN Development Programme are required to work out plans for economic improvement. The outside help fits into these plans which have sometimes taken years to put together and bring to operation. An influx of refugees of any size forces a readjustment of such plans. It tends to cut into the local resources which form the base for the supplemental external aid. Salient parts of the national administration will certainly become preoccupied by a severe refugee crisis. Furthermore, the adjustment of plans and operations means undoing interlocked decisions. A typical development project in which the foreign exchange component is funded from outside sources takes two to five years to put into place, requires extensive documentation and planning and decisions by international organs. Bilateral programmes sometimes require less forward planning, sometimes more. As the usual hope on the part of governments at the beginning of a refugee flow is that it is temporary and reversible, development managers have little incentive to make immediate, sharp readjustments, even when they are able to do so. If the refugee flow reaches large proportions or cannot be diverted, they may find that their programmes have been overwhelmed.

At the same time, refugees have a theoretical potential for helping with economic development while advancing their own self-sufficiency, either in situations of first asylum or as settlers. But unless additional resources can be assembled for development and self-sufficiency programmes for refugees, provisions for existing projects will have to be diverted. No immediate responses can be expected from the intergovernmental development agencies, whose programme cycles run into years. In an effort to turn these theoretical potentials into actual programmes, UNHCR in 1980 created a Fund for Durable Solutions. It was strongly encouraged by the United States, the leading donor for all refugee and development programmes. The new fund sought to identify low-cost supplementary development projects which would benefit refugees and the local economy. Thus, the fund would not compete with existing programmes but rather supplement them. Its work would be attractive to host governments because it would add to the total of development projects and presumably reduce the local costs incurred by handling refugees. For the donor countries, it promised some slight reduction in contributions in the near future and, possibly over a longer period, an important diminution of them. The projects would be identified and planned with support from UNHCR. If attractive enough, they would presumably find additional funding. In fact, the United States Congress declined to fund the American share of the fund, and this alone was enough to discourage other potential donors. The fund was in essence stillborn, although a few of its genes linger in the bureaucratic shade.[15] The Fund as such therefore neither stimulated the international development agencies to act on behalf of refugee projects nor did it creatively compete with them — as some feared — for scarce financing.

In a less firmly institutionalised way than the creation of the Fund for Durable Solutions suggested, the hope that the economic development and care of refugees could be mutually helpful lives on. UNHCR officials continue earlier approaches made to development agencies. Voluntary agencies oriented towards development — such as Oxfam and the Mennonite Central Committee — mount some of their own projects with developmental aims. These typically aim at leaving behind working facilities, such as water supplies, when the refugees depart; the host government thus benefits from the investment which has meanwhile helped with the maintenance of the refugees. After 1980, the World Bank began to show at least some interest in the long-term potential, as with the UNHCR development project for Pakistan. In scattered resolutions that reflected UNHCR's ideas, the General Assembly continued to endorse the developmental approach.[16] Nevertheless, experience of deliberate programmatic stimulation of joint development projects for refugees and host governments remains limited, although the effort to use its potential continues, especially in the African context.

A bold effort by Sudan to expand its development programme to provide a promising future for refugees offered the first clear, major example of this approach.[17] Despite the unquestioned developmental possibilities in its eastern province, where refugees from Ethiopia have been housed since the mid-1960s, Sudan's existing programme had not prospered. Recently its economy has suffered severely from the sharp increases in energy prices and from insufficiencies in management and leadership. The burden of refugees had an increased impact in these circumstances. The largest in Africa, the UNHCR programme included support for many projects designed to promote self-sufficiency and economic development for refugees.[18] These aimed at reducing the costs of refugee care in both camps and rural areas for both UNHCR and the government as well as at creating more favourable conditions for the foreigners. These programmes yielded few dramatic results and were inherently incapable of fulfilling their objectives. The Sudan government, which follows a general policy of providing asylum for those who flee oppression in their own country, had always permitted the

Ethiopians — including Eritreans, Tigreans and certain others — first asylum; in other parts of Sudan, Zaïreans, Chadians and Ugandans also found asylum. As many Eritreans, according to Sudanese officials, concentrated in towns in eastern Sudan and Khartoum, where they absorbed a disproportionate share of the social services and engaged in prostitution and other undesirable activities, better programmes were needed. In these circumstances, the Sudan government sought to take a major step forward, treating its refugee populations as an opportunity and seeking to promote development on the land so as to lessen the impact of refugees on the towns.

The medium chosen by Sudan for launching its development-refugee plan was an international conference it summoned for 1980 in Khartoum. The government presented to the attending representatives and to international organisations its own sheaf of development plans, somewhat hurriedly put together for the conference with the aid of outside consultants. To put these plans into effect would have required $280 million in new financing. The conference resulted in pledges of some ten million dollars, some of which was transferred by donors from existing programmes in Sudan. Certain donors showed only slight confidence in the Sudanese government, while others had little interest in making new commitments. International organisations also failed to show an unusual degree of enthusiasm for the effort. UNHCR agreed to attend the conference and to help support planning, but its officials approached it with some scepticism. The effort probably had some salutary results in sharpening Sudanese development planning, making clear to others that a certain amount of specific planning could help with the disposition of refugees, and posing more clearly than before the immensity of the refugee situation for Sudan. The conference was also followed by a far-reaching reorganisation of the Sudanese refugee administration and doubtless some salutary restraint with regard to the fostering of huge development schemes and the disposal of refugee problems in one blow.

A similar approach was employed in the already mentioned pair of International Conferences on Aid to African Refugees, summoned in 1981 and 1984 by the United Nations. Altogether ICARA I resulted in pledges amounting to $570 million, much of which simply represented switching from one national donor account to another. By 1983, any new money was close to exhaustion, and the new conference produced no windfall. Instead, donors examined 128 projects put forward by the African countries to help with infrastructural and developmental projects intended to benefit both refugees and the economies in question. Of these, the donors expressed interest in about a third but declined to make any financial commitment at the conference. They saw the meeting as one step in a process on which there was general agreement that existing machinery should be used. Nor was the mandate of UNHCR to be broadened. The UN Development Programme agreed to take on the new projects, materially expanding its interest in the results of forced migration. Some donor governments preferred to keep any aid projects within their bilateral programmes rather than allot them to the multilateral agencies. Criticism of the quality of certain proposals was followed by requests from some governments for additional feasibility studies before going ahead. ICARA II could hardly be seen to represent a major step towards practical development projects from which large numbers of refugees in Africa would benefit.

Countries of immigration, where resettlement takes place, do not as a rule specifically connect entering refugees with economic development. In part, this is because, as in affluent or rapidly growing economies, development — in the sense that the Third World approaches it — is not an issue. Yet their economies necessarily feel some impact from newcomers, especially if these are numerous or have difficulties in adjusting. In the largest and richest of the immigration lands, the United States, a sharp inflow of refugees may have mostly local consequences. These can include the creation of new businesses, the construction of housing, other kinds of social investment, the introduction of new products, techniques and working habits, and new artistic and cultural manifestations. When the stimulus of refugee influxes comes at a time of financial stringency, the adaptation of the local economy may be slow. The impact on the social welfare system will then be proportionately higher. It will also be higher in the case of refugees whose cultural background demands a lengthy period of adjustment. However, it can be argued that immigration in general and refugees in particular stimulate the economy, as was the case in the Miami area of Florida when the initial phase of entry was complete.

Even if it were generally accepted (it is not!) that economic development offers a readily usable path for clearing up or at least easing refugee situations, whether accompanied or not by on-the-spot resettlement, the possibility remains that successful development might prove so attractive to neighbouring populations that increasing numbers would be led to seek asylum. This is an aspect of the 'pull' effect that has entered discussions of refugee affairs in the United States. It postulates that many who claim asylum seek a better economic future rather than an escape from persecution. Although a case for the 'pull' effect can be made, it relies on the proposition that migrants move as easily on the basis of economic advantage as on that of pressures. This proposition seems facile. It seems more useful to concentrate on the margins that make displacement more attractive than enduring further local pressure. Stating the issue in this way makes it clear that refugees nevertheless believe themselves to be forced into exile, not merely attracted by a relatively flourishing economy. Those asylum-seekers — such as the Haitians — who face threateningly lean times at home and little future in terms of employment or entrepreneurship, also feel themselves to be driven by forces beyond their control.

Unresolved refugee situations

When those people left over from resettlement or repatriation pro-grammes prove to be an acceptable burden to a country of asylum, a refugee incident is deemed to have been resolved. Such integra-tion usually takes place quietly, often in the country of first asylum, and may include the aged and infirm, those whose psychological make-up has altered so much in the course of the time spent in refuge that they are unable to cope with another shift, and those who simply have been offered no alternative to staying where they are. In-dividuals may, of course, combine several of these characteristics.

Absolute liquidation of refugee situations in the sense that every entrant into asylum without exception returns home or finds unchal-lenged permanent asylum and personal independence seems highly unlikely in the light of experience since the First World War. Well after the Second World War, for example, a few refugees from the Soviet revolution still had no nationality, while others developed no ability to earn their own living. Instead, they became lifelong charges of various organisations, some of them voluntary associations. Similarly, the effort on the part of IRO to find places for all those in its camps left some who were obliged to depend on the new UNHCR for protection and a degree of material assistance. Such incidents of 'hard core', or remnants, hardly constitute a major preoccupation for governments and voluntary agencies, compared with the appearance of hundreds of thousands of new refugees, but the circumstances in which individuals find themselves may be par-ticularly tragic. They then require organisational and financial resources over a considerable period and often some kind of diplomatic activity before permanent refuge can be arranged.

Any substantial flow of refugees carries with it an undertow of fear that their situation will rigidify into a permanent presence of indigestible size. The refugee situations in Somalia, Pakistan and eastern Sudan, as well as in parts of South-East Asia, create such fears. There local political relationships among the governments promise little in the way of immediate change, and when it eventually comes it probably does so at a glacial pace. The possibilities of self-sufficiency are limited, even when refugees are allowed to settle. Officials working with these situations often refer in open horror to the possibility that the refugees will become frozen in place, as the Palestinians in the UNRWA camps have been.

The 700,000 refugees who left Palestine in 1948, and the smaller numbers that have since joined them, constitute the best recent historical example of a rigid situation. By now, of course, many of the original asylum-seekers have died, but their children and grandchildren live on with support from an international network. As has been noted, their future was soon tied to a general political settlement in the Middle East. Camps in the Gaza Strip, Jordan and Lebanon, moreover, changed hands with the ebb and flow of fighting and invasion between Israel and its neighbours. What never changed was the claim on the part of the Palestinian leaders that their people were refugees, not permanent residents, and needed appropriate treatment. These claims found support among the governments of the Arab countries, who demanded retribution for the material and psychological damage done the asylum-seekers. Donors to UNRWA, however, in general support the organisation as a humanitarian gesture and a means of avoiding a worsening of political relationships in the area. Little financial support for UNRWA has ever come from the Middle East area; the United States has been the biggest single donor.

Many Palestinians have worked their way out of UNRWA refugee status over the years, although the figure given is very doubtful because of the well-known inflation of camp registries. Some of them have achieved either full or partial integration, while others have moved away to places such as the Persian Gulf or the United States where their skills were in demand or where welcoming families had already settled. The schools in the refugee installations, incidentally, have trained a substantial number of people for higher education and good employment in the Arab world. Yet despite their inherent discomfort, the refugee camps now house a third generation

156

of inhabitants. Unless a substantial change occurs in Middle Eastern politics, a fourth generation will dominate the camps before long.

The rigidity in the situation of the Palestine refugees derives from the attitude of their leaders on the one hand and the policy of Israel on the other. The Palestinian leaders insist on a return of the exiles to long-since appropriated properties in what is now Israel. The Israeli government has no intention of letting them return under the conditions they want. All other arguments, including those about rights and about offers Israel may have made earlier, are merely secondary to these principal facts. Attempts, inspired from within the area and from outside, to build permanent places in the countries of first asylum through the route of economic development have also failed for various — mainly political and security — reasons. In these circumstances, only the most energetic, ambitious and lucky of the original Palestinians and their descendants have achieved a reasonable resettlement and level of integration. The fact that substantial numbers have nevertheless been able to become self-sufficient suggests that if the humanitarian content of the Palestinian refugee situation could be detached from political bargaining, the populations would diminish spontaneously. At the same time, it is likely that many of UNRWA's clients have become so accustomed to receiving extra support that they would give it up only under pressure.

The general intransigence that shaped the fate of the Palestinians could come to dominate other refugee incidents. Governments driven by fear, political orthodoxy, military insecurity and social prejudice are capable of brushing aside the plight of foreigners on their soil. They are able to force the humanitarian responsibility for their unwanted guests on to other authorities. The refugees will soon be bound into a rigid pattern of existence without a future. Humanitarian impulses that lead to third-country resettlement, especially if not bound to acceptable political goals, may soon reach their limits. The populations of prospective host countries may reject settlers of alien culture or who bring with them political zealotry of an exotic kind. Their governments may strive to remain at a distance from a political situation for which they want no responsibility. Nor can much be expected from machinery designed to promote the transnational protection of human rights: a determined government can face down criticism from that quarter. Furthermore, it is simpler for distant governments to contribute to the relief of refugees than to come closer to them. Finally, the temptation is strong to demonstrate the wickedness of another government's policies by insisting on the repatriation of refugees as the only acceptable end, whatever other possibilities may be in sight.

The fear that another refugee flow may turn into an untreatable social ulcer like that formed by the Palestinians is no idle nightmare. Quite real potentials for such an outcome exist both in the causal circumstances and the political atmosphere surrounding some of the most important of recent refugee incidents.

Prevention

In a broad sense, all activities intended to protect human rights also work to prevent the creation of refugees. Yet their frequent violation only tends towards the production of refugees and the impact of short-term needs to cope with the presence of asylum-seekers. The extended network of experts and organisations offering humanitarian relief bears witness to the imperfection of the long-term human rights system. Governments and other authorities are thus logically encouraged to give attention to the prevention of refugee flows, if only in order to ease the burden of coping with their result.

Demands for first asylum by refugees in South-East Asia and the United States prompted those in government circles to devote some thought to the subject of short-term preventive measures. In both areas these appeared to be of a somewhat incidental nature, when contrasted with a permanent system of prevention. In both instances, government officials speculated on the importance of a 'pull' factor in refugee flows and treated some asylum-seekers as mere economic migrants seeking to exploit a sudden opportunity for profit.

Preventive measures took three main forms. Firstly, governments of origin were pressed to restrict what they themselves regarded as illegal immigration. Secondly, programmes of orderly departure were explored. And thirdly, refugee reception centres were made as unattractive as possible within the limits of humanitarian treatment. All these methods also led to controversy.

The 1979 Geneva Conference on the refugee situation in South-East Asia produced a clear example of what was an attempt to shut off a refugee flow at its source. The Vietnamese government was asked to undertake a moratorium on the outflow of people; it accepted the request, originally framed by France. The already diminishing flow of refugees originating there declined further as

Vietnam began actively to enforce laws which it had systematically overlooked during the previous two years. In fact, it is widely accepted that the government had a direct hand in allowing the departure of the 'boat people' and that its policies encouraged the flight of those ethnic Chinese who left on foot for China. It clearly became more difficult for Vietnamese to leave, although the diminished flow still continued into 1986.

Similarly, during the Mariel crisis, the United States attempted by various methods to persuade Cuba that it should not 'dump' people abroad. This line of communication, was, however, contradicted by a more general, ideological stance to the effect that the United States welcomed victims of oppression. In fact, in the initial stages of the Mariel crisis, the United States based its ground-level reaction on the ideological stance, but this quickly began to erode as the impact on local authorities increased.

With regard to the Haitian refugees, the United States undertook more Draconian measures. As these asylum-seekers arrived in often unseaworthy boats on the beaches of Florida, usually directly from Haiti but sometimes from the Bahamas, they could be diverted while still at sea. Accordingly, the United States began employing its (armed) coast guard vessels to intercept boats thought to be carrying Haitian asylum-seekers. They were warned not to proceed, and if the boats were unseaworthy the passengers were taken off and returned to their place of origin. Haitians who had landed in the United States complained that they would be subject to prosecution for illegal departure if they were returned. The Haitian government reacted to American representations by announcing that anyone who returned was left unmolested. This procedure raised a series of legal questions. It was not clear that the United States could legally stop on the high seas the boats suspected of carrying asylum-seekers. The rejection by the United States of Haitian claims to asylum was based on the further controversial view that they were economic migrants who had no reason to fear persecution. Moreover, turning back asylum-seekers at sea involved a summary decisional process that was left to the coast guard, not to the usual administrative services. Yet these methods unquestionably reduced the flow of migrants, or at least of those who came under the eyes of officials.

The orderly departure method was most fully worked out with Vietnam and by the end of 1984, involved more than 1,000 people per month.[19] UNHCR led the way to this agreement. Its officials, especially the then Deputy High Commissioner, Dale de Haan, negotiated directly with the Hanoi government an arrangement by which those Vietnamese who claimed the possibility of family reunion with relatives in the United States could enter their names on a list. The United States would compile a similar list. Where the names matched, Vietnam undertook to allow departure in conventional ways. The operation of the procedure began very slowly and later gathered momentum. It was intended to help prevent unorganised departure by providing an alternative, more attractive method. It thus offered immigration to presumably potential refugees. No first-asylum phase elsewhere in South-East Asia would be necessary for those permitted to depart for immigration in the United States.

For a considerable period in the early years following the Cuban revolution led by Fidel Castro, an orderly departure programme was in fact in operation. Those wishing to depart for the United States were permitted to do so from Havana Airport by ordinary commercial means. In 1962, the Cuban government stopped commercial air services to the United States and any departure from then until late 1965 was accomplished in a clandestine manner. After that date, however, the US Department of State administered an airlift that brought 800 to 900 people per week to Miami. For the first few weeks it was supplemented with departures by small boats from ports in Florida. This programme, however, fell victim to the increasingly bad relations between Cuba and the United States, which were not improved by the hasty departures of the Mariel incident after emigration had been blocked for several years. The orderly departure from Cuba and entry into the United States took place under less rigid conditions than those applying in Vietnam. In this case the governments made no claims to be preventing a flow of refugees, although the United States described the new entrants as victims of oppression.

A somewhat similar pattern of migration from the German Democratic Republic to the German Federal Republic is in constant use. The West German government accepts immigrants from the East and gives them asylum as a matter of right. The East German government, however, usually demands payment of a substantial amount of hard currency for each exchange. These payments supposedly cover the cost to East Germany of the loss of valuable manpower. In the sense that an established process for departure is involved and that positive, physical barriers discourage unauthorised exit, this programme resembles that used in Vietnam.

Discouraging refugee departures by advertising the unpleasant conditions they are likely to encounter on arrival has been used by the Hong Kong government and Thailand in order to stem immigration from Vietnam. The general method consists of depositing unauthorised entrants who decline to return to their places of origin in camps that permit almost no contact with the surrounding society. Conditions in these camps have a cruel edge to them. Severe discipline is maintained. Little opportunity for creative activities and none for work in the surrounding society is available. The inmates may see very few or no visitors. They are permitted to leave for resettlement if they can arrange it, but they do not have the privileges normally given to refugees allowing them to come into easy contact with sponsors of third-country resettlement.

Hong Kong, which had offered asylum to all who reached its shores and had a plausible story of repression to tell, began to change its policy with regard to Vietnamese in 1979 and put it into full effect from then onwards. Its government complained that too few Vietnamese were leaving the Crown Colony for repatriation or resettlement and that no space was available there. By 1984, Hong Kong officials claimed that the flow of people from Vietnam was nearly at an end, though an occasional boatload of fisherfolk or farmers still turned up. Whether a similar policy, instituted in Thailand in 1980, has had a similar effect is not clear. The first inmates of a 'hard camp' were lowland Lao people who had been living in virtual assimilation with the surrounding society in northeast Thailand. New asylum-seekers from Laos went to these camps. In any case, no notable wave of repatriation followed their establishment.

All these managerial devices for reducing refugee flows attract certain criticisms. Moratoria and physical prevention of departure seem a prima facie violation of the right to leave one's country, as set out in the Universal Declaration on Human Rights and made part of the UN Covenants on Human Rights with certain reservations. Interception and summary blocking of movement in a search for asylum arouses similar objections as well as the question of whether it is permissible under international law to interfere with a vessel. In any case, neither of these methods offers much change to the would-be refugee making his case for asylum.

Orderly departure programmes seem to legitimise the claim of a possibly repressive government that it has the right to retain subjects who may believe themselves under sufficient threat to want to leave. In the cases of Cuba and Vietnam, there is little question that some of the migrants were driven by acute fear. But as both cases demonstrate, the emigrants' country of origin has the last word on whether they may depart. This, too, seems to legitimise a violation of an important human right which the receiving countries claim to uphold. It can be argued that getting some people out of danger is better than leaving all to the mercies of a repressive government. Yet those who suffer most may be the least able to depart under such programmes, which nevertheless permit the government to deflect the criticism that its society is not much different from a prison.

The method of 'hard camps', or 'humane deterrence', raises similar issues. People in such camps are deprived of the treatment that the UN Refugee Convention seeks. They are unable to earn their own living, unable to work, unable to move about, and they lack the means of attracting attention to their difficulties. These are circumstances that encourage camp neurosis and permanent dependence. Tough methods of prevention, which are open to the accusation firstly that they violate the spirit of the regime for refugees built up so painfully over three generations and secondly that they leave individuals to the mercy of arbitrary decisions by governments cannot yet be matched by incentives to behave otherwise. As has been shown here, refugees represent a duty placed on governments of asylum, require special attention and may turn into a permanent obligation. Governments faced with such a duty, not to mention the various irrationalities with which nationalists confront foreigners, find little incentive, beyond that of behaving humanely towards probably innocent people in difficulties, to continue to receive asylum-seekers. This encourages short-term approaches which may have detrimental long-term effects.

Notes

1. These approaches serve as the standard terminology in most discussions of refugees by government and international personnel. It depends primarily on a legal conceptualisation, which looks towards a settled status for each refugee. But a legal limbo can also be conceived. In it, the refugee would in fact never have the legal right to remain where he has settled yet would none the less not be disturbed by the authorities.

2. A recent series of incidents of this kind has involved Tamils, who have been appearing in Western Europe since 1984. They claim asylum on the grounds that it would be dangerous for them to return to Sri Lanka. In the Netherlands, decisions on their precise status involved a long political process during which the government pointedly stated the opinion that the Tamils were not in fact refugees and could return home without danger. They were isolated from the host society but given food and shelter. The

West German authorities meted out similar treatment. In 1986, serious riots among the Tamils took place in shelters in the Netherlands in which uncertainty, rumours and lack of occupation were factors. Similar tension built up in camps in the United States, where Cuban asylum-seekers were held after the exodus from Mariel. These are mere illustrations of situations that have been encountered in many countries on many occasions.

3. A common practice in repatriation involves the establishment of reception centres. These get support in Laos and Ethiopia, for instance from UNHCR. Nevertheless, no rush of returnees has occurred. As usual, the numbers do not quite agree. UNHCR reports, for instance, that from September 1983 to December 1984, over 7,400 people were transported from Djibouti to Ethiopia by train (United Nations, Office of the High Commissioner for Refugees; *Report on UNHCR assistance activities in 1984-85*, p. 84). A 'large-scale repatriation program' was ended, however, in December 1984, by which time more than 13,000 refugees were reported to have been moved by rail in organised trips since September 1983 and another 19,000 had returned spontaneously (Ibid., p. 99.) A careful report in 1983 estimated that 31,500 refugees were in Djibouti (US Committee on Refugees, *World Refugee Survey 1983*, Washington, 1983). Somehow more went back to Ethiopia, if these numbers are compared, than had been reported. By the end of 1984, more than 16,000 refugees were still in camps, according to UNHCR (UNHCR, *Report 1984-85*, p. 82).

My interviews underlie the remarks about re-education camps. For a brief comment on repatriation to Ethiopia, which gives rise to concern for Somalis and Eritreans among others, see Roberta Aitchison, 'Repatriating Refugees to Ethiopia: A Model Calling for Assessment', in US Committee on Refugees, *World Refugee Survey 1984* (Washington, 1984), pp. 44-5.

4. See reference in note 3 on Djibouti and Somalia. Flows of refugees into Zaïre and out again have occurred repeatedly, depending on local military conflicts and on maladministration of various sorts. 'An estimated 82,000 Zaïreans remain in exile. A series of amnesties has led to the return of 190,000 since 1978, and the May 1983 amnesty brought several thousand more back without incident (US Committee on Refugees, *World Refugee Survey 1984*, p. 48).

5. The General Assembly implied a request to the Secretary-General to attempt conciliation in the Afghan conflict by asking that it keep them informed of progress towards withdrawal of the Soviet forces (UN General Assembly Resolution ES-6-2, 14 January 1980). It later made the request specific on 20 November 1980. Secretary-General Kurt Waldheim subsequently appointed Javier Perez de Cuellar as his representative. Perez later succeeded Waldheim as Secretary-General. Neither Perez nor his successor found that Afghanistan (or, presumably, the Soviet Union) or Pakistan had any urgent desire for face-to-face negotiations. Six years later it remains doubtful as to who accepts whom as a party, although the UN effort continues. Few Afghan refugees have returned from either Iran or Pakistan.

6. The notoriety surrounding the Moskito Indian refugees from Nicaragua in the early 1980s and the emergence of guerrillas among them appears to have been followed by a shift in that country's policies. Nicaragua has often stated that anyone who fled is free to return, but no mass movement seems to have followed. In 1983, some 12,000 of these people were in

UNHCR-supported camps in Honduras (US Committee on Refugees, *World Refugee Survey 1984*, p. 54). UNHCR planned a programme of local integration and self-sufficiency that included provision for more than 15,000 persons, continuing into 1986 (United Nations, High Commissioner for Refugees, *Report on UNHCR assistance activities for 1984-85*, p. 238).

7. The United States at first welcomed the Mariel asylum-seekers, but after convicts and inmates of mental hospitals appeared on the Florida docks, restrictive policies came into effect. The 'undesirables' were regarded as having been dumped on the United States. 'The Cuban influx came to be regarded as a formidable instrument in the hands of a hostile regime' — Mark J. Miller and Demetrios G. Papademetriou, 'Immigration and US Foreign Policy' in Papademetriou and Miller, *The Unavoidable Issue: US Immigration Policy in the 1980s* (Institute for the Study of Human Issues, Philadelphia, 1983), p. 174. Some sending countries have come to view out-migration as a 'national resource', to be exploited like any other resource . . . with sending countries coming to perceive the benefits of manipulating out-migration as a policy . . . the benefits . . . may be . . . malevolent in intent . . . [t]o destabilise neighbouring adversaries (Vietnam and Cuba)' — Michael S. Teitelbaum, 'International Migration and US Foreign Policy' in Lydio F. Tomaso, *In Defense of the Alien*, vol. 6 (Center for Migration Studies, New York, 1984), p. 221.

8. The results of ICARA I, which combined the idea of the UNHCR and the Organization for African Unity, are summed up in a report of the Secretary-General on the conference in UN Doc. A/37/522, 19 October 1982. The document outlining the plans is UN Doc. E/1982/76. Altogether, ICARA I resulted in pledges of $572,807,000, of which $159,275,000 was to go through bilateral channels. Not every pledge represented new money, as some simply redirected earlier contributions. The United States was the largest single donor for refugees, although its contribution for other humanitarian programmes was exceeded by the European Communities by a factor of two.

The principal planning document for ICARA II, which was inspired by the relative success of the earlier conference, was UN Doc. A/CONF.125/2, 23 March 1984. It identifies 128 projects in 14 African countries, beyond those already planned by UNHCR, which would have cost $362,260,000. Five more countries later sought another $66,678,000 (UN Doc. A/CONF.125/2/Add.1, 8 November 1984). A year later, ICARA II had resulted in donor interest or commitment for some one-third of the 128 projects (UN Doc. a/40/425, 16 July 1985). ICARA II was intended as a continuation of the first conference and a consolidation and furthering of its work. Individual donors would select worthy projects and support them, either bilaterally or multilaterally.

9. A three-way agreement on a $20 million, three-year project aimed at creating employment in Beluchistan and the North-West Frontier Province and at generating self-sufficiency among refugees was signed in 1984 by Pakistan, the World Bank and UNHCR (United Nations, General Assembly: 39th Session, *Report of the High Commissioner for Refugees*, p. 6). High Commissioner Hartling told the Executive Committee in 1985 that the World Bank had offered to pay for consultants to develop similar projects in Sudan but that no financing was then available there(UN Doc. A/AC.96/SR.393, pp. 3-4).

10. See brief summary in Joseph Cerquone, 'Ahead for the US — The Asylum Debate' in US Committee for Refugees, *World Refugee Survey 1982* (Washington, 1982), pp. 53-4.

11. Aspects of this process are treated in Robert G. Wright, 'Voluntary Agencies and the Resettlement of Refugees', *International Migration Review*, XV, 1-2 (spring-summer 1981), pp. 157-74; Barry N. Stein, 'The Commitment to Refugee Resettlement', *The Annals of the American Academy of Political and Social Science*, 467 (May 1967), pp. 187-201; and Dennis Gallagher with Susan S. Forbes, *Refugees in South-East Asia: Toward a More Comprehensive Strategy* (Refugee Policy Group, Washington, 1985). When an active resettlement programme is in progress, the diversion of refugee-camp routines in its direction is palpable, if my direct observations are accurate.

12. An extended description and analysis of the way voluntary agencies serve in the United States can be found in David S. North, Lawrence S. Lewin and Jennifer R. Wagner, *Kaleidoscope: The Resettlement of Refugees in the U.S. by the Voluntary Agencies* (New TransCentury Foundation, Lewin Associates, and National Opinion Research Center, Washington, 1982). This report was prepared for the US Department of State.

13. For example, Algeria remarked in the 1980 meeting of the Executive Committee that countries of asylum were also donors, because they had to bear the burden of the introduction of refugees in their societies. This was not covered by international contributions. 'It was particularly unjust, under the circumstances, for Africa, the poorest continent, to be relatively less favored in the matter of aid from the international community' (UN Doc. A/AC.96/SR.318). High Commissioner Hartling later remarked that comments on burden-sharing had gained ground after the Arusha Conference of African states on refugee issues in 1979. He said African problems were becoming better understood (UN. Doc. A/AC.96/SR. 321, p. 7). Decoded, these remarks mean that UNHCR had become sensitive to the growing intensity of African complaints. These had diminished by 1985, when the African drought and the consequent movement of masses of people in great need did indeed get widespread sympathy and response in the donor countries.

14. Göran Melander, 'Refugees and International Cooperation', *International Migration Review*, XV, 1-2 (spring-summer 1981), pp. 39-40. In 1984, UNHCR spent $38.44 per person on the estimated 96,500 refugees in Zambia. In Thailand, UNHCR had 128,429 Indo-Chinese refugees in its care and maintained a programme costing $32,497,000, an average of $253 per person (United Nations, Office of High Commissioner for Refugees, *Report on UNHCR Assistance Activities in 1984-85*, pp. 193-8, 372-80). It is dangerous to draw a normative conclusion from these primitive comparisons. Not every refugee situation poses the same demands, and local prices are never easy to compare. Yet such comparisons make splendid material for debaters in UN deliberative organs.

15. The Fund was created with considerable enthusiasm in the Executive Committee of UNHCR (UN Doc. A/AC.96/SR.322 and 323). The proposal was set out in UN Doc. A/AC.96/582 and 583. By 1984, no mention of it could be found in the High Commissioner's Report to the General Assembly. Nevertheless, the whole subject of development as an assistance to what UNHCR calls 'durable solutions' — usually resettlement in the

country of first asylum in this case — continues to be discussed and worked at. On this subject, see also Charles B. Keeley, *Global Refugee Policy: The Case for a Development-Oriented Strategy* (The Population Council, New York, 1981); 'Refugee Aid and Development', submitted by the High Commissioner for Refugees (UN Doc. A/AC.96/645, 26 August 1984); and Poul Hartling, 'Refugee Aid and Development: Genesis and Testing of a Strategy', in US Committee on Refugees, *World Refugee Survey 1984* (Washington, 1984), pp. 17-19.

16. For instance, in the General Assembly's resolution on the High Commissioner's report in 1985, it expressed warm satisfaction for his application of 'the concept of development-oriented assistance to refugees and returnees, as initiated at the Second International Conference on Assistance to Refugees in Africa, and urges him to continue the process', mentioning the World Bank and UNDP (UN General Assembly Resolution 40/118, Dec. 13, 1985).

17. On its own initiative, Sudan summoned an international conference to consider refugee problems on its territory. Its government, assisted by outside consultants, prepared several volumes of documentation, including specific development plans. See [Sudan] National Committee to Aid Refugees, *Documentation for the Conference* and *Final Report*. See also Gordenker, 'Refugees in Developing Countries and Transnational Organization', *The Annals* (May 1983), pp. 74-5. The Conference failed, as was anticipated, to provide anything near the financing sought by the Sudanese government. Some governmental representatives and officials of international institutions made clear their lack of confidence in the Sudan government's ability to administer the proposed projects. Some additional funding was made available, sometimes by realigning existing programmes.

18. As the programme for Sudan is very large, its range of self-sufficiency projects is broad and provides a good example. The World Food Program covered settlements in southern Sudan during 1984; in 32 of 47 settlements, a level of self-sufficiency in food was reached and no further WFP aid was needed. Co-operatives, irrigated vegetable gardens and poultry farms have been developed in eastern Sudan; a suburban settlement was being constructed near Port Sudan. In all these projects, one or more international agencies and voluntary agencies was associated with UNHCR and the Sudanese government. In the case of refugees based around cities, UNHCR helped train individuals for occupations and to obtain driving licences. Meanwhile, other refugees were arriving. United Nations, High Commissioner for Refugees, *Report on UNHCR Assistance Activities in 1984-85*, pp. 150-1.

19. 'In 1984, the number of departures under the ODP increased significantly. Under this Special Programme, implemented under the terms of a Memorandum of Understanding signed by the Vietnamese Government and UNHCR in May 1979, 29,154 Vietnamese nationals departed for resettlement during the year. This is the highest annual number of departures under the Programme to date and represents a 55 per cent increase over the 1983 departure rate . . . In October 1984, a Vietnamese delegation . . . visited UNHCR Headquarters . . . to discuss . . . the Programme and its future development . . . UNHCR's operational partner in Viet Nam is the Vietnamese government.' United Nations, High Commissioner for Refugees, *Report on UNHCR Assistance Activities in 1984-85* p. 383.

Writing of humane deterrence to seeking asylum in Vietnam, Astri Suhrke says that an expansion of the orderly departure programme offers one such means: 'This requires agreement by the sending and the receiving countries, and the problems on both sides have complicated the ODP for the Vietnamese. Continued hostile relations between Vietnam and the United States is one major factor, as evidenced by the much larger number of ODP cases that have departed for countries with which Vietnam has diplomatic ties and overall better relations, mainly France, Canada and Australia' — Suhrke, 'Indochinese Refugees: the Law and Politics of First Asylum', *The Annals*, p. 112.

7

Looking Ahead

By tracing the way in which refugees are set in flight, given relief and protection and eventually returned to their homelands or provided with new ones, issues are raised which suggest means of coping with forced migrants in the future. This chapter sets out those issues and some of the difficulties in resolving them. It also makes incidental suggestions as to how such difficulties may, at least in part, be overcome. Given the frequent appearance of refugees, the ease with which they can be set on the move and the tangled consequences of their migration, it would be promising far too much to claim that the difficulties they cause can always be overcome. No once-and-for-all permanent resolution of such issues can be expected. Rather, the aim of this examination is to indicate possible openings for more effective approaches to refugee situations.

Forecasting refugee flows

The forecasting of refugee flows, to the degree that it has occurred at all, has relied primarily on *ad hoc* guesses. Individuals close to developing refugee situations have speculated about what the days and months ahead may bring. Their information has been of a fragmentary nature. Caution about the reaction of authorities, whether in the originating or the receiving territories, has impeded the publication of factual material in the hands of intergovernmental organisations and voluntary agencies. National officials hesitate to admit that their decisions lead to flows of refugees or that they may be obliged to offer asylum. In the former case, the possibility of moral opprobrium or tacit admission of brutality or incompetence accompanies a discussion of refugee flows. In the latter, officials may fear that premature discussion of refugees may attract more of them and also draw down on them the wrath of the originating state.

All these discrete reactions owe much to a concentration on short-term difficulties. Inevitably, bureaucracies react to the immediate challenge. This is particularly true of the police and security services, which are usually among the first to have knowledge of a flow of refugees. Political leaders, so the analysis here suggests, tend to react after the bureaucracies have made their reports. The structure of the state, among other things, dictates this pattern of response. But reaction, rather than anticipation, however understandable it may be in terms of administering a policy, does little to obviate human suffering before it occurs. Nor does it suggest much about the treatment of the underlying causes of forced migration.

A general standard

A longer-term approach to forecasting would rest on a general standard of measurement or basis of estimate. This could apply to any refugee situation, whether it involved only a few people or large numbers. It would help to reduce some of the politico-bureaucratic caution with regard to forecasting by dimming the aura of *ad hoc* handling which accompanies the initial phases of refugee movements, especially large-scale ones. Such a standard would also increasingly lend itself to comparative studies and perhaps eventually to rather more exact prediction. Before that point is reached, the use of such a standard would encourage more focused international negotiation.

The basis of a general standard for forecasting forced migration already exists in the system established for the international protection of human rights set up after the end of the Second World War, primarily under the auspices of the United Nations.[1] This work stimulated important parallel efforts in the Council of Europe, the Organization of American States and the Organization for African Unity. The contemporary system for the international handling of refugees, however much it may have been an improvisation to cope with human emergency, continues on the basis of treaty regulation and networks of organisations that foster the human rights of refugees. This organisational approach can be understood as a special case of the international protection of human rights.[2]

Violations of human rights, as the analysis in Chapter 4 shows, can be symbolized by a heavy red line linking all refugee situations. Coping with the results of this deprivation in the short term calls into being the processes analysed in Chapter 5. The longer-term processes needed to restore human rights are the subject of Chapter 6.

Refugees in the familiar political definition of the UN Convention on Refugees suffer the deprivation of basic human rights. It is their fear of arbitrary, threatening actions on the part of governments or their neighbours which prompts their departure; alternatively, they may find themselves surrounded by a form of military activity which deprives them of their basic human rights, including that of staying alive. Similarly, the movement of those who claim to be driven by hunger or lack of future economic security also implies that they are denied the basic economic and social rights embodied in the UN Universal Declaration of Human Rights. Viewed from this perspective, forced migrants are persons who act to protect their physical existence by flight on perceiving an extreme threat to their normal way of life at home. They suffer from a denial of precisely what the widely accepted undertakings to protect human rights try to ensure. However broad and abstract the statements of human rights in the UN Universal Declaration of Human Rights and the binding UN Convenants on Political and Civil and Economic and Social Rights may seem at first glance, they are exceedingly concrete to those who have found their existence so threatened that they choose the uncertainty of flight. That concrete quality as seen from the perspective of forced migrants makes a human rights standard a suitable basis for forecasting movements.[3] It identifies the deprivations which become intolerable. If the scheme of human rights set out in the international instruments were in fact enforced, then presumably refugees would not appear. But that Utopian day has not yet arrived. Between it and the contemporary world, a sketch of what might ultimately come can now serve as a yardstick of change. The rate and character of change could warn of impending forced migrations. Further research might make it possible to assign quantitative values to these deprivations and their rates, making possible reasonably accurate forecasts.

The link between refugee incidents and the international protection of general human rights usually finds hesitant expression among those who use doctrines of non-political humanitarian assistance as the basis of their organisation and work. Despite the doubtful logic of separating the two issues, the humanitarian approach has helped to ward off the hot breath of international political strife from substantial activities on behalf of refugees (but not all, as illustrated by the case of Palestine). Whether this shield can long stay in place becomes ever more doubtful under the pressure of mass exoduses caused by controversial national policies.

If the study[4] ordered by the UN Commission on Human Rights from Sadruddin Aga Khan, former High Commissioner for Refugees, is an accurate portent, a rising sensitivity to the deeper implications of refugee incidents is emerging in some government circles. Moreover, at the time this report was being prepared, the General Assembly expressed concern over the repeated appearance of masses of fleeing people and organised what six years later was still a futile inquiry into means of preventing such flows.[5] Taken together, these reactions at the beginning of the 1980s, when the famine experienced in African countries stimulated a greater awareness, broadly speaking, of forced migration, may be promising in terms of initiatives for the reduction of future suffering.

Prince Sadruddin's report argues that violations of human rights cause mass exoduses. Despite the withdrawal of four case-studies[6] after hypersensitive governments got wind of them, the report, coinciding with the analysis here, makes the significant point that mass exoduses involve political issues and cannot be dealt with only on technical grounds. At the same time, it makes clear that substantial organisational resources already exist for the co-ordination of relief, early warning of refugee situations, rules and diplomatic contacts. Prince Sadruddin recommended a rather grandiose revision and update of international rules and the creation of a Special Representative for Humanitarian Affairs operating within the UN framework to promote better co-ordination.

Existing machinery[7]

Refugee issues can be brought to light in several existing organisational contexts other than that of UNHCR. These include the UN Commission on Human Rights, sponsor of Prince Sadruddin's report, and the UN Economic and Social Council and General Assembly. The International Labour Organisation, the UN Educational, Scientific and Cultural Organisation, the Council of Europe and its highly developed European human rights structure, the regional organisations for Africa and Latin America, the European Communities, the International Committee of the Red Cross and even the World Intellectual Property Organisation all touch on human rights as part of their broader responsibilities. In short, the international machinery now in existence provides ample fora for discussion among governments and sometimes for concerted preventive action, such as co-ordinated pressure to halt violations of rights or well-documented studies of the misconduct of specific authorities. Moreover, these organisations have the duty of supervising the application of existing treaties and offer the possibility of revising or expanding legal rules.

Whatever this machinery does, it neither constantly progresses towards its stated goals nor offers much concentration on forced migrants. Its use, however, does shed light on the national policies which tend to lead to forced migration. Moreover, its generality of interest means that the doctrine of humanitarian assistance can continue to shelter the more specialised institutions from the full blast of political strife, which more often than not wells up in human rights issues. Its use encourages a wider public of governmental and voluntary organisation officials to learn more about activities on behalf of both refugees and human rights. It could lead eventually to the development of additional protections under treaties for persons involved in many kinds of man-made disasters and to firmer administrative and diplomatic practices.

At the same time, the intergovernmental machinery for the protection of human rights cannot be expected to give full satisfaction to every government or observer at all times. On the contrary, its work falls under the restraints of nationalism, repressive approaches to governing, sheer lawlessness and other harmful practices that are used to injure innocent people. The procedures followed by intergovernmental organisations are cumbersome and slow. The introduction of self-serving claims and hobby-horse topics proceeds with the assurance with which governments exercise their sovereign rights. Some of the statements in the UN Commission on Human Rights, for instance, have an unmistakeably meretricious quality. The representatives of governments on the deliberative bodies associated with the international protection of human rights do the bidding, whenever it is transmitted, of their national capitals. They do not necessarily respond to persuasion, cajolery or threats, even from the mightiest organisations on earth, the major powers. Yet sometimes these representatives are faced with the need to explain why their governments behave in a way likely to endanger the lives of their subjects. Sometimes, moreover, they do respond to criticism, either public or private, in such a way as to temper harshness. Without wishing to excuse the foolishness of some of the gestures that active governments have extracted from this machinery, it can yet be argued that a useful potential remains to be developed for coping with forced migration on the basis of the broad protection of human rights.

Additional capacity

For the moment, the limit of easy intergovernmental construction has probably been reached, but the continued interest of transnational voluntary agencies and national groups in many countries of asylum suggests that additional capacity might be found or built in that direction. Although such arrangements require a great deal of co-ordination and present inherent difficulties as far as management is concerned, they can nevertheless sometimes vault over the narrow limits of action on which the organised international community insists.

The non-governmental groups could perhaps organise a systematic surveillance of those violations of human rights likely to lead to forced migration. This could begin with an attempt to set out recent refugee incidents in as quantitative a profile as possible: the impact of violations of human rights could be defined in terms of numbers of incidents, gravity of incidents, economic impact of violations and social impact in terms of discriminatory closing of opportunities to participate in the social process. A continuing survey and analysis of information and propaganda in places where threats to rights emerge would also offer indicators. The activities of a number of capable organisations in the human rights field — such as the Refugee Policy Group in Washington — have already collected some data. Other data would be available from groups with defined geographical interests, such as those concerned with South Africa or with Cambodia. The drab documents of the intergovernmental organisations, carefully read, would also provide additional data. In addition, a determined, systematic effort to interview samples of incoming refugees in each fresh incident and a comparative study of the views of refugees of less recent times would provide insights into what those in flight believe to be driving them. The systematic nature of such an investigation would differentiate it from most available information, as would the fact that it is carried out without direct reference to the aims of any particular government or organisation of governments. It should be noted that while some reporting of this sort now occurs, it depends primarily on initiatives by individual groups or persons. Standards may vary greatly over time and between organisations. Reports therefore lack reliability and cumulativeness. The possibilities of collating information and encouraging research as a basis for early warning will be discussed in the next sections.

Early warning

The human rights standard could provide a basis for the early warning of forced migration. Early warning comprises only information and projections from that information, not the distribution of material goods or other forms of assistance; nor does it set out a programme. The relevant information concerns those activities defined by the human rights standard as likely to have disastrous consequences for specific people in particular places at given times. These consequences might be expressed by the affected people in the belief that they cannot further sustain their lives where they are; it might be set out by qualified experts; or it might include reports of an actual case of forced migration whose consequences are still being felt.

Early warning includes information which is not otherwise easily gathered, formulated and analysed by organisational leaders capable of reacting to incidents of forced migration or other kinds of man-made disasters. Such information, impartial but not neutral in purpose, could be used as a basis for the framing of policies and programmes to cope with forced migration.

The employment of early warning would bear on two main kinds of specific situation. In the first, no significant outflow of people has yet occurred but is likely to do so, whether very soon or at some more distant time in the future. The prevention or containment of an outflow of people would still be possible. In the second category, the migration has begun. Prevention is no longer possible, but amelioration may be. In either case, early warning would be directed at governmental organisations and relevant groups in the voluntary sector. Man-made disasters could perhaps be prevented if action were taken early enough, although timely notice cannot in itself forestall action on the part of a determined government, however costly its results in terms of forced migration. Warning of a refugee flow in progress may make it possible to prepare assistance of the most useful kind before the migrants overwhelm local administrations. Yet early warning alone does no more than provide a stimulus and an informed basis for action on the part of relevant organisations.

Fundamental factors

Most early warning of forced migration is likely to be concerned with proximate rather than fundamental causes. Nevertheless, indications of an approaching migration could in principle be amassed at a very early stage. The information gathered by such a system would probably lead to a prediction of future disaster should current activities be continued. Among the causative factors would be those treated in Chapter 6.

Surveillance of such background factors could well lead to a warning that applied to a whole geographical region rather than a single polity. Had an early warning system of universally recognised persuasiveness then been in existence, it could credibly have warned, for example, of the impending, partly man-made disaster which occurred in 1984-85 in the sub-Saharan and Horn of Africa regions where forced migration, government failure and lack of rainfall coincided.

Warning for relief

The possibility that early warning could be used to strengthen efforts to cope with the presence of forced migrants has perhaps attracted most attention to the idea. This emphasis follows from the fact that organisations of some sort must be engaged to feed, shelter and care for migrants, especially when these appear in large numbers and in conditions of distress. Early warning of the need for relief efforts would provide an informational basis for more systematic advance planning for the extension of aid to those forced to flee. It would increase the time available for designing programmes and putting them to work. Supplies could be assembled where they were needed and personnel summoned for the tasks ahead. Information gathered from earlier experiences with analogous relief efforts could be consulted by responsible officials. Policy and executive decisions could be prepared and some of the latter could be taken in advance. By reducing the time-lag between the appearance of refugees and the response in the form of delivered services, the amount of human misery involved would be reduced.

A useful response to early warning of the need for relief would require accurate information, both on the character of those on the move and on the precise causes. If, for example, government error or malfeasance led to mass starvation, those affected would be in need of supplementary nourishment and the women and children among them in need of a kind of attention that is rather different from that given to refugees from short, sharp communal violence or war. Furthermore, the direction of movement would also form an important part of the early warning, for that knowledge would help alert the organisations most likely to have contact with the migrants. Early warning of this sort could even be issued while forced migrants were still within the borders of the state of origin.

Warning, prevention and politics

The use of early warning, the creation of facilities for it and the prevention of flows of forced migrants all have unavoidable political implications. As forced migrations result mainly from what governments either do or fail to do, political factors inhere in early warnings. The use of a human rights standard as the basis for early warning also entails political causes and consequences. Moreover, governments and intergovernmental organisations have to provide the main reactions to a flow of migrants, as the earlier chapters of this study make clear. Accordingly, the mere voicing of an early warning, however convincing, would not in itself prevent a flow of refugees; it would merely provide the basis for urging — or possibly even imposing — changes in the government policies responsible for causing forced migration.

As a consequence of the political overtones of early warning, the construction of a reliable working system depends on more than a mere demonstration that it would benefit forced migrants. In fact, political obstacles explain why the considerable existing capacity for early warning in intergovernmental and other organisations has never been shaped into a reliable, standing institution. At the same time, the range and nature of data available have constantly increased both as refugees and other aspects of disasters have been given more attention and as modern technology — such as earth satellites and other developments in telecommunications — is put to work. At the same time, the exclusivity of national authorities inhibits the full use and expansion of this capacity.

A more effective early warning organisation would need to meet strict political and technical standards. Such a body would have to be beyond easy reach of governmental authority, possibly located within the private sector in a country with an excellent record on freedom of information and of political activity. It would have to assemble authentic information, the more precise the better. It would require access to the most up-to-date technical means of gathering and analysing information, including computer facilities, modern telecommunications and earth satellites. It would need the collaboration of sensitive, expert analysts, including some in the field.

The early warnings themselves would have to meet the highest standards of accuracy and authority in order to gain acceptance by bureaucracies, governments and voluntary groups. The estimates would have to be reasoned and defensible as well as insightful. They would have to come from sources that cannot be presumed to be doing the work of political movements. They would have to be produced in a form that consumers are able to accept. These consumers would be governments, public bureaucracies, voluntary agencies, specialised publics and the general public, depending on the situation. Existing organisations, such as UNHCR or ICRC, would have to have confidence in both the early warning facility and its product; on that basis, they would both support its existence and make use of its product.

Preventing forced migration

As with early warning, the mechanisms for stopping refugee incidents before they start suffer from a number of important weaknesses and defects. Nevertheless, from the point of view of refugees, governments of countries of asylum and financial contributors, the most desirable means of dealing with forced migration would be to render it unnecessary. Prevention at any price, however, could conceivably prove just as inhumane as the circumstances that give rise to forced migration.

Obviating departure

Removing the causes of flight, which are primarily to be found in the actions or failures of governments, would mean an end to refugees and to most forced migrations. Refugee flows would also decline if governments could be persuaded to avoid international strife and other actions not intended to harm particular persons or groups but nonetheless forcing migration. Given the manifold and virtually eternal causes of forced migration, to hope for their complete elimination demonstrates either a talent for circular reasoning or a witless utopianism.

At the same time, forced migrations of the future need not simply reproduce the past either in intensity or numbers. Moderating measures on the part of governments, intergovernmental institutions and other organisations may be possible. What governments do of their own accord or with their eye on other governments will have the greatest effect in encouraging or obviating forced migration.

Few governments can altogether ignore criticism from abroad. Forced migrants can cause sympathetic publics to react sharply, even in countries where the flight-provoking policies are put into effect. It may not be hopeless in every instance to appeal to the government responsible to moderate its policies. Such appeals may have special impact if they carry with them the promise of assistance in dealing with the causes of human outflows. Not every moderating appeal will succeed in the future any more than it has in the past. However eloquent outside appeals may be, deep-rooted racial hatred or severe religious orthodoxy will not usually soften. Yet governments can sometimes be moved to discourage unofficial pressure against hated minorities, giving them time to depart with a minimum of molestation or to adjust their relationships with the surrounding community. As for economic policies that threaten particular groups sufficiently to induce them to flee, these can sometimes be moderated by assistance from abroad during a transition period. Alternatively, in some cases, rapid economic development might conceivably ease the pressure on sections of the population that might otherwise become refugees. However, even these modest means of obviating refugee flows depend on diplomatic initiatives on the part of influential governments. Those governments claiming to respect the international standard of human rights would logically lead in making representations.

The use of the human rights standard would provide a definite basis for one government to urge another to alter its policies so as to preclude a forced migration. It would also link any initiative on forced migrations with other aspects of foreign policy. Furthermore, the degree to which initiatives for obviating the production of migrants became a matter for general public knowledge would have to be considered in the light of each situation.

Any government has the choice of emphasising the formal machinery available in international institutions for the promotion of human rights and the settlement of disputes or of relying on its own resources in bilateral discussions. When international violence or the threat of likely violence leads to refugee movements, a variety of multilateral and bilateral dispute-settling methods could be invoked. Alternatively, or simultaneously, recommendations could be made by one or other human rights organ, or by UNHCR or the UN Secretary-General, with regard to a particular group of refugees or a relevant programme of assistance and protection. Such recommendations have a natural locus in the UN system because of the experience of UNHCR, UNRWA and UNICEF and its other activities connected with humane response to refugees and other disaster-related events. Regional organisations can sometimes be similarly involved. The European Communities and NATO could help in concerting the policies of the Western European and North American governments.

These intergovernmental agencies encourage reactions from a broad spectrum of governments and are able to base their programmes on the protection of human rights. Moreover, the international institutions may be able to offer in an impartial manner the inducement of economic assistance and other kinds of comfort to the migrant-producing government in return for undoing the decisions that caused the flow of migrants in the first place.[8]

Involving intergovernmental organisations offers both advantages and difficulties in an effort to obviate refugee movements. An obvious advantage lies in the internationalisation of a particular refugee incident. If governments voice their common opposition to the policies that force migrations, the authorities responsible will sometimes be led to moderate their conduct. Short of that, a discussion involving many governments within an institutional framework will sometimes help to clarify the nature of a refugee incident so that additional steps follow without undue difficulty. The collaboration of an early warning centre at the beginning of such a discussion could be of great value. A broad consensus would give support to assistance programmes for refugees. If the migration is the result of the use of violence in international relations,[9] then a discussion may provide the basis for an effort at conciliation or, in extreme cases, for the use of punishment in the form of economic or military sanctions. Even if such sanctions did not bend a recalcitrant government into a new posture, they could conceivably serve as one of the instruments needed to encourage the correction of a serious human rights violation that caused people to flee.

In the case of a rich and powerful country — especially the United States — the likelihood is that its diplomacy will be concentrated on bilateral relations, no matter what steps to obviate forced migrations are suggested in the United Nations or other international institutions.[10] However, the fact that one channel is open does not mean that the other is blocked; representations made along bilateral lines can be used to support initiatives taken in multilateral settings and should as a rule be capable of enhancing both procedures. Bilateral channels ensure a longer period during which persuasion can be kept confidential, while similar initiatives on the part of international agencies tend to become public knowledge very quickly. Yet it cannot be argued that public discussion of forced migration leads ineluctably to undesirable results in all instances. On the contrary, where some hope exists of deflecting a refugee-producing policy by means of public appeal, shame or scorn, international assemblies have considerable value.

Public efforts also involve the indisputable risk that certain members will use the situation to advance their own political line. They may convert what began as a humanitarian gesture into an argument to demonstrate the perniciousness of an antagonist's course of action. They may also link refugee situations with broader political goals that are not necessarily germane or pressing. The history of the Palestinian refugees furnishes ample illustration of how a migration can become a focus for political pressure. A similar outcome can be seen in the cases of Hungary and other flows of refugees from Communist countries, which have led opposing governments — the United States included — to claim that such is the normal outcome of Marxism-Leninism and the use of military instruments of repression by Communist regimes.

The linking of barely relevant claims to a particularly dramatic incident involving a violation of human rights can hardly be avoided, but it can be contained through a careful preparation of positions, the mobilisation of friendly governments and offers of suitable cooperation to supporters.

Preventing departure

When a government prevents its subjects from departing to a new situation where they are likely to claim asylum, a refugee incident is clearly unable to develop. This does not mean that causes which otherwise might have induced flight have somehow been swept away, but only that the rest of the world will not have refugees on its hands. Both the application of human rights standards and the use of early warning indicators suggest that, in the absence of any restraint on departures, forced migrations are likely to occur.

Some governments do in fact try to control their subjects in order to prevent them from becoming refugees or, for that matter, to prevent them from departing at all. In order to make controls work effectively, governments go to extraordinary lengths to supervise the movements of their nationals. This violates the right of departure from one's own country, as set out in the Universal Declaration of Human Rights and given binding form, under certain reserves, in the Covenant on Political and Civil Rights. Yet such violations occur daily. Very few Soviet nationals or East Germans, for instance, are able to leave their countries, either temporarily or permanently, whatever the Universal Declaration, the UN Covenants and the Helsinki accords may promise. Any proposed travel abroad comes under restrictive control and as a rule only a very small proportion of the population are able even to dream of applying for permission to go abroad, for whatever reason. Clandestine exit is physically obstructed, and probably succeeds only occasionally. Similar comments could be made about such widely separated, different regimes as South Africa and North Korea.

Were democratic societies in North America, Western Europe and elsewhere to co-operate with regimes that police their subjects heavily in order to prevent departures, and thus the development of refugee situations, the former would clearly be acting in violation of their own ethical precepts. The democratic governments led the way to establishing the principles of civil and political rights under international supervision and the special status of refugees; it would hardly be logical for them to brush aside these rights by locking up potential fugitives within national enclosures. It is conceivable that a right to travel abroad — as intimated in the Helsinki accords — could be separated from a right to emigrate, but this division would clearly make it easy to protect what is a relatively trivial right compared with that of emigration, particularly under the pressure of destructive government policies.

A somewhat softer approach to the prevention of floods of refugees and one that nevertheless depends on restricted exit can be seen in the agreement signed in 1979 by the UNHCR and Vietnam for the purpose of creating a system of 'orderly departure'. This system in effect builds on the idea of family reunification in order to secure legal permission for certain Vietnamese to leave their country. In practice, during most of the period the agreement was in force the Vietnamese regime allowed only a trickle to leave — at times far fewer in a year than the monthly intake of the South-East Asian holding centres. Since 1984, a higher rate of departure has been allowed under the programme. Whatever the numbers, the control of departures rests just as firmly in Vietnamese hands as it does when no orderly departure procedure existed. For those able to use it, the system is certainly more attractive than braving pirates in the Gulf of Thailand.. At the same time, the special procedure seems to have had relatively little effect on the high number of clandestine departures.

While the orderly departure system was developing, the Vietnamese government also agreed to the suggestion — made by France — of a moratorium on departures. Announced at the 1979 Geneva Conference on South-East Asian Refugees by the UN Secretary-General, it had at least the implied tone of an acceptable — if not obviously legitimate — international agreement. Some governments praised Vietnamese willingness to co-operate for the purpose of coping with the refugee situation in South-East Asia.

Both these preventive programmes applied by Vietnam raise serious questions about human rights in the long term. The orderly departure programme implicitly supports the notion that refugees would not appear if only formal arrangements were made among governments to channel departures. In effect, it dismisses the fact that refugees are driven by fear and, as is usually the case, immediate peril, not by a lack of procedural facilities to select migrants. Forced migrants are neither able to wait to depart in some legally approved manner nor do they have much capacity to ensure that orderly methods will in fact be applied to them. The orderly departure programme also raises the question of whether those who have good reason to believe that their rights and lives are under threat ought to take second place to those whose conduct has given no offence to an oppressive regime and who have the good fortune to have a relative in the United States.

The moratorium is open to equally serious doubts. The Vietnamese government certainly did little to eliminate the causes of fear on the part of those who became or tended to become refugees. The ethnic Chinese living in Vietnamese society understood only too clearly that they were unwanted; they left by the thousands. The government also permitted — or even connived at — profiting from clandestine departures by boat.[11] It is hardly conceivable that a regime so expert in directing its people to re-education camps and new economic zones would not have been able to exert more effective restraints over those who loaded the fugitives aboard leaky, but quite visible, tubs in a dozen ports. In the midst of an international conference called for the purpose of dealing with the refugee situation its policies had caused, the Vietnamese government agreed to do what it usually did in controlling the departure of its nationals; in this way it obtained a measure of international legitimation for conduct that reeks of a harsh violation of human rights. The successful application of police methods may go some way to staunch an outflow of human beings, but it scarcely eliminates the causes. The moratorium was actually followed by a thinner stream of refugees, but failed to dam it. During the fiscal year ending 30 June 1982, the refugees were still arriving at the rate of 4,200 per month. Hundreds more were rescued at sea. At the end of 1984, some 2,000 Vietnamese per month were still arriving across the Gulf of Siam and the South China Sea in their wallowing, overloaded vessels.

Discouraging entry

Those preparing to flee seriously threatening situations would presumably wish to avoid entering equally menacing conditions. Or, given the choice, they would presumably prefer a more comfortable and promising place of asylum to that which offered forbidding circumstances. The prospect of a lengthy period of unpleasantness might provide the marginal factor which makes them decide against leaving at all.

Such reasoning underlies the past and present policies of several governments faced with influxes of refugees. Thailand, for instance, adopted in 1982 a system of 'humane deterrence' in which Lowland Lao entrants face a year of confinement at subsistence level in rather unpleasant, isolated camps before they can even be considered for removal to third-country resettlement. Hong Kong stores recent refugees in isolated, crowded camps with minimal facilities. In these clean, monotonous, heavily disciplined camps they can neither have visitors nor expect to work in the British colony. They can either return to their points of origin or await rescue by seldom available resettlement. The United States held many Haitian asylum-seekers in chilly, snow-covered camps until it was decided whether they could remain in the country or had to return to their tropical island slum. Some Cuban asylum-seekers found themselves in what amounts to penitentiaries.[12]

National authorities adopt policies of discouraging entry either in specific, open terms or else implicitly by their reaction to asylum-seekers. Hong Kong, Malaysia, Singapore and Thailand took the former course, the United States and others the latter. Decisions on deterring asylum-seekers rest largely on the judgement and moral standards of the government from which asylum is sought. International standards hardly specify precisely what conditions should apply, although as a rule the Geneva Conventions can be taken as a minimum, Spartan standard. Criticism of or attempts to influence such practices involve sensitivities of the same kind that apply to other aspects of immigration policy. As UNHCR raises no public objection in principle to the Thai policies, under which it gives financial support for camps and other facilities, a rudimentary international approval for this means of discouraging entry could be claimed. As for the Hong Kong camps, UNHCR has opposed them, but the local authorities also note with satisfaction that the number of Vietnamese arriving by boat has fallen off sharply.

UNHCR does have the power and the precedent for arguing against the imposition of really punitive conditions, as do other bodies concerned with human rights. Even if determined national authorities, acting consistently with local mores, are frequently capable of weathering such criticism, in some instances it has a moderating effect. It can also be used in legal processes initiated by asylum-seekers to obtain their release. Any moderating of the policies may discourage the wasting of the lives of innocent, useful individuals in endless confinement in neurosis-breeding conditions. It may prevent the development of future difficulties at both the international and personal level.

Preventing entry

Taken literally, the UN Convention on Refugees prohibits those governments that adhere to it from sending asylum-seekers back into danger. If persons claiming to be refugees have a well-founded fear of persecution, then the government is legally obliged to grant them asylum. Nobody has a right to asylum, however, merely on the basis of his own assertion. National authorities determine whether the fear of persecution is well founded. The good faith of the government in fulfilling its legal obligations is taken for granted. UNHCR and sometimes other agencies interested in human rights can attempt to add their voices during the process of determination, but with few exceptions they have no guaranteed place in the deliberation. In fact, a legal process of some kind is generally carried out by immigration or border officials — or, at least, it is supposed to take place. But such processes often involve a great deal of local discretion, possible arbitrariness and even neglect and prejudice.

In fact, the nature of immigration controls militates against persons claiming refugee status, just as it serves to exclude certain or all entrants from abroad. Border officials routinely begin with the examination of an entrant's documentation. He must have identification, such as a valid passport and visas. Asylum-seekers generally have none of the necessary documentation, or only part of it; they can be easily rejected at that point. Furthermore, uncontrolled land borders can be brought under tighter surveillance when a government has reason to fear an influx. Where stringent conditions operate on a border, refugees will not receive the benefit of the doubt. As it becomes widely known, reaching even populations that include putative refugees, this stringency deters flights, at least towards some possible havens.

Asylum-seekers who use sea routes can be subjected to additional kinds of discouragement. The well-known, continuing operations of rapacious pirates in the Gulf of Thailand may be presumed to discourage some forced migrants from attempting to use water routes. A lack of zeal in suppressing criminal activities at sea is likely to prolong the inhibiting effect of pirates. The United States has developed its own special technique for discouraging Haitian *émigrés* from sailing to the Florida beaches: specially posted Coast Guard vessels stop boats on the high seas in order to send persons hoping to land as refugees back to Haiti.

Other discouraging devices that may be used are radio broadcasts warning against illegal immigration into a target country for forced migrants. Widely publicised trials of those violating local regulations may also have a similar effect. Deportations may be handled summarily and rapidly. Complaints about illegal migration can be made in international fora, such as the UN General Assembly. Finally, those individuals who manage to slip through the outer control could be subjected to lengthy searches, questioning and detention.

Measures taken by national governments to prevent the entry of forced migrants can easily endanger the foundations of the international regime to protect refugees. If a receiving government leans heavily in the direction of restriction, then the marginal cases at least are likely to be decided to the disadvantage of asylum-seekers.

In other cases, the possibility of unjust restriction during a lengthy decisional process is strong. Interference with passage on the high seas has historically caused a great deal of friction among governments. Its use to prevent the movement of people who claim to be fleeing dangerous oppression projects a new rationale for what has usually been regarded as a high-handed activity on the part of powerful naval states. Furthermore, preventive measures can easily shade into discriminatory police practices which run contrary to fundamental justice.

Preventive actions thus tend to fall into a grey area between the protection and promotion of guaranteed human rights and the unrestrained exercise of legal and administrative powers for the carrying out of state policy. Within this area germinate important controversies concerning the exercise of personal rights in those countries where they are in fact available. In other countries, it can easily lead to scandals, where people already under extreme pressure are simply forced to fend for themselves in conditions that practically ensure the deaths of most of them.

In either case, some witnesses will perceive the conduct of the government concerned as brutal and inhumane. The national officials involved will almost certainly be called upon to formulate political and moral defences of actions likely to prove hard to justify. Additional cynical argument may be spun out. Some of the asylum-seekers will probably end up in orbit, unable to land anywhere and causing administrative flurries and emergencies wherever they appear. Others will seek yet farther, and some will eventually find asylum. Yet others will have no choice but to return to the misery which sent them into flight. All of them will have endured a great deal of wasted time and effort, and many will have suffered mental and physical injury. The rest will go to unremembered death.

'Push' and 'pull'

Forced migrants leave home for reasons that have an unmistakable urgency. The precise causes vary from individual to individual, from family to family, from social group to social group; but the coercive nature of the cause is common to every case. Yet when the causes are multiplied in intensity, extend over only a few days or exist in a narrow geographical context, the question naturally arises of whether all those fleeing feel the same threat to the same degree. When some migrants admit to police and border officials to having left because they were unable to make a living or because they saw an opportunity to escape from mounting deprivation, the question might be asked as to whether they were attracted abroad, rather than pushed. In either case, the causes of their departure are by no means trivial even if they do not add up to an indisputable claim to refugee status.

Haitians, for example, who may have spent their youth under pressure from the official police and party activists and who in their country of origin could not expect a future much above the starvation level, have good reason to complain — if sophisticated enough to do so — of a deprivation of their human rights. They will be able to identify this derogation with the more dramatic proceedings leading to the Mariel outflow which was greeted with notably more warmth by the American authorities. Those of Chinese extraction who leave Vietnam illegally and run the pirate gauntlet in the Gulf of Thailand sometimes manage to arrive ashore with money or valuables. They tell stories which indicate that they could possibly have remained at home had they been willing to adapt to the new regime. Lately, similar stories have been told by an increasing number of former Vietnamese peasants and fishermen who also claim that they were hardly able to survive at home and say that they knew that as emigrants they would succeed in finding some help. Such tales have been repeated elsewhere. Yet the emigrants' causes for departures are serious, the risks they take enormous and the uncertainties of their futures daunting.

Individuals among a group of forced migrants can be expected to vary considerably in their estimates of how heavily coercion had affected them. Their motives will therefore seem mixed. It can hardly be doubted that many individuals would prefer the uncertainty of quitting Cuba for the United States in a small boat to the assurance of continued imprisonment for an offence that would be recognised as such anywhere in the world. A claim of persecution by such a person falls flat and can be legally rejected without further ado. In other situations, such as that of the Somali refugees, it was doubtless the pressure of drought and severe hunger which led some of them to the shelter of the camps. Wherever the normal economy fails to provide sustenance and the refugee economy provides a living, it is likely that some magnetism will draw people to claim refugee status. In cases of severe famine, such as that of Sudan in 1985, it becomes difficult to begin to separate refugees with legal claims to that status from those primarily seeking food.

Are undeserving claimants to relief as refugees numerous? Does aid to refugees exert a 'pull' effect? If so, how important is it? The analysis here makes it easy to argue that in general the pull effect is distinctly subordinate to the pressure exerted by the denial of human rights. Not all those who depart under such circumstances fit the definition of the UN Convention, but the actual broadening of the scope of concern of the UN system through directives given by the General Assembly and through practice has contributed to a blurring of that definition. Moreover, it does not fit well with contemporary situations of mass flows of refugees from and into very poor countries.

At the same time, empirical research of a kind that demonstrates convincingly why individuals leave their homes has rarely been available and has not been a characteristic part of operations to assist refugees. Claims that a large proportion of asylum-seekers are actually economic refugees must thus be viewed with some scepticism. Furthermore, merely asking asylum-seekers why they left their homes serves little purpose, for if they are unsophisticated they may well reply that they were terrorised by fighting that took place in their localities, that they were unable to find work, that their land was taken from them or that they feared generally for the future and hoped to ensure security for their families. This has been the case in Somalia, eastern Sudan, South-East Asia and Honduras, to give some examples. But if the migrants are sophisticated, they will certainly emphasise those elements in their histories that support claims for refugee status under the international definition. Moreover, with modern transportation, claims from some people from poor countries for refugee status on the basis of sophisticated argument can now be heard in the airports of western Europe and the United States. The arrival of small groups of Sri Lankan Tamils in the German Federal Republic, the Netherlands and the United Kingdom in 1985 illustrates this phenomenon. Doubtless they are driven and attracted simultaneously, just as the poorest, most ignorant and desperate refugee from intense governmental oppression is attracted to the place where asylum is offered.

Expulsion as a weapon

A sudden wave of forced migrants can prove a powerful source of embarrassment to a reluctant host government. To refuse all asylum would call forth international opprobrium and inspire frenzied scenes in which refugees were driven away by force. Should the numbers involved be very large, the effort would probably fail. Decisions about how to react would be attended by confusion and possibly serious quarrelling within the host society. To accept such decisions mutely would imply *de facto* acquiescence in dictatorial interference from abroad in the immigration policies of the host country. Between these extremes, governments and local populations could choose accommodation, and face a range of difficulties along the lines of the various patterns described earlier.

The embarrassment and hardship that a wave of humanity can induce for its hosts could in principle be deliberately exploited by one government against another. Cynicism of a like degree can, alas, all too easily be located in the recent annals of politics. Yet this specific weapon for impelling a wave of humanity appears to have been employed only rarely — fortunately for mankind.

The only major refugee incident that comes close to an expulsion of citizens for the purpose of embarrassing a host is to be found in Cuba's handling of the Mariel exodus. What began as an embarrassment to Cuba ended as disarray in the United States. Other governments besides Cuba have expelled nationals in order to rid themselves of irritating personalities or demonstrate to their own populations that they refuse to tolerate certain types of conduct. The Soviet Union and Poland appear to have dealt with dissidents in this way. Alexander Solzhenitsyn was deprived of citizenship and virtually expelled after his literary work had brought him fame and cast a baleful light on the way in which the Soviet Union handled dissidents and others thought to be dangerous. Poland put pressure on leaders of the Solidarity trade union movement to leave the country in possession of valid travel documents.

These cases in the Soviet realm can be distinguished from the situation of the Khmers who fled the murderous Pol Pot regime in Cambodia. Official military forces and police tried to interfere with their headlong border crossing, but once they were out of the country no effort was made to retrieve them. The effect on the Thai host government would have been the same had the Khmer been deliberately expelled from their homes for the purpose of creating embarrassment, but in fact this result attended other aims on the part of Cambodia. Similarly, the Ethiopian government was conceivably glad to rid itself of troublesome Somalis who left Ogaden, but they were not deliberately driven away in order to upset the Mogadishu government.

Even the Mariel exodus does not perfectly illustrate the use of expulsion to embarrass another government. Some of those who left for the United States during the tumultuous few days when the improvised fleet of small boats crossed from Florida certainly had been expelled. This apparently small minority comprised prison inmates and former offenders who were of little significance to Cuba. The vast majority seemed anxious to depart for reasons of family unification, unhappiness with the political and social situation and sheer frustration with an economic system that excluded them from any current benefits or promise for the future. Unlike previous exoduses from Cuba, when the United States had found ways of co-operating on a minimal basis with the Castro government to give the outflow an appearance of reasonable order, the Mariel exodus had no organisational fibre. It was simply a wider opening of the gate that had been forced by the 10,000 Cubans who had sought asylum in the grounds of the Peruvian embassy only a few days before.

In retrospect, it appears that the Castro government turned a shaming episode in which it publicly lost control of a discontented section of its population into a gesture that shoved responsibility on to the antagonistic United States.[13] This opportunistic improvision embarrassed the United States and diverted attention from the causes of pressure to leave Cuba. In the process, the government in Havana washed its hands of those it viewed as undependable or undesirable. Whether it paid a commensurate price in terms of infamy for its cynical treatment of its own people is doubtful.

Cuba avoided the full blast of international opprobrium partly by controlling the information that was released about what it was doing, partly by refusing to allow any significant organised international involvement in the incident and partly by passively profiting from the normal attention given by the proficient American mass media to the dramatic armada bearing the asylum-seekers. Once the emigrants came within range of the media lenses, the main attention shifted to them as individuals and to their plight. This was followed by detailed reporting on difficulties in providing them with assistance, legal status and integration into the society.

The test of policy towards refugees implicit in the Mariel exodus showed up a number of deficiencies in the American understanding of what refugee status meant. Furthermore, the administration of an untested policy in an emergency led to a variety of strains. Interpretations of the policy varied from a wide open door to refugees to prevention of landing and prohibiting as a criminal act the transporting of Cubans. Responses at state and local levels showed similar variations. In the process, some of the entrants encountered unsympathetic handling as well as fumbling. Furthermore, the outflow from Cuba encouraged a similar if somewhat smaller one from Haiti. The presence of the Cubans also cut across the immigration policies applying to refugees from Indo-China, for had the Cubans been treated as refugees the number of approved immigration places would have been used up. Thus, one incident potentially threatened a major line of the whole refugee programme in the United States.

Among the questions raised by the Mariel incident, perhaps two are outstanding. These are whether a government may be expected to employ expulsion as a weapon against another; and whether such practices can be brought under control.

The paucity of historical examples of mass expulsions intended primarily to cause embarrassment to other governments may be taken as comforting. As has been suggested here, although many governments have the capacity to drive large numbers of their subjects away, most large-scale incidents have resulted from actions carried out with little regard for what would happen to those affected or to the governments that offered asylum. Such a generalisation would apply, for instance, to the South-East Asia and Afghanistan situations. In both of these cases, the governments producing refugees imposed costs on the host states, but that was not the principal intention. Expulsions of small numbers of people do not cause embarrassment of the kind resulting from the Mariel incident, though occasionally an expellee may be as repulsive politically or socially to his putative hosts as he was to his country of origin.

In fact, severe limitations apply to the use of mass expulsion as a weapon. To begin with, expulsions entail substantial costs to the country of origin. Unless the people involved can be clearly identified as alienated, unproductive and irreconcilable, their departure is likely to involve significant long-term costs in terms of production and social organisation. The expulsion of the Asians from Uganda by the Amin government is a case in point. Mass departures lead to heavy one-off costs in the short term, evidenced by social disruption, a decline in economic production and sometimes in political stability. Substantial administrative effort may also be required to select those who must depart and to exile them.

The costs in international relations are also likely to be considerable. A government that simply expels part of its population inevitably causes an international scandal and, very likely, a hue and cry about violations of human rights. The government suffering damage by receiving the expellees would get material support from others if that were needed. The source state would become the object of suspicion on the part of its neighbours — even those not directly affected by the exodus — for it would raise questions about the limits of its policies in other respects. A distinct cooling of relationships with other governments would follow, and so might a possible loss of material and political support.

A target government will almost certainly retaliate in some fashion for the use of a wave of refugees against it. Such retaliation could conceivably even include armed action and a host of lesser measures. Furthermore, the launching of a wave of expellees would put far into the future the opportunity for a betterment of relations, especially when the newcomers use their asylum as an opportunity to encourage tough policies against the government that threw them out.

Nor can the precise outcome of a policy of expulsion be predicted. While it is conceivable that so great a wave of people could be set in motion that the target government would collapse, that outcome seems rather far-fetched. It is inconceivable that such a campaign would succeed against the United States or another highly developed country, or that the attempt to mount it would not call forth a punishing reaction. Moreover, the repeated use of expulsion also seems unlikely in view of the costs to the user, and also because the supply of expellees is subject to natural limits. Not even the most pathologically violent regime would attempt to push its people away in very large numbers over a short period of time, for it would be eroding its own base. Moreover, with each forced exodus more of the remaining population might choose to turn their grievances concerning the loss of their relatives into resistance.

It can be concluded that mass expulsion as a weapon could probably be used only rarely, even by extremely cynical governments. The effects on a target government would usually be limited and the costs to the expelling government telling.

Notes

1. The primary documents are the UN Universal Declaration of Human Rights and the two consequent Covenants on Civil and Political and Economic and Social Rights. They have been conveniently reprinted as *The International Bill of Rights XXX* (United Nations, New York, 1978). For a few of many useful commentaries, see David P. Forsythe, *Human Rights and World Politics* (University of Nebraska Press, Lincoln, Neb., 1984); Louis Henkin, *The Rights of Man Today* (Westview Press, Boulder, CO., 1978);

A.H. Robertson, *Human Rights in the World* (Manchester University Press, Manchester, 1972); and Henry Shue, *Basic Rights: Subsistence, Affluence and U.S. Foreign Policy* (Princeton University Press, Princeton, NJ, 1980). Shue argues that rights concerning the preservation of human life, such as those to food and security, are so interlinked as to be impossible to separate from one another. Thus it follows that what he identifies as basic economic rights cannot be treated as being of second order any more than can political rights.

2. Although the Universal Declaration of Human Rights does not constitute an explicit and incontrovertible legal obligation on governments, it is widely accepted as a standard, that is, as means of judging distance from a goal that ought some day to be reached. Article 13 says that '[e]veryone has the right to leave any country, including his own, and to return to this country'. Article 14 states: 'Everyone has the right to seek and to enjoy in other countries asylum from persecution.' Refugees clearly attempt to exercise these rights, which supposedly pertain to every individual. They are also caused to flee by an inability to satisfy such rights as those to freedom of thought, conscience and religion and to opinion and expression. Moreover, life is hardly possible for any human group if it is barred from employment or if the standard of living it experiences is inadequate to sustain life. The elaborate construction of institutions, networks and legal obligations to benefit refugees — who are a particularly carefully defined section of humanity — can be understood as an attempt to restore basic human rights which have been so gravely denied or restricted as to cause flight.

3. Whether these rights are legally enforceable or whether they are susceptible to close definition in individual cases is not at issue. In fact, refugee situations usually involve not marginal but gross failures to achieve the human rights standard.

4. UN Doc. E/CN.4/1503.

5. In 1980, the General Assembly adopted a resolution, introduced by the Federal Republic of Germany, calling for a study of the prevention of mass exoduses (UN General Assembly Resolution 35/124, 11 December 1980). It was opposed only by the Soviet group. A year later, the General Assembly asked the Secretary-General to appoint a seventeen-state committee of experts to look into the matter (UN General Assembly Resolution 36/148, 16 December 1981). The report had not yet been submitted by the 1985 General Assembly.

6. These were later reprinted in 'Four Case Studies', *Transnational Perspectives*, Special Study (1982), pp. 23-41.

7. This section draws on Gordenker, 'Early Warning of Disastrous Forced Migration'. For a careful elaboration of some of these ideas, see Refugee Policy Group, 'Early Warning of Mass Refugee Flows' (mimeograph, 1986), prepared for the Independent Commission on International Humanitarian Issues.

8. The use of incentives by international institutions does not seem to be a highly developed art. Sovereign equals are presumably given equal treatment. Yet the UN Charter, for example, carefully outlines only a series of punitive measures and institutional arrangements to be used in the event of a breach of the peace. See UN Charter, Chapter 7.

9. Even in a world riddled by military activity of a destructiveness that

long ago would have seemed outrageously lethal, as with the Iraq-Iran conflict or the fighting in Afghanistan, Lebanon or Ethiopia, it may be worth remembering that members of the United Nations have voluntarily agreed to be bound by the legal obligation not to use violence in their international relations and to settle disputes without resort to violence. UN Charter, Article 2 (3) and (4).

10. The Reagan administration has emphasised its preference for bilateral negotiations and for unilateral action when it does not find support for its proposals in multilateral councils. The Soviet Union is itself hardly a novice at this type of behaviour. The most dramatic expressions of the bilateral preference are the summit meetings continually proposed by the United States and the Soviet Union as well as negotiations on the control of nuclear weapons.

11. Wain, *The Refused*, Chapter 4.

12. Such policies may prevent entry to a specific place, but if the impelling reason for departure remains, people will still flee but seek asylum in other locations. The entry of Lowland Lao declined in Thailand but increased when pressure rose in Laos. Thailand began in 1985 to push some would-be entrants back across the border. United States Department of State, *Report of the Indochinese Refugee Panel*, Publication 9476 (Department of State, Washington, 1986), p. 25. For an account of the situation in Hong Kong, which asserts that boats containing refugees from Vietnam now either avoid Hong Kong altogether or leave it hurriedly, see 'Living in Limbo: The Boat Refugees of Hong Kong and Macao', mimeographed paper prepared by Allen K. Jones for the United States Committee for Refugees (Washington, May 1986).

13. Some observers have suggested that a new political instrument, 'migration politics', has been developed around refugee flows. 'The Cuban influx came to be regarded [in the United States] as a formidable policy instrument in the hands of a hostile regime. Meanwhile, reports from the Far East suggested that the United States was encouraging a refugee outflow as part of a deliberate policy to undercut the Communist regime of newly reunified Vietnam' — Mark J. Miller and Demetrios G. Papademetriou, 'Immigration and US Foreign Policy' in Miller and Papademetriou, *The Unavoidable Issue*, p. 176.

8

Conclusions

The current state of affairs for refugees and other forced migrants could blandly and inconclusively be described as mixed but not entirely dismal. Millions of refugees, though not all, do get attention. A substantial international structure sustains them. Evidence of sympathy, even for those denied official status, comes from influential quarters. In any case, refugee status implies uncertainty. The mixture of succour and threat, humaneness and indifference, only mirrors a hard world.

Summary treatment of this kind is seriously misleading. It fails to perceive the nuances, the complexities, the interconnections that this study has emphasised. It gives the impression that the simplicity that all too often characterises news reporting on refugees actually represents a summary. It omits to differentiate between various kinds of forced migrant, the causes of their departure and the effects on others that this study seeks to elucidate. Yet misleading though such simplicity may be, it may, alas, lend itself to the sort of political decision-making in which numerous groups and their ideas compete for attention and resources.

Political decisions concerning forced migrants sometimes rest on thoroughly considered, integrated reasoning. Sometimes — perhaps more often than governments would care to admit — their decisions are based on acquiescence, near-indifference, muddling along, misinformation and misunderstanding. Yet in certain incidents of forced migration, impressive responses have emerged. Their impressiveness can be measured by the number of those assisted, the amount of expenditure involved, the rapidity with which administrative structures have been set up where little had been known to function previously and the sheer length of the lists of programmes. Possibly never in history has so much effort been made by such a wide proportion of mankind to succour strangers in trouble.

The existing organisation that is required to react to the entry of refugees and secure their ultimate departure can certainly be described as elaborate. It includes the relatively familiar tokens of co-operation among governments in the form of permanent institutions equipped with standing secretariats, deliberative organs, consultative mechanisms, budgets, legal foundations and diplomatic procedures. It also comprises lengthy chains of personal relationships — or networks — built around common experience, defined expertness and the bureaucratic discipline required for organisation. These networks form and re-form in response to the specific demands of particular refugee situations. They can be understood as the informal counterparts of the more formal institutions. Yet neither the institutions nor the networks would be able to exist one without the other.

The elaborateness of the organisation can be traced in part to the safeguards on which governments of modern nation-states insist in order to maximise their abilities to make autonomous decisions. This urge towards the safeguarding of autonomy has concrete expression in the limitations set on legal responsibilities. The lengthy organisational chains and involved processes are in part a reflection of the need to bring some flexibility to the way in which the international machinery deals with specific situations. Also, the machinery itself, and the engagement of the ever-changing networks, derive from the idealism and charity of the individuals and organisations involved. The ethical norms of individuals cannot be brushed aside as mere eccentricities in a world of power politics. Normative notions drive not only the saintly but also the less-than-perfect in their execution of programmes designed to save lives and provide futures for those who see flight from their homes as their only salvation. At state level, these ethical-normative concepts find partial expression in the still-evolving system for the international protection of human rights.

For those who oppose the wanton wasting of human lives, who sympathise with the women and children huddled in tent openings in the turmoil of refugee camps, who are disquieted by the summary justice meted out by border police, who have sensed the despair of those who feel compelled by the spectre of destruction or starvation to leave home, it would be comforting to imagine that the elaborate machinery would always grind out assistance and protection and, eventually, a stable existence. Yet the organisation set up for the handling of forced migrations operates under a variety of severe limitations, which have been indicated above.

Limitations on responses

The characteristics of the modern state and the nature of the decisional processes attending it constitute an overarching limitation. On the one hand, the modern state limits the potential for organisation that institutional experience and technological developments — such as electronic communication and rapid transportation — imply. The personnel of existing institutions that have dealt in the past with the man-made disasters of forced migration and natural disasters, such as earthquakes, probably have little of real significance to learn about delivering assistance; it can be done quickly and efficiently. That is not to say that each disaster is brilliantly handled. Nor does it mean that institutions can be depended upon to apply the lessons of their earlier campaigns. But no one needs to reinvent, for instance, the organisation of a refugee camp or its facilities, such as sanitation or a dispensary. Even the difficulties of bringing supplies to a mass of refugees in the nether regions of the world can be overcome.

On the other hand, what is possible and what is permissible vary enormously in the international reaction to refugees. Governments generally show little enthusiasm for long-term commitments to foreigners who are largely without influence and form a possibly intractable group within the place of asylum. Financial consequences of asylum, too, may discourage commitment. Reluctant governments can only be persuaded — not compelled — to conform to international standards regarding refugees. No amount of pleading or logic will necessarily move a government that has decided otherwise. The decentralised nature of international relations thus constitutes a perpetual limitation of uncertain extent on the reaction to forced migration.

This decentralised set of relationships, moreover, includes varied perceptions on the parts of governments — really those few officials charged with the relevant tasks — and less official organisations of what a forced migrant is, when a response is desirable and what should be undertaken. In essence, therefore, each refugee incident calls forth a reaction with a somewhat different tone. The ideological preoccupations of authorities and organisations clearly have much to do with the resulting approach to refugees. The definitions in treaties, the tried-and-tested techniques, the bureaucratic and institutional memories all condition the ultimate tone of reactions to refugees. But the decentralised nature of international relations ensures a considerable degree of uncertainty.

The play of political opinion within states strongly conditions responses to refugees. Some governments — such as those of the Scandinavian countries, the Netherlands and Japan — give generous financial, diplomatic and moral support to co-operative international efforts to cope with the flow of forced migration. The smaller European countries have led the way over the years to the creation of sound legal procedures and a clear understanding of what an internationally recognised refugee is. Nevertheless, this decent and humane attitude does not mean that refugees are welcomed in these countries as permanent residents; on the contrary, individuals and groups who turn up at airports or arrive at border crossings usually find themselves beaten down by the meticulous application of domestic law. Unexpected asylum-seekers, who could become claimants for permanent residence, do not automatically receive a cheerful welcome. This exclusiveness finds support among national political organisations.

The United States appears at first glance to have followed a markedly different policy. It has taken in more refugees in third-country resettlement programmes than any other single country in the world. In contrast with, say, Japan, another rich polity, the United States has shown almost unimaginable generosity in giving homes to the homeless. But this superficial view does not sustain buoyant conclusions.

The United States has not simply welcomed all of those who have the label of refugee. It has only recently formally adhered to the international standard for determining refugees, and even since then has continued to treat different groups of forced migrants differently, depending on their national origins and political relationships with the government of their country of origin. It has generally favoured asylum-seekers from countries dominated by Communist goverments and offered them permanent asylum in third-country resettlement programmes. In this regard, it has strong support from domestic groups.

Like many other countries, the United States operates a highly restrictive formal immigration policy. That the execution of this policy may not be satisfying either to the authorities or to those groups and individuals in the society interested in controlling immigration in no way alters the restrictive intention of the laws.

These restrictions, too, have widespread support in both organised and unorganised opinion in the United States. Similar comments can be made about most of the wealthy countries of North America and Western Europe. The United Kingdom, for example, has openly restricted the immigration of Indians, Pakistanis, Chinese and others of darker skins even when they have close family connections with legal residents in Britain. As for Eastern Europe, the notion of asylum is for all practical purposes unknown, except for the occasional political or espionage operative forced to decamp or the soldier from the West who seeks escape from one or another irritant in his own surroundings. But forced migrants almost never seek or expect asylum in the Soviet bloc.

Thus, with its emphasis on setting policies with the local political circumstances as the primary consideration, the nation-state confronts forced migrants and those who would come to their aid with a cross-hatching of practices that recall the turmoil of an abstract expressionist painting. This jumble of local practices and policies offers many opportunities for temporary and permanent asylum, but it does not unquestioningly hand over to all who ask a general pass to a secure future. Nor is there any reason to expect, given the strength of the contemporary state, that strict uniformity of practice will soon develop. In fact, as the weaker states of the world continue with their ceaseless extension of administration to every patch of land and water that exists within their borders, it can be expected that the remaining tranquillity of neglect will vanish.

Responses to forced migrations are limited not only by local political configurations. The primitive facts of available resources also condition reactions. Resources for forced migrants are usually denominated in currency units and arranged in budgets. Such budgets for refugees and other forced migrants have, as noted above, sometimes reached amounts that are impressive compared to the usual expenditures on co-operative transnational programmes. But often in social welfare programmes, not every need can be covered: the formal budgets seriously understate reality. A lengthy chain composed of the ancillary effects of forced migration claims resources that cannot easily be provided for when drawing up accounts. Social services, such as police and fire protection, soon come to be affected. Demands on schools and hospitals can perhaps more easily be forecast and sometimes recompensed through co-operative means, but even the process of repayment depends on the time and effort spent by authorities that have other tasks. The experience of resettlement in third countries shows, too, that newcomers make claims on the social welfare apparatus until they become fully self-supporting. It would be hard to deny that in the short run refugees can impose costs on their hosts. As for the economy as a whole, the result of the displacement of people from active employment to idleness in exile piles up irretrievable losses in production. Yet refugees, by their very presence and humanity, make effective demands for some scarce resources.

To consider the limited resources available for forced migrants is to refer by implication to psychological and organisational boundaries. Psychological limitations concern the ability of both forced migrants and those responsible for receiving them to understand the situation with which they are jointly coping. The refugees usually enter exile in a desperate frame of mind. They leave behind them an intolerable situation in which the normal circumstances of their lives have given way to threat and danger. Their new surroundings are generally unfamiliar, difficult to fathom, limited by the orders of local authorities and frequently quite unpleasant in appearance, smell and intention.

Those responsible for refugees feel pressure from the migrants. Here are people who have all the usual human requirements but who for the moment have little or no ability to provide for themselves. What is more, they may speak a foreign language, so that their needs and requests cannot be easily comprehended. Some of their number may die, go insane, suffer illness or be either too young or too old to act independently. All of this must be kept in some order by the receiving authorities, whose experience may be of a quite different character. Not all officials have the mental flexibility to adjust to this new group. Moreover, the higher authorities are required to set policies. They may also have difficulty in accurately perceiving the nature of the migration and how to cope with it. In addition, local opinion must necessarily bear heavily on their reactions. In some instances, humaneness and good will may give way to hostility dictated by the surrounding community. The pressure on officials and those who want to help can mount dangerously.

Closely allied to psychological limitations are cultural predispositions. Some cultures leave little room for charity to those beyond the recognisable family. Others incorporate xenophobia, colour prejudice, unique notions concerning the role of women, children or employment, or special norms. Imbedded in the culture may be powerful religious injunctions that shape reactions.

Organisational reactions may reflect limiting psychological and cultural factors. Because organisations draw together individuals whose work becomes joined to reach a common goal, personal psychological limitations are necessarily injected into the organisational framework. Also, organisations may set limitations when defining their goals, whatever process may apply. Very little existing organisation, as we have seen, concentrates on refugees and other forced migrants. Most has to do with the day-to-day life of a society in which the forced migrant is by definition alien. Little organisation is therefore adapted to the needs of the newcomer. When the number of refugees is small, adaptations to the existing organisation cause relatively little difficulty, but larger numbers rapidly overwhelm the existing capacity for dealing with newcomers and swamps any ability there may be for the making of minor adjustments in standard procedures. Organisational memories may fail to find precedents. The well-known bureaucratic phenomenon of responding to the familiar and stiffening in the face of anything new comes into play.

A related kind of organisational limit concerns legal capacity. State organisations depend on rules adopted to regulate the societies in which they operate. Therefore, the responses of organisational bureaucracies take place within a framework of social rules determined largely by government. Both intergovernmental and voluntary organisations depend ultimately on the approval or acquiescence of governments in their programmes. They require permission from a government in order to put their programmes for the assistance and protection of forced migrants into effect and to enlist the assistance of national governmental and voluntary agencies. The intergovernmental and foreign voluntary agencies have no legal or — for that matter, material — power to act if a territory is not opened to them by the government in charge; they can only make representations to the governments involved. The legal system of independent states necessarily entails this limitation. It is given extra emphasis by the restrictions built into the international instruments which provide some specific legal authority for dealing with certain forced migrants.

An obsolete standard?

The idea of an international legal standard of general applicability to determine who is a refugee seems to have wide — though not universal — support among governments. The adherence of over

100 governments tò the UN Convention on Refugees demonstrates a broad level of support for such a standard. But, as has been pointed out here, decisions about asylum tend to vary among national authorities and localities, even where the international definition of a refugee is incorporated as a baseline into local law. The differing points of view of those — national government officials, local officials, voluntary agency personnel, international officials, clan members and so on — who have contact with persons seeking asylum affects the way the standard is applied in different incidents. Furthermore, as has been argued here, the nature of refugee flows has altered in comparison with the expectations of those who drafted the convention. Practice and reinterpretation have led to the filling in of some gaps. Nevertheless, some governments and observers have begun seriously to question the usefulness of the present international definition of refugees and the regime that it establishes.

One main line of critical argument suggests that the entire existing legal framework should be revised. A rebutting argument insists that opening a discussion of the existing arrangements would unleash more difficulties than now exist. Another line looks to a rationalisation and systematisation of existing practice. Given the variety of interests involved in refugee affairs both within and among states, it seems highly unlikely that a definition to suit every need could be found. This uncertainty increases in proportion to the amount of pressure exerted on governments by incidents of forced migration, especially the more notorious situations involving large numbers of people. In any case, narrow, exclusionary approaches imply a lessening of responsibility for the governments concerned. Such governments are more likely to agree on a fragmentary or limited international standard than on a comprehensive system of definition, administration and centralised decision-making. This generalisation about likely future reactions is one that conforms to historical experience of refugee situations.

Meanwhile, crises and recent practice have repeatedly demonstrated that the exclusionary definition of the 1951 Convention either does not adequately fit specific situations or that the range of causes, development and scope of forced migration makes a broader approach desirable for the purpose of avoiding worse difficulties. The reasons for a broader approach include: real human need on a large scale; a varying degree of political acceptability on the part of host governments and those governments giving aid to particular groups of asylum-seekers; the firm establishment of basic international machinery; and the importance of legitimation based on international rules.

As for revising the existing legal framework, built around the 1951 Convention and its various interpretations, this could proceed in one of two main directions. One line would be to tighten up the definition so as to restrict the possibilities of asylum. Another would be to give formal status to recent practice, for instance extending asylum under the category 'refugee' to large groups of people without subjecting them to individual examination. The extension of the 1951 definition that is set out in the African refugee convention could also be applied universally, especially for the purpose of providing asylum to those who flee internal disorder. The divergences between these points of view — both of which have partisans — imply that a new definition would certainly not emerge smoothly from international negotiations.

The probable shape of such a negotiation can perhaps be sketched in advance. The countries of immigration, such as the United States and Canada, would probably seek narrower, or at least still more precise, guidelines in order to reduce the numbers of those asylum-seekers who have legitimate refugee status. This restrictive tendency reflects a resistance to continuing the historical practice of accepting the immigrants that each succeeding forced migration brings with it. Likely countries of first asylum would probably join in the arguments for restrictions in order to make it easier for them to reject asylum-seekers.

On the other side, humanitarian organisations can be expected to press for a broader definition so that the stamp of legitimacy on their area of concern would encompass a yet greater segment of forced migrants. As organisations, they would then have more scope. Their charitable rationale would gain support from those who deplore human suffering of any kind. The officials of African governments would probably seek a broader definition along the lines of the convention to which their governments are committed. If nothing else, this would give more force to their claims on outside help for the region.

The diversity of suggested remedies for the deficiencies of the legal framework gives cogency to the argument that no revision ought to be attempted in order to avoid calling into question certain current practices which do in fact make it possible to extend aid and protection to many thousands. A full-dress negotiation, it could be argued, would sharpen the views of already critical governments and reduce the scope for improvisation in the next serious refugee incident. It might even end with more restrictive instructions to UNHCR and ICM.

The argument for a rationalisation of current practice — in contrast to a reopening of the formal, legal arrangements — is based on the assumption that the present structure has enough elasticity to serve well in almost all asylum situations. Moreover, at least some governments do come forward to help. The UN General Assembly and other international deliberative bodies have time and again sanctioned the expansion of UNHCR and given legitimation to the creation of the existing refugee network. At any one moment, that network represents something like the maximum possible range of practical agreement on refugees. That it expands and contracts in response to particular situations may seem organisationally untidy, but it roughly meets the needs. It might be supported by further study, with careful discussions within UNHCR and in non-governmental contexts such as universities and research centres. The experience of officials who have dealt with refugees should be given an unofficial hearing and subjected to systematic analysis. It might even be found that an international standard of convincing sturdiness already exists and serves the purpose better than any likely change.

Formal revision of rules and strict codification of practice seem to hint that the handling of forced migration as an international issue can be given a final or nearly fixed form. Recent incidents of forced migration to unlikely places create a contrary image of persuasive line. Both the nature of forced migrations and the lack of converging opinion therefore suggest that the possibility of fixing more strict international rules is probably rather limited. At the same time, flexibility without guidelines can lead to erratic behaviour. Flexible reactions to emergencies would, ideally, have a normative basis that obviates rewarding those who cause hurt and hurting those who have already been affected.

A normative basis for such responses could be further developed from the international standard to protect human rights. This human rights standard, as has been suggested here, fits with little difficulty into the vaguer notion that human beings should be rescued from difficulties that are not of their own making. This notion, embellished over the decades with legal obligations, practices and doctrine, underlies humanitarian activity at the international level. Such activity typically emerges in the event of an earthquake, a famine, a flood or a fire.

Refugees too suffer from pernicious situations beyond their control, but because the causes of their distress are man-made, political and persecutive, they have historically been separated from those struck by natural disaster. The relevant causes presumably result from choices on the part of authority and could be controlled. Nevertheless, the classic refugee has immediate requirements similar to those of the disaster victim. His long-term needs resemble those of someone whose way of life has vanished either because of a changing social or economic structure or due to a land-consuming natural catastrophe, such as a flood of lava on fertile fields.

From a humanitarian point of view, it could be argued that all persons sent into flight by disaster should be cared for immediately. To separate out the refugees on the basis of political persecution misses the point. Refugees are people who have suffered political or social disasters, but they are not the only ones who have been dealt blows. An improvement in the transnational arrangements for the handling of all human disasters would result in important short-term benefits for every category, including refugees. The authorities on whom the burdens of care are imposed would also benefit. In their emergencies, they would receive help sooner as less effort would be spent on patching together a consensus on policy and improvising the necessary organisation.

Some additional forward planning would also be possible. The general tone of improvisation — even of reinventing the wheel — that dominates the treatment of large-scale forced migrations, especially those associated with such threatening local causes as famines or mounting government oppression, could almost certainly be dampened by forecasting. Such forecasting would require the construction of an early warning system. It could conceivably operate both on the basis of economic and natural data — for instance, shifts in market conditions or an unusual weather pattern — and on the basis of violations of civil and political rights. Early warning, if used properly by state authorities, would almost certainly lead to a reduction in the amount of expenditure needed to cope with forced migration, for it would at least forestall the waste and confusion of improvised responses and would encourage serviceable policies towards forced migrants. At the same time, the use of early warning would hardly be likely to proceed very far if governments tried to pretend that forced migrations were so unlikely that no preparation need be made.

The argument for treating refugees and related forced migrants as disaster victims and de-emphasising the man-made nature of the causes implies new responsibilities for governments. A large number of those fleeing brutal, incompetent or repressive governments in less developed countries would gladly accept asylum in richer areas where an opportunity for an easier life seems available. The short-term option of resettlement would appear far more attractive than the hope of ultimate repatriation into a situation that might well be even less attractive than the one that caused them to flee in the first place. The taxpayers of the countries of asylum would doubtless react angrily if the charges imposed on them were to continue for long periods or to involve large sums. In short, all the negative reactions associated with resettlement might be activated.

The issues posed by forced migrations thus differ, depending on the time involved, the numbers, the causes, the immediate impacts and the long-term expectations. In principle, firmer and more responsive organisation is possible. It seems obvious that concepts now employed in connection with forced migrations strain against the limits of state autonomy and changing social and technological circumstances. Finally, it seems certain that forced migrations will continue to pose difficulties which cannot be wiped away in a single burst of innovative planning or a whirlwind of creative imagination.

The benefits of internationalisation

The internationalisation of refugee issues and of some of those posed by forced migration as a whole has rendered a long list of benefits (traced in the earlier chapters of this study) to the human beings involved, the governments affected and the individuals and groups willing to assist those in need. In fact, in refugee incidents of more than minor scale, the internationalisation of treatment may be the principal reason why any substantial effort is made to save lives.

From the standpoint of a government, internationalisation may offer an indispensable means of effective action at the time of forced migration. The resources may have to come from abroad, and their provision through established international channels may be the most attractive, or even the only, available method. Moreover, the receiving government can justify its reaction on the basis of international standards. For governments that provide resources, either in the form of financing for relief and resettlement or in the form of actual places for resettlement, internationalisation distributes the burden on a generally acceptable pattern. It reduces friction over 'fair shares' issues and spreads risks. It also spreads the responsibility of participating governments so that no single one of them is capable of being blamed for every misdeed or omission. For all who participate in an internationalised programme of the sort analysed here, there is an ethical benefit in acting according to widely sanctioned humanitarian values. All these factors determine the existence of a transnational mode of formal and informal, governmental and private organisation in a world of nationalistic governments.

Even if governments were blanketed with legal obligations to treat forced migrants consistently with the human rights standard, a global Utopia would hardly emerge. Such obligations would have to be executed in such a manner that would give them full effect and to internationalise the treatment so that efficient transnational co-operation would replace episodic reaction. The numbers of refugees in the world during the last three decades offer only partial comfort to those who hope for an unviolated international regime and generous national policies.

Enough in the way of legal obligations and administrative precedents probably now exists for a hue and cry about the harm done to human beings that ensues from many — perhaps almost all — forced migrations. This clamour could include complaints to intergovernmental agencies, such as the UN, the OAS and the OAU, on the part of governments and, less directly, private groups. Similar furores could be aroused within national governments. Supporting studies and reports could be produced by governments and citizens' groups. In short, a powerful campaign could develop to make the violators and their sponsors notorious moral outcasts in the world community.

The hue and cry could be accompanied by national governmental actions to put pressure on the violator of human rights to alter its conduct. Such measures, short of violence, have an arguable legal and political basis as a form of self-help within a decentralised system. They might include persuasion in the form of private admonition; support for private representation on the part of such international agencies as UNHCR; public declarations; cooler diplomatic relations; the withdrawal of consular facilities and the shrinking of diplomatic establishments; a reduction in the amount of assistance given for development and military forces; a refusal to be associated with the violating government in coalitions within intergovernmental bodies; and many other gestures of displeasure, both individual and co-operative. To this, like-minded governments could add initiatives in intergovernmental agencies, the seeking of suitable publicity, admonitory resolutions and even organised coercive pressure.

Few governments can remain altogether oblivious to this sort of pressure, especially if it is well co-ordinated. When it is led by power-ful and respected states, such as those that have traditionally sup-ported international co-operation on behalf of refugees, it has all the more likelihood of getting a serious response.

The hue and cry, however, does not carry with it any guarantee of success; political measures are always chancy and complex. They may subtly result in desirable changes, even if they lack the simplicity of military destruction. If there is no change, as a rule not a great deal is lost, for such measures imply that extreme violations of rights are already taking place at relatively little international cost to the causal agents. If well managed, the hue and cry will at least raise the ideological costs of such violations and perhaps do a great deal more.

If violators faced the virtual certainty that their activities would draw wide attention, they might be dissuaded at an early stage, before their programmes had hardened into vested, irrevocable commitments. Such dissuasion would require early warning of massive violations of rights and forced migrations as well as the necessary political will among those in a position to read the signs of inhumanity.

Limits and potentials in organising internationally

That organising internationally for the purpose of coping with forced migrations and even with narrowly defined refugees from unmistakeable persecution soon encounters hindrances must be obvious. As this study has shown, these limitations are consistent with the workings of the contemporary state, the principal force in international relations. They arise from the specific circumstances of forced migrations and the internal socio-political order of the countries where migrants seek asylum. The very weakness of migrants as influences on the life around them tends to limit responses.

Yet governments — sometimes acting alone and sometimes co-operating in intergovernmental bodies — and voluntary agencies have repeatedly responded to the needs of forced migrants. Despite the large numbers of asylum-seekers that exist, the general reaction to them has been notably more humane than, say, the behaviour of guerrilla raiders driven by holy zeal. Expectations, however vague, of some chance of finding assistance helps to cause once-settled people to take to the roads and the seas in desperate search of asylum.

How can this reaction be understood in a world that puts power and coercion so high on the agendas of governments? What does it have to say in a more general sense about organising internationally? Does the treatment of forced migrants stretch expectations about international co-operation?

Refugees represent an awkward fact for governing authorities and others who encounter them. They bring with them little of immediate value and, whatever their own notions about their activities, implicitly or explicitly make demands on the host society. Yet they are also people, not inanimate objects guided by some objective force. They have some will of their own, some ability to act on their own initiative and to reason. They do not disappear in an explosive instant or have the brutish simplicity of, say, a column of tanks or an automatic rifle. Thus, they are an uncertain and even a mysterious quantity against which no relatively simple, familiar defence — such as a raid by baton-wielding policemen — can be made. Moreover, those who encounter refugees may come to understand that, for all their alienness, these people nevertheless do not constitute an enemy to be feared and hated.

Governments, it has been argued here, face certain imperatives in the very awkwardness that refugees create. Their impact on life around them impels reaction. But so does the view that other governments and voluntary agencies take about them. Similar views may well be held by part or all of the population in the country of asylum. Too cavalier or too punitive a treatment of refugees calls down the wrath of both powerful and sentimental interests. It poses for governments the question of what is to be gained by declining to observe the widely accepted norms that have painfully been formulated in the light of hundreds of incidents.

Mere human need, however, can hardly be said to pose a perfectly convincing argument in the eyes of all governments or perhaps even of most. The shameful spectacle of young children with hunger-bloated bellies ought to furnish enough evidence, as convincing as it is frequent, that need alone does not induce either vigorous organisation or unselfishness in international relations. Yet the needs of refugees do meet with sympathy, expressed in the form of relatively durable organised international policies and programmes. How can this case be distinguished from others?

The destruction brought about by two world wars and the revolutionary upheavals that accompanied them were fresh in the minds of the statesmen and the masses alike when the norms for the protection of refugees were first drafted. It is perhaps justifiable to suggest that a feeling of shame broadly affected the victors in the Second World War when they understood what the German government had done to the Jews and others marked out for death by the Third Reich's racial policies. Staggering out of the death camps, secret attics and farm lofts, those who survived needed precisely the kind of help that refugees require. Indeed, many of them would have been refugees earlier had there been a way out and somewhere to go. There was neither.

To this retrospective political basis was added a novel element. Many of the next wave of refugees, flowing in at a time when the direct experience of the Second World War remained acute, came from Eastern Europe, where the Soviet Union had deepened its penetration. This fact fitted neatly within the reaction in favour of refugees that followed the First World War. That, too, had concentrated on the migrants from Communist control, from the 1917 revolution and its aftermath. Those governments that led the way in coping with the refugees of 1945-50 were the same ones who had reacted after 1917. They were also the governments most likely to commit themselves to humanitarian activities in order to satisfy local opinion.

Thus, in the time of the Cold War, as in the days of the 'Bolshevik menace', hard political doctrine coincided with softer notions about charity, brotherhood, rescue and human rights. Interest groups at the national level, it seems fair to surmise, furnished at least the critical shove, if not the driving force, to governments which as usual were dominated by specialists in the application of power. Moreover, this crystallisation of policy twice took place amidst ambitious attempts to reorganise world politics by the means of institutionalisation, first in the League of Nations and then in the United Nations.

The global international institutions supplied a vehicle which enabled the normative conventions establishing legal protection for refugees to be enhanced by permanent bureaucratic supervision. The international bureaucratic supervisors served their national counterparts by providing extra legitimation for positions taken in domestic contexts, where appropriations of funds had to be sought. Together the national and international functionaries soon formed a network whose members needed each other's activities and competence in order to carry all or significant parts of their mandates. Voluntary agencies then became part of the operating structure as well as an essential element in securing respect for international standards.

Because refugees as a rule did not form the most pressing items on governmental agendas, work to protect and eventually to give material assistance to migrants only occasionally emerged as a national issue and certainly not at the same time everywhere. Yet transnational networks of politicians, officials, voluntary agency personnel and simply interested persons took shape. The operation of the national bureaucracies — far larger than the international group — ensured that wherever the United Nations and other humanitarian conventions were accepted in fact or in law, refugees would be dealt with by officials who had at least some relevant charges and had perhaps been influenced by activities at the international level. Moreover, these officials would eventually help shape the national policies towards refugees.

The establishment of the global international institutions also resulted in the creation of a menu of practices for governments that intended to take a full part in influencing their opposite numbers. Respect for international law and its extension was among these practices. It was particularly persuasive both in the immediate postwar situation and at the times when new members joined the institutions. Therefore, when the flood of new members entered the United Nations, some of them looked sympathetically at the refugee assistance system which had been created immediately after the Second World War and whose roots went back to the earlier conflict. In considerable numbers but not universally, they too acceded to the international instruments and began to take part in the policy processes.

New refugee incidents also encouraged governments to work cooperatively and bore with special effect on national bureaucracies embattled by sudden, large-scale flows of refugees. Even when formal accession to the international conventions did not obtain, governments hoping for assistance through international routes in the handling of refugees could hardly avoid following what had become increasingly firm international practice. And in the case of any sizeable emergency, they had little choice but to rely on internationally organised assistance.

If the abstract argument that bureaucratisation provided a protective screen behind which assistance for refugees could be nurtured seems straightforward, the concrete events of administering the policies manifest the confusions, frictions and evasions analysed in this study. For any particular refugee or group of forced migrants, the system could fail and too often did. At the same time, bureaucratisation assured that a standard for measuring performance was available, even if in the end it was ignored. If nothing more, it has become much harder than ever before to conceal the presence of refugees or regard their treatment with indifference. At best, a new standard of compassion governs the reaction.

In many important respects, the international treatment of refugees is specific to the issues posed and to the time in which these issues were perceived by authority or those with access to it. Refugees receive protection and assistance because they pose difficulties by their very presence and because they stimulate non-governmental responses. The main construction of legal obligations and institutions, coming at the end of world wars and in an atmosphere charged with the confrontation of ideologies, lent the presence of refugees a special tone. While general ethical predispositions doubtless played an important part in the decisions on the part of governments to act, it could hardly be claimed that they did so in order to achieve a better world order or to use co-operation on behalf of refugees as a first step towards further organisation or some brand of integration. From the point of view of governments, co-operation for dealing with refugee issues was more convincing for its short-term practicality than for its long-term effect. The separation of the treatment of forced migrants from national migration policies emphasises the point.

It would be hard to argue, therefore, that the example of the international treatment of refugees can be used as a universal guide to constructing additional organised international relationships. Nor could it be claimed that the structures created to deal with refugee situations could simply be converted to cover international duties of a broader scope, such as coping with man-made disasters of every kind and natural disasters as well. While those who have managed the aftermaths of large-scale forced migration have a technical proficiency that could be applied elsewhere, other conditions, including the nature of governmental support for refugee assistance, have not yet been met. Among these conditions are a willingness to provide yet greater financial support on a standing basis for an international establishment and a system of legal commitments to act on behalf of certain classes of injured people or in specific emergencies. In fact, some governments which could be expected to lead such an effort — especially the United States during the Reagan administration — have shown strong hostility to multilateral organisation.

A more appropriate question would concern the viability of the existing organised structure for coping with refugees. It is easy to see the accumulated experience of refugee flows being used as the basis for a continued readiness to serve on the part of the present network of organisations and specialists. Organisational imperatives alone would tend in that direction. Yet a technical approach would leave untouched the deeper impulses that drive forced migrations. It would do little to eliminate mounting fears that some of the largest forced migrations — such as those from Afghanistan and Ethiopia — might begin to resemble the permanent misery of the Palestinians, unaccepted where they are, unable to return whence they came. It could stir up foreboding that the use of the technical facilities in new incidents might open the way to repetition of past frustrations.

Viewed from another perspective — that of regimes theory — what has happened in the case of organising to cope with refugees fits with many other examples of organised international relations. A clear set of basic norms came into existence. These norms emerged, as a result of complex demands, from decisional processes in international institutions, some of which were created for the purpose. This same set of processes adjusts and supplements the norms for particular incidents, seeks to settle disputes and helps to provide for permanence. It results in a specific material output in the form of legal protection, relief and settlement. The intention in creating the refugee regime was that it should continue until refugee matters had diminished to an insignificant level. As refugees can be expected to continue to appear, the refugee regime can now be considered long-term if not permanent.

The application of this analytical mode doubtless helps to identify the organisation set up to deal with refugees with other international arrangements established for the handling of specific issues, such as tariffs or financial stability. Yet the identification remains at a very abstract level. The particularities of handling refugees as an international issue loom large indeed if one compares its relative success with, say, the failure to establish a general regime to control nuclear weapons. In addition, the bureaucratic skills required for maintaining the refugee network would appear to be of a different order from those involved in the designing and negotiating of safeguards for international peace and security. Perhaps the principal difference has to do with the fact that handling refugees within an international structure provides immediate, positive benefits to suffering people and to governments wanting material help or legitimation for their decisions. The process of the refugee regime turns out such benefits at a reasonably reliable tempo. It does so, moreover, by involving extra-governmental groups as well as state bureaucracies. This feature of the network for refugees differs substantially from the usual intergovernmental efforts and may be uncommon among international regimes in general. It may also help to explain the persistence of governmental commitment to aid to refugees.

If organisation on behalf of refugees does not convincingly serve as a seedbed of ideas which quickly and efficiently bring peace, security and prosperity to the whole world, it does at least give protection and relief to a number of human beings. It has developed professional skills and made use of these to bring help to many millions of people; this suggests a possible expansion to include at least some additional migrants. It demonstrates that the notion of international co-operation has continuing value as well as insuperable short-term limitations. Perhaps above all, it shows that short-term political goals can sometimes be combined with compassion for those individuals deprived of basic rights. The whole of humanity thus benefits.

Bibliography

Note: Sources consulted for this work include the official documents of intergovernmental organisations, especially the United Nations, of which the documentation of the High Commissioner for Refugees forms a part; informal publications of intergovernmental agencies, including press releases and other public information materials; secondary studies of a scholarly nature; journalistic books; and newspapers and magazines. These sources were supplemented with interviews (see Preface).

General references

For complete bibliographical references pertaining to refugees, see Barry N. Stein, 'A Bibliography on Refugees', *UNHCR: News from the United Nations High Commissioner for Refugees*, 4 Oct./Nov. 1980, supplement; International Refugee Integration Resource Center, *International Bibliography of Refugee Literature* (working edition), (Geneva, IRIRC, 1985); International Refugee Integration Resource Center, *A Selected and Annotated Bibliography on Refugee Women* (Refugee Documentation Center, UN High Commissioner for Refugees, Geneva, 1985); the bibliographical section of *World Refugee Survey: 1985 in Review* (US Committee for Refugees, Washington, 1986), pp. 73-6; and *Refugee Abstracts*, also published by IRIRC. The special issue of *International Migration Review*, 15, 53/54 (spring-summer 1981), entitled 'Refugees Today' and edited by Barry N. Stein and Sylvano M. Tomasi, contains a lengthy bibliography, p. 331 ff.

Official documents

Intergovernmental Committee for [European] Migration, *Report of the Director for the Work of the Committee for the Year . . .* (annual).

—— *International Migration* (quarterly), United Nations, Department of Public Information, *Yearbook of the United Nations* [1945-46, 1947 etc.] (United Nations and others, New York, annual)

United Nations, General Assembly, Official Records: Sixth [to 41st] Session, *Report of the High Commissioner for Refugees*, Supplement no. 12 and *Addendum to the Report of the High Commissioner for Refugees*, Supplement no. 12A.

United Nations, General Assembly, Official Records: First [to 41st] Session, *Report of the Secretary-General on the Work of the Organization*, Supplement no. 1.

United Nations, High Commissioner for Refugees, *Collection of International Instruments Concerning Refugees* (UN High Commissioner for Refugees, Geneva, 1979).

—— *Handbook for Emergencies* (UN High Commissioner for Refugees, Geneva, 1982).

—— *Handbook on Procedures and Criteria for Determining Refugee Status under the 1951 Convention and the 1967 Protocol Relating to the Status of Refugees* (High Commissioner for Refugees, Geneva, 1979).

—— *Refugees* (monthly magazine). (Replaces *UNHCR: News from the United Nations High Commissioner for Refugees*).

United States Department of State, Bureau for Refugee Programs, *World Refugee Report* (Department of State, Washington, 1985).

United States Senate, Committee on the Judiciary, *World Refugee Crisis: The International Community's Response* (Government Printing Office, Washington, 1979) (Produced by the Congressional Research Service).

—— , Subcommittee on Refugees and Escapees, *Aftermath of War: Humanitarian Problems of South East Asia*, Staff Report, 94th Congress, 2nd sess., 17 May 1976.

Periodicals

Disasters
ICVA News
International Migration
International Migration Review
Migration Today
Refugee Abstracts

Books

Baehr, Peter R. and Leon Gordenker. *The United Nations: Reality and Ideal* (Praeger, New York, 1985)

Bethell, Nicholas. *The Last Secret: Forcible Repatriation to Russia 1944-47* (André Deutsch, London, 1974)

Brooks, Hugh C. and Yassin El-Ayouty, eds. *Refugees South of the Sahara: An African Dilemma* (Negro Universities Press, Westport, CT, 1970)

Brownlie, Ian. *Principles of Public International Law*, 3rd edn. (Oxford University Press, Oxford, 1982)

Buehrig, Edward H. *The UN and Palestinian Refugees: A Study in Nonterritorial Administration* (Indiana University Press, Bloomington, IN, 1971)

Chandler, Edgar H.S. *The High Tower of Refuge: The Inspiring Story of Refugee Relief Throughout the World* (Praeger, New York, 1959)

Cox, Robert W. and Harold K. Jacobson. *The Anatomy of Influence* (Yale University Press, New Haven, CT, 1973)

Divine, Robert A. *American Immigration Policy, 1924-1952* (Yale University Press, New Haven, CT, 1957)

Druks, Herman. *The Failure to Rescue* (Robert Speller & Sons, New York, 1977)

Forsythe, David P. *Human Rights and World Politics* (University of Nebraska Press, Lincoln, NE, 1984)

Garcia-Mora, Manuel R. *International Law and Asylum as a Human Right* (Public Affairs Press, Washington, 1956)

Goodwin-Gill, Guy S. *The Refugee in International Law* (Clarendon Press, Oxford, 1983)

Gordenker, Leon. *International Aid and National Decisions* (Princeton University Press, Princeton, NJ, 1976)
—— *The United Nations in International Politics* (Princeton University Press, Princeton, NJ, 1971)
—— *The UN Secretary-General and the Maintenance of Peace* (Columbia University Press, New York, 1976)
Grahl-Madsen, Atle. *The Status of Refugees in International Law* 2 vols. (Sijthoff, Leiden, 1966, 1972)
—— *Territorial Asylum* (Institute of International Affairs, Uppsala, Sweden, 1979)
Henkin, Louis. *The Rights of Man Today* (Westview Press, Boulder, CO, 1978)
Hirschman, Albert O. *Exit, Voice, and Loyalty: Responses to Decline in Firms, Organizations, and States* (Harvard University Press, Cambridge, MA, 1970)
Hoeksma, J.A. *Tussen vrees en vervolging* (Van Gorcum, Assen, Netherlands; 1982)
Holborn, Louise W. *The International Refugee Organization. Its History and Work 1946-1952* (Oxford University Press, London, 1956)
—— *Refugees: A Problem of Our Time* 2 vols. (Scarecrow Press Inc., Methuen, NJ, 1975)
Jacobson, Harold K. *Networks of Interdependence: International Organizations and the Global Political System*, 2nd edn. (Alfred A. Knopf, New York, 1984)
Keller, Stephen L. *Uprooting and Social Change: The Role of Refugees in Development* (Manohar Book Service, Delhi, 1975)
Keohane, Robert O. and Joseph S. Nye, Jnr. *Power and Interdependence* (Little, Brown & Co., Boston, 1977)
—— and Joseph S. Nye, Jnr., eds. *Transnational Relations and World Politics* (Harvard University Press, Cambridge, MA, 1972)
Krasner, Steven D., ed. *International Regimes* (Cornell University Press, Ithaca, NY, 1983)
Kritz, Mary M., ed. *U.S. Immigration and Refugee Policy: Global and Domestic Issues* (D.C. Heath Co., Lexington, MA, 1983)
Kulischer, Eugene M. *Europe on the Move: War and Population Changes, 1917-47* (Columbia University Press, New York, 1948)
Loescher, Gilburt D. and John Scanlan. *Calculated Kindness: Refugees and the Half-Opened Door* (Free Press, New York, 1986)
Lyons, Gene M. *Military Policy and Economic Aid: The Korean Case* (Ohio University Press, Columbus, OH, 1961)
March, James G. and Herbert Simon. *Organizations* (John Wiley & Sons, New York, 1958)
Melander, Goran. *Refugees in Orbit* (International Universities Exchange Fund, Geneva, 1978)
—— and Peter Nobel, eds. *African Refugees and the Law* (Scandinavian Institute of African Studies, Uppsala, Sweden, 1978)
Morse, Arthur D. *While Six Million Died: A Chronicle of American Apathy* (Random House, New York, 1967)
Oliver, Thomas W. *United Nations in Bangladesh* (Princeton University Press, Princeton, NJ, 1978)
Papademetriou, Demetrios G. and Mark J. Miller, *The Unavoidable Issue: U.S. Immigration Policy in the 1980s* (Institute for the Study of Human Issues, Philadelphia, 1983)

Proudfoot, Malcolm J. *European Refugees: 1939-52: A Study in Forced Population Movement* (Faber & Faber, London, 1957)
Robertson, A.H. *Human Rights in the World* (Manchester University Press, Manchester, 1972)
Schechtman, Joseph B. *European Population Transfers 1939-45* (Oxford University Press, New York, 1946)
—— *Postwar Population Transfers in Europe 1945-1955* (University of Pennsylvania Press, Philadelphia, 1962)
—— *The Refugee in the World: Displacement and Integration* (A.S. Barnes, New York, 1963)
Shawcross, William. *The Quality of Mercy* (Simon & Schuster, New York, 1984)
Shue, Henry. *Basic Rights: Subsistence, Affluence and US Foreign Policy* (Princeton University Press, Princeton, NJ, 1980)
Simpson, John Hope. *The Refugee Problem: Report of a Survey* (Oxford University Press, London, 1939)
Stoessinger, John George. *The Refugee and the World Community* (University of Minnesota Press, Minneapolis, 1956)
Tolstoi, Nikolai. *The Silent Betrayal* (Scribner, New York, 1978)
Tomaso, Lydio F. *In Defense of the Alien*, vols 5-7 (Center for Migration Studies, New York, 1983-86)
Van Dyke, Vernon. *Human Rights, the United States, and the World Community* (Oxford University Press, New York, 1979)
Vernant, Jacques. *The Refugee in the Post-War World: Preliminary Report of a Survey* (Geneva, 1951)
—— *The Refugee in the Post-War World* (Yale University Press, New Haven, CT 1952)
Wain, Barry. *The Refused* (Simon & Schuster, New York, 1981)
Weiss, Thomas G. *International Bureaucracy: an Analysis of the Operation of Functional and Global International Secretariats* (D.C. Heath Co., Lexington, MA, 1975)
Woodbridge, George. *The History of UNRRA* (Columbia University Press, New York, 1950)

Articles and monographs

Bach, Robert L. and Lisa A. Schraml. 'Migration, Crisis and Theoretical Conflict', *International Migration Review*, XVI, 2 (summer 1982)
Beyer, Gunther. 'The Political Refugee; 35 Years Later', *International Migration Review*, 15,53/54, (spring-summer 1981)
Carruthers, Norman and Aidan R. Vining. 'International Migration: an Application of the Urban Location Choice Model', *World Politics*, XXXV, 1 (October 1982)
Clark, Lance D. and Barry N. Stein. 'ICARA II and Refugee Aid and Development', *Migration Today*, 13, 1 (1985)
Cohon, J. Donal, Jnr. 'Psychological Adaptation and Dysfunction Among Refugees', *International Migration Review*, 15, 53/54 (spring-summer 1981)
Forbes, Susan. *Adaptation and Integration of Recent Refugees to the United States* (Refugee Policy Group, Washington, 1985)

Forsythe, David P. 'The Palestine Question: Dealing with a Long-term Refugee Situation', *The Annals of the American Academy of Political and Social Science*, 467 (May 1983)

—— 'UNRWA, the Palestine Refugees and World Politics', *International Organization*, 25, (winter 1971)

Gallagher, Dennis with Susan S. Forbes. *Refugees in South-East Asia: Toward a More Comprehensive Strategy* (Refugee Policy Group, Washington, 1985)

—— *The Refugee Situation in Thailand* (Refugee Policy Group, Washington, 1985)

Gordenker, Leon. 'Refugees in Developing Countries and Transnational Organization', *The Annals of the American Academy of Political and Social Science*, 467 (May 1983)

—— 'The United Nations and Refugees', unpublished paper prepared for the annual meeting of the International Studies Association, 1985

—— 'Early Warning of Disastrous Population Movement', unpublished paper prepared for the Independent Commission on International Humanitarian Issues, Geneva 1984. Revised version with same title in *International Migration Review*, 20,2 (summer 1986)

Huyck, Earl E. and Leon F. Bouvier. 'The Demography of Refugees', *The Annals of the American Academy of Political and Social Science*, 467 (May 1983)

Jones, Allen K. 'Living in Limbo'. mimeographed paper, United States Committee for Refugees (Washington, 1986)

Keeley, Charles B. *Global Refugee Policy: The Case for Development-oriented Strategy* (Population Council, New York, 1981)

Kunz, Egon F. 'Exile and Resettlement: Refugee Theory', *International Migration Review*, XV, 1-2 (spring-summer 1981)

Lindijer, Koert. 'UNHCR faalde bij hulp in Soedan', *NRC-Handelsblad* (11 February 1985)

Melander, Göran. 'Refugees and International Co-operation', *International Migration Review*, XV, 1-2 (spring-summer 1981)

North, David S., Lawrence S. Lewin and Jennifer R. Wagner. *Kaleidoscope: The Resettlement of Refugees in the U.S. by the Voluntary Agencies* (New TransCentury Foundation, Washington, 1982)

Putka, Gary. 'The tragedy of Sudan's spreading starvation is that it's caused by man's errors, not nature's', *Wall Street Journal* (22 January 1985)

Stein, Barry N. 'The Commitment of Refugee Resettlement', *The Annals of the American Academy of Political and Social Science*, 467 (May 1983)

—— 'Indochinese Refugees: The New Boat People', *Migration Today*, 6, 5 (December 1978)

Suhrke, Astri. 'Indochinese Refugees: the Law and Politics of First Asylum, *The Annals of the American Academy of Political and Social Science*, 467 (May 1983)

Taft, Julia Vadala, David S. North and David A. Ford. *Refugee Resettlement in the U.S.: Time for a New Focus* (New TransCentury Foundation, Washington, 1979)

Weiss, Patricia Fagan. *Refugee and Asylum Issues in Inter-American Relations* (Refugee Policy Group, Washington, 1983)

Winkler, Elizabeth. 'Voluntary Agencies and Government Policy', *International Migration Review*, XV, 1-2 (spring-summer 1981)

Wood, Charles H. 'Equilibrium and Historical Structural Perspectives on Migration', *International Migration Review*, XVI, 2 (summer 1982)

Wright, Robert G. 'Voluntary Agencies and the Resettlement of Refugees', *International Migration Review*, XV, 1-2 (spring-summer 1981)

Zolberg, Aristide. 'The Formation of New States as a Refugee-Generating Process', *The Annals of the American Academy of Political and Social Science*, 467 (May 1983)

Index

administration, national 50-1
Afghanistan 15
    mass exodus from 43
Algeria 39
Allende, Salvador 79
Amin, Idi 76, 127
Angola 67, 79, 85
Argentina 75, 77
Armenians 13, 20
asylum 30, 66, 74-90 *passim*,
    94, 125-6
    discouraging 183-5
    draft convention on 41-2
    East European 199
    for Haitians in United States
        159
    Hong Kong 161
    immigration policies and
        138-41
    Latin America 79
    national decisions on 202
    OAS and 100
    OAU and 100
    'pull' effect on 154, 168-9,
        188
    refusal of 98, 188, 191
    resettlement and 131-41
    revision of concept 203-4
    social aspects of 110
    Sudanese 152-3
    UNHCR requests for 101,
        103, 106
    West German 160
    see also High Commissioner
        for Refugees, refugees
asylum seekers
    see forced migrants, refugees
Australia 27, 145
Austria 24, 26, 34, 83

Baha'i 70
Baltic states 68
Bangladesh 14, 72, 90
Berenstein, Alexandre 3
Berlin 93

Black, Prof. C.E. 8
boat people 98, 112, 159
Botswana 14
Burundi 74, 75, 132, 150

Cambodia 101-3, 189
    Heng Samrin government
        15, 102
    Pol Pot regime 15, 189
    see also refugees, Thailand
Canada 27, 145, 203
Carlin, James 7
Carter, Jimmy 17
Castro, Fidel 86, 160
Catholic services 16, 104
Central America 85, 131-2
    see also Cuba, El Salvador,
        Guatemala, Nicaragua
Chadians 108
Chile 70, 75, 79
    see also asylum, *coups d'états*,
        refugees
China 39, 132-3, 159
Commonwealth of Nations 97
concepts 16, 116, 196, 206
Council of Europe 169, 171
coups d'état 68-71, 131
Cuba 15, 128
    broadcasting to 85
    expulsions from 159, 189-91
    mass exodus from 43, 75,
        83
    orderly departure from 160
    propaganda from 84
    'pull' effect on 132
    sanctions against 85
    social change 77-8
    support for Nicaragua 85
    US treatment of refugees
        from 91-3, 137, 141, 183
    see also Intergovernmental
        Committee on Migration,
        refugees, United States
Cyprus 40
Czechoslovakia 14, 66, 139

de Haan, Dale
disasters 12, 96, 172, 174-5,
   197, 204-5
displaced persons 19, 25, 66,
   103, 113
dissidents 75, 77, 82-3, 189

elites 69, 78-81
El Salvador 75, 85, 91, 122
England 9, 144
Equatorial Guinea 76, 113, 127
Ethiopia 15, 102, 116, 129, 148
   attacks from 147
   friction with Sudan 132
   Ogaden Province 15
   re-education in 129
   social change in 77
   see also refugees
Europe 22, 69, 139-40
   eastern 24, 27, 34, 71, 84
   war in 65-8
   western 14, 68, 91-3, 181
European Communities 57, 99,
   120, 171, 179
expulsion 67, 73, 188-92

Food and Agriculture
   Organisation 57, 97
   see also World Food
      Programme
forced migrants
   see forced migration, refugees
forced migration 12, 13, 15
   attracting 186-8
   caused by war end 67
   discouraging 183-4
   early warning of 174, 205
   forecasting of 168-77, 205
   nature of recent 49-60
   political decisions on 195
   prevention 177-88
   remarkable aspects 52-9
   transnational response to 95
   see also expulsion, refugees
Ford Foundation 34
France 39, 103, 139, 158-9

Geneva Convention 16
Germany 20, 24
   east 14, 34, 71, 84, 160

federal republic 71
   west 34, 83, 84, 160
Gordenker, Leon 1, 2, 3
Guatemala 73, 75

Haiti 81, 122, 159, 185, 191
Hartling, Poul 7, 43, 117
van Heuven Goedhart, G.J. 33,
   43
High Commissioner for
   Refugees 1, 16, 117
   activities expanded 34-6
   authority 29-33, 58-9
   budget 17, 29, 35, 37-8,
      118-20
      donor meetings 45
      issue 44-5
   capacity of 97-8, 100
   concept expanded 36-42,
      59-60
      geographical limit 37
      legal limit, 39-41, 59-60
      refugee-like situations
         40-1, 59, 113
      time span 37
   diplomatic role 29, 58
   emergency fund 97, 100
   emergency unit 97
   executive committee 44
   executive role 42, 117
      expanded 42-6
   Fund for Durable Solutions
      151-2
   good offices 39
   narrow design 33
   nomination of 29
   operating partners of 99
   requesting aid of 102
   statute of the office 28, 59
   see also refugees
Hitler, Adolf 14
Hmong 133
Hocke, Jean-Pierre 117
Holborn, Louise W. 21
Honduras 85, 98
Hong Kong 39, 133, 161, 183-4
Horn of Africa 91, 122, 132,
   147
hue and cry 207-8
human rights 87-8, 126, 130-1,

158, 169-73, 210
as standard 174-8, 204
denial of 63, 67-8, 71-80
    passim 133
incorporated in ethics, 196
of emigration 181
see also refugees, inter-
    national protection of;
    UN Covenants on
    UN Universal Declaration
    on;
Hungary 14, 34-5

IC[E]M *see* Intergovernmental
    Committee for [European]
    Migration
ICRC *see* International Com-
    mittee of the Red Cross
immigration 30, 138-41
    economic effects of 154-5
    large-scale 55
    national policies 30
    restrictions on 58-60, 184-6,
        189-91, 198, 203
India 14, 26, 72, 80, 84
Indo-China *see* Cambodia,
    Laos, refugee, Thailand,
    Vietnam
Inter-governmental Committee
    on Refugees 21-2, 28
Intergovernmental Commission
    for [European] Migration 7,
    16, 23, 117-18, 120, 139
    design 33, 204
    initiatives of 43-5
    provision of travel 35, 99, 143
International Catholic Migra-
    tion Commission 16
International Committee of the
    Red Cross 7, 101, 105, 111,
    113, 171
    repatriation aid 130
    Thai border programme
        101-5
International Confederation of
    Voluntary Agencies 45
International Labour Organisa-
    tion 87, 171
International Red Cross 16
    see also International

Committee of the Red
    Cross, League of Red
    Cross Societies
International Refugee Organiza-
    tion 16, 25-9, 155
Iran 66, 70, 83-4
Iraq 66
Israel 14, 16, 33, 66
    asylum in 95, 104
    forces 76
    Palestinians and 130, 156-88
    see also refugees, UN Relief
        and Works Agency
Italy 14, 26

Jackson, Sir Robert 103
Jacobson, Harold K. 1
Jews, 14, 15, 210
    leaving Germany 14
    Soviet 73, 83
Jordan 156

Kampuchea *see* Cambodia
Kenya 26, 79, 80
Khaddafi, Colonel 77
Khan, Prince Sadruddin Aga 7,
    40, 43, 171
Kingsley, J. Donald 26
Korea 67-8, 85

LaGuardia, Fiorello H. 23-4
Laos 79, 149, 161
law, international 12
League of Nations 16, 19-21,
    26
League of Red Cross Societies
    7, 44
    see also International Com-
        mittee of the Red Cross
Lebanon 76, 156
Lehman, Herbert H. 23
Lesotho 14
Libya 77
Lindt, August 7, 39, 43
Lutheran World Services 104

Malaysia 147, 184
Mariel crisis 159, 190-1
    see also Cuba, forced
        migration, refugees,

United States
mass exodus 43, 53-5
  see also forced
    migration, refugees
Médecins sans Frontières 44
Mennonite Central Committee
  152
Middle East 14, 156-8
migration 55-6, 63-4, 68, 80
  see also forced migration,
    immigration
minorities 72-4, 144, 160
Moskito Indians 98
Mozambique 14, 67, 79, 103,
  150

Nansen, Dr. Fridtjof 20, 23, 42
Nansen office 20, 27
nationalism 50-1, 72-3, 141,
  172
Netherlands 91
networks, international 2, 11,
  15, 196, 204, 213
  ad hoc construction of, 96
  expansion, 56
  functions, 56-8
Nicaragua 69, 98, 127
Nobel Prize for peace 34, 43
non-refoulement 31, 89, 97-8
non-governmental organisations
  1, 11, 39, 103-5
  as communications channels
    93
  functional modes of 104-5
  generalisations on 103-5
  influence 45
  leadership 43
  resettlement role 145
  see also organisations, trans-
    national agencies
norms 16

OAS *see* Organization of
  American States
OAU *see* Organization for
  African Unity
Ogaden 91
opposition groups 85
organisations 16
  intergovernmental 6, 99-102,

111-12
  see also non-governmental
    organisations
Organization for African Unity
  40-1, 64, 99, 169
Organization of American
  States 100, 169
Oxfam 16, 152

Pakistan 15, 72, 77, 84, 91, 136
Palestine 26, 72, 156, 171
Palestine Liberation Organ-
  ization 76
Papadopoulos, Colonel 87
Peron, Juan Domingo 77
Pitt, David 3
Poland 14, 79, 83, 189
propaganda 66-7, 84-5

Reagan, Ronald 17
Red Cross, national 93
  see also International
    Committee of the Red
    Cross, League of Red
    Cross Societies
refoulement, see non-refoulement
Refugee Policy Group 173
refugees 5
  Argentinian 15
  causes *see* refugees, causes of
  Chilean 15
  concepts of 19, 29-31, 63,
    201-6
  definition in convention 31,
    49-50
    insufficiencies 59-60
  early warning of 118
  Eritrean 15
  flows 17, 77, 210
    blocking 180-3
    early warning of 174-7
    forecasting of 168-74
  German attacks on 65-6
  Greek 14
  group status 39
  humane deterrence of 161-2,
    183-4
  international handling of 1,
    196, 206-14
  international protection of

16, 26-8, 97-8, 124-5
  by League of Nations 16,
    20-2, 27
Jewish 20-1, 210
Lao 15
Nicaraguan 15
number of 11, 52-3
Palestinian 16, 33, 156-8
  see also UN Relief and
    Works Agency for
    Palestine Refugees
Polish 93
political 13
political reasons for 2, 31
prevention of 158-62, 180-3
regions affected by 14
responses to 11, 195-201
  internationalising 206-14
  national limits of 196-201
Russian 22
Salvadorean 15
Tamils 92-3, 188
travel documents 31
urgent assistance 90
Vietnamese 15
see also forced migrants; High
  Commissioner for
  Refugees; refugees, assistance to; refugees, causes
  of; refugees,
  liquidating situations of
refugees, assistance to 89-111
  bilateral 95-6, 111-12
  boundaries of 91
  camps 105-6
  continuing phase 105-7
  efficiency 116
  financing 113-14, 118-21
  food 107-8
  from intergovernmental
    agencies 96, 111-12
  general standard 149
  health services 108-9
  housing 107-8
  institutional co-ordination
    110-11
  leadership 118
  legal obligations 93-4, 112-13
  management of 115-17
  numbers 91-3

qualitative differences 146-7
schooling 109-10
UN General Assembly
  recommendations 94, 103
refugees, causes of 62-8 *passim*
  161-2, 178
  denial of human rights 63-4
  forecasts 62
  turbulence in states 68-77
  war 64-8, 82
refugees, liquidating situations
  of 125-67 *passim*
  authoritarian handling 134-5
  confusion in United States
    137
  costs 135, 148-9
  development 136, 149-50
    asylees impact on 150
    international conferences
      on Africa 153-4
    Sudan initiative 152-3
  hostile reactions 133-4, 144
  initiatives 130-1
  integration 137
  local effects of 144-5
  political values 145
  remnant groups 155-6
  repatriation 126-31, 135-6
  resettlement 131-45
    family reunion in 139
    in first asylum 131-8
    organised 139-40, 181-3
    preparatory programmes
      143
    readjustment for 141-2,
      144
    relation to causes 132-8
    relation to immigration
      138, 140-1, 144
    self-support 135-6
    spontaneous 131-2
    third-country 138
  standard approaches 125
repatriation, forcible 24, 28,
  126
revolution 68, 69-70, 78, 82,
  85, 131
  Chinese 78
  Cuban 78
  Iranian 70

Nicaraguan 69
Russian 13, 69, 77-8, 211
Zimbabwean 70
Rhodesia 86-7
Rikhye, Maj.-Gen. Indar Jit 9
Roman Catholic church 44
Roosevelt, Franklin 21
Rwanda 74, 75, 133

Schnyder, Felix 7, 43
security 51
Singapore 184
Solzhenitsyn, Alexander 189
Somalia 15, 72, 117
    government 17, 105
    mass exodus from 43, 90
South Africa 14, 71, 77, 88
South-East Asia 15
Soviet Union 14, 17, 95-6
    contributions 122
    during Hungarian exodus 35
    forced repatriation to *see*
        repatriation, forcible
    influence on refugee issues
        29
    invasion of Afghanistan 15
    Jews in 73, 83
    relations with United States
        28
    support for opposition 85
Sri Lanka 91 .
Sudan 15, 93, 135-7, 147-8,
    152-3
Swaziland 14

Thailand 97, 101-3, 184
    border friction 92
    Cambodian border 66, 105
    camps in 15, 146, 161
    government 17
    holding centres 97, 101, 105,
        143
    local resettlement 147
    voluntary agencies in 105
transnational agencies 90
    see also non-governmental
        organisations
Turkey 14, 20, 67

Uganda 67, 73, 191

UN Children's Fund 57, 97,
    100, 105
UN Commission on Human
    Rights 26, 171
UN Convention on Refugees
    27-9, 41, 64, 89, 170
    aid under 94
    application in humane deter-
        rence 162
    protocol of 1967 38, 41
    revision 202-4
    Soviet attitude towards 29
    see also High Commissioner
        for Refugees, refugees
UN Covenant on Economic
    and Social Rights, *see* UN
    Covenant on Human Rights
|UN Covenant on Human
    Rights 94, 161, 170
UN Development Programme
    100, 120
UN Disaster Relief Organisa-
    tion 96
UN Educational, Scientific and
    Cultural Organisation 97, 171
UNHCR *see* High Commis-
    sioner for Refugees
UNICEF *see* UN Children's
    Fund
United Kingdom 26, 199
United Nations 1, 86-7
    Commission on Human
        Rights, *see* UN Commis-
        sion on Human Rights
    Convention on Human
        Rights, *see* UN
        Convention on Human
        Rights
    Convention on Refugees, *see*
        UN Convention on Refugees
    Disaster Relief Organisation,
        see UN Disaster Relief
        Organisation
    Economic and Social Council
        of 25, 32, 171
    Educational, Scientific and
        Cultural Organisation,
        see UN Educational,
        Scientific and Cultural
        Organisation

General Assembly of 25, 27, 28, 32, 44, 89, 171
  recommendations on refugee aid 94
High Commissioner for Refugees, *see* High Commissioner for Refugees
military forces of 14
refugee-like situations and 40, 89
Relief and Rehabilitation Administration *see* UN Relief and Rehabilitation Administration
Relief and Works Agency for Palestine Refugees *see* UN Relief and Works Agency for Palestine Refugees
Secretary-General 17, 58
Security Council 87
system 1
Universal Declaration on Human Rights *see* UN Universal Declaration on Human Rights
United States 17
  Central American clients of 85
  contributions 120
  Cuban asylees in 159, 160
  Geneva mission of 45
  immigration and naturalisation service 142
  lobbying 2
  local aid to refugees 92
  Mariel refugees 159, 160
  political values 120
  refugee act of 1980 137-8
  refugees resettled 15, 137-8 ✓
  relations with Soviet Union 28
  Soviet Jews resettled in 83
  treatment of Haitians 92, 159
  Vietnamese resettled in 83
UN Korean Reconstruction Agency 113
UN Relief and Rehabilitation Administration 16, 22-5, 36, 156-7
UN Relief and Works Agency for Palestine Refugees 16, 156-7, 179
  Agent-General 43
  camps 106, 156
  initiative 43
  see also Palestine, refugees
UNRWA *see* UN Relief and Works Agency for Palestine Refugees
UN Universal Declaration on Human Rights 34, 161, 170

Vietnam 14
  limits refugee flows 103, 158-9
  moratorium on departure 182-3
  orderly departure program 159-60, 181-2
  re-education in 79
voluntary agencies *see* non-governmental organisations

Waldheim, Kurt 40, 102-3
Weiss, Thomas G. 3
WFP *see* World Food Programme
WHO *see* World Health Organisation
World Bank 150, 152
World Council of Churches 16
World Food Programme 57, 97, 100
World Health Organisation 97, 100
World Intellectual Property Organisation 171
World Wars 13, 19

Yugoslavia 14, 34

Zaïre 39, 76
Zambia 14, 80
Zimbabwe 14, 78, 80, 127